LEGENDARY LOCALS

OF

# KENT COUNTY

## MARYLAND

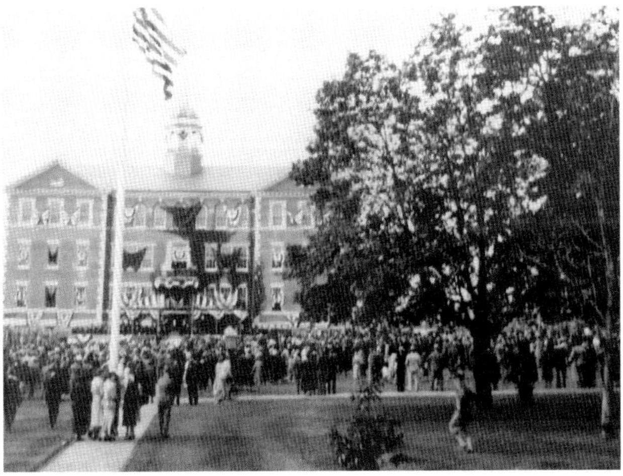

I0805811

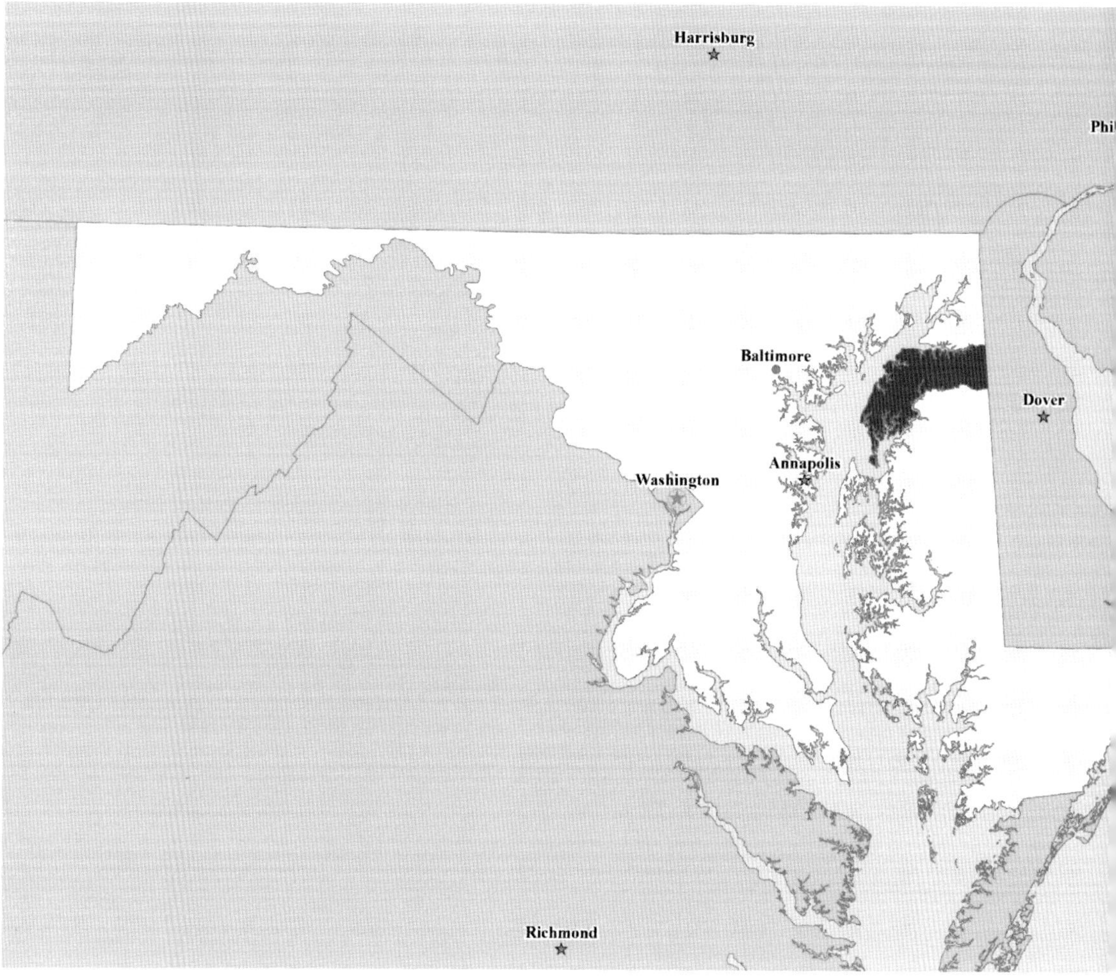


**Map of Maryland**

Kent County (in black) is bordered by the Chester River to the south, the Chesapeake Bay to the west, the Sassafras River to the north, and its namesake, Kent County in the state of Delaware, to the east. (Courtesy of Kent County, Maryland Planning Commission.)

**Page 1: Washington College Welcomes Pres. Franklin D. Roosevelt**

Thousands of spectators are shown in front of William Smith Hall at Washington College welcoming US president Franklin D. Roosevelt when he attended the inauguration of Washington College president Dr. Gilbert W. Mead in 1933. (Courtesy of Washington College.)

LEGENDARY LOCALS

OF

# KENT COUNTY

## MARYLAND

PATRICIA JOAN O. HORSEY

LEGENDARY LOCALS

ISBN 978-1-4671-0218-6

Legendary Locals is an imprint of Arcadia Publishing
Charleston, South Carolina

Printed in the United States of America

Library of Congress Control Number: 2015935313

For all general information, please contact Arcadia Publishing:
Telephone 843-853-2070
Fax 843-853-0044
E-mail sales@arcadiapublishing.com
For customer service and orders:
Toll-Free 1-888-313-2665

Visit us on the Internet at www.arcadiapublishing.com

**Dedication**

*To the people of Kent County, both past and present*

**On the Front Cover**: Clockwise from top left:
Randolph Waddell "Jazz" Johnson, local jazz musician (Courtesy Eloise Johnson; see page 39), Milford Dukes and Francis M. "Gibby" Gibson, well known to many generations who patronized Chestertown's landmark bar, the Blue Bird (Courtesy Beverly and Francis Gibson, Jr.; see page 79), Sue Dunning Matthews, jazz vocalist (Courtesy Michael G. Stewart Photography, see page 42), Alonza Copeland "Cope" Hubbard, Kent County waterman and business owner (Courtesy Donna Hubbard Edwards, see page 74), Clarence Hawkins, Kent County educator and elected official (Courtesy Clarence Hawkins, see page 28), Mabel Deringer, teacher of dancing and etiquette (Courtesy Mary Deringer Phelps, see page 86), and Bartus O. Vickers, Kent County sheriff for 32 years (Courtesy Pat Vickers Smith, see page 14).

**On the Back Cover:** From left to right:
Earl Kennard Jones, popular Still Pond business owner (Courtesy of Willis K. Jones; see page 63), Edward Lee "Sonny" Townsend (left) and Robert Lee "Bozy" Robinson Jr., Kent County game wardens (Courtesy of Sally Robinson Lane; see page 14).

# CONTENTS

# ACKNOWLEDGMENTS

It was not easy putting together a book of people, past and present, who have had an impact on our community throughout its history, because space is limited, and there are many. I am grateful to the many individuals, families, and organizations who shared photographs and stories and to those who helped me make the final selections for this first volume.

In addition, I would like to thank Joan Andersen and Karen Emerson of the Historical Society of Kent County, Bernadette Bowman and Jen Davis from the Kent County Tourism Office, Annie Coleman, Mackey Metcalfe Dutton, Connie Godwin, Barbara Heck, Kevin Hemstock, Beth Horsey, Gary Horsey, Bill Ingersoll, Bayly Janson-LaPalme, Betty Lockwood, Robin Wood Kurowski, Tracye S. Landon, Trish McGee, Amy Moredock from the Kent County Planning Office, Scott Smith, Todd Smith, and photographers C. Dudley Reed, Trixie White, Ralph H. Usilton Jr., Francis Connolly, and Austin Walmsley.

Special thanks to my husband, Elmer E. Horsey, for his understanding of the time needed to complete this, and to my grandchildren, Frank Ozman Smith, Kathryn Macey Smith, Carli Crew Smith, James Thomas Ozman Landon, Baker Fallon Horsey Landon, and my step-granddaughters, Jennifer Ashley Horsey and Lauren Nicholson Horsey, who have provided the inspiration for me to write about our county's people.

# INTRODUCTION

Kent County is often called "the land of pleasant living." The Chesapeake Bay region of Maryland was first explored by Capt. John Smith in 1608 and 1609, including the areas of the Sassafras River in the upper part of Kent County, Maryland. Kent County was named for the shire of Kent, which borders the English Channel in the southeast of England. It goes back to William Claiborne's settlement on Kent Island in 1631 (now part of Queen Anne's County, which adjoins Kent County). Kent County was represented in the legislature in 1638–1639 and mentioned in 1642 when the governor and council appointed commissioners for the Isle and County of Kent. The first settlement in what is today Kent County was established in 1675 on Gray's Inn Creek outside of Rock Hall and named New Yarmouth. The original county court house and jail were located in New Yarmouth along with two shipyards. The population declined after the county government was moved to New Town (now Chestertown).

Kent County is the smallest county geographically on the Eastern Shore and is Maryland's second-oldest county. It is bordered by the Chester River to the south, the Chesapeake Bay to the west, the Sassafras River to the north, and Delaware's Kent County to the east. The coastline varies from historical waterfront towns with marinas to acres of farmlands. Kent's economy continues to be based on agriculture and water-related activities. It is noted for its beauty and its traditions, which are still very much in evidence today.

There are five incorporated towns, including Chestertown, Rock Hall, Betterton, Galena, and Millington. In addition to Kent's incorporated towns, there are a number of census-designated places where generations of residents have grown up, including Butlertown, Edesville, Fairlee, Georgetown, Kennedyville, Lynch, Massey, Still Pond, Tolchester, and Worton. The population of Kent County is diverse. The communities are a mix of generations of families who have lived in Kent County all of their lives and residents who have moved to Kent County more recently. *Legendary Locals of Kent County* includes only a few from a cross section of people from all parts of the county who are unique individuals, past and present, and who have contributed in some way to Kent County's way of life. There was not enough space to name everyone in just one volume. Please contact the author if you know someone who could be noted, should another volume be compiled.

Chestertown, originally called New Town, and sometimes referred to as the "gem city on the Chester," was founded in 1706. It is located on the Chester River and serves as the county seat. It was granted the port of entry for Kent, Queen Anne's, and Cecil Counties in Maryland and stood as the center of trade with Great Britain and the West Indies. Between 1756 and 1793, George Washington made eight known visits to Chestertown. Chestertown was designated the first geographic center of population in the United States in 1790. It is also the location of Washington College, the 10th-oldest college in the nation and named for George Washington, who was a member of its Board of Visitors and Governors and gave the college permission to use his name. Chestertown's historic district is the second oldest in Maryland.

Rock Hall, referred to as the "pearl of the Chesapeake," dates back to 1707. It was a tobacco port and fishing and crabbing center. The first news of the Revolutionary War victory over Cornwallis at Yorktown was carried through Rock Hall to the Continental Congress meeting at Philadelphia. In 1814, the War of 1812's only land battle on the Eastern Shore took place at Caulk's Field near Tolchester, just outside of Rock Hall, where the British, under Sir Peter Parker, were defeated and their commander killed. Tolchester Amusement Park on the Chesapeake Bay near Rock Hall is remembered as a destination for steamboats bringing visitors from Baltimore to enjoy amusement rides, swimming, and picnicking. Today, Rock Hall remains important to the fishing and crabbing industry and has become a destination for sailors, boaters, and visitors.

Betterton, located on the Chesapeake Bay at the mouth of the Sassafras River, is known as the "jewel of the Chesapeake." It began in 1698 as Fish Hall, became Crew's Landing in 1715, and was given its present name in 1851. It was once a popular destination for steamboat excursions. Its location on the Chesapeake Bay and its many amusements once drew visitors by water and land. Its focus now is on its architectural, cultural, and historical importance. A Betterton Historic District was approved and is now listed in the National Register of Historic Places.

Galena was founded in 1763. It was once called Downs Crossroads. Legend says silver was once mined from the Galena area, and that may be where the name "galena" (a mineral) came from. Galena is a small rural community. George Washington stopped in Galena at a tavern owned by William Downs in 1774 en route to and from the Continental Congress, and he traveled this road on his eight visits to Kent County.

Millington was originally called Head of Chester. The Chester River runs through the town, and the town shares shores with both Kent and Queen Anne's Counties. Its name was changed to Bridgetown in 1724, and the town became known as Millington in 1818. Millington was located in the center of a large corn-, wheat-, and fruit-growing area and also boasted an active commerce trade, including mills. The Kent and Queen Anne's Railroad enabled Millington to become one of the largest peach shippers in Kent County for many years. Millington continues as a small rural town with a rural atmosphere.

Kent Countians are proud of their past. It is truly the "land of pleasant living."

# CHAPTER ONE

# Service

Kent Countians serve in many ways, including in the military, as government officials, and as elected officials. They have served in wars and at times of conflict, like Sgt. Preston Ashley of Rock Hall, who died at age 23 in North Africa during World War II; Lt. Gen. Robert Richard Dierker, who served in various operational and staff positions in the United States, Southeast Asia, Northeast Asia, and Europe; Charles Samuel Jacquette Jr., who was one of only 44 survivors on the first US Navy ship to be torpedoed and sunk by German forces in 1941; Betty Lussier, who helped the British Air Transport Auxiliary set up a chain of double agents and transmitted misinformation to the enemy; and identical twins Joseph Wilbur Strong Jr. and Robert H. Strong Sr., who both served as US Navy pilots during World War II.

Kent Countians who have worked in government have dedicated themselves to serving the public over the years. William Stevens Ingersoll has served as Chestertown's town manager for 40 years, under four mayors; Marcellene Beck was the first female police officer in Chestertown and the first female African American police officer in Chestertown and Kent County; Margaret Mulford served as postmaster at Galena for 41 years; Medford Capel served the town of Chestertown for 53 years, retiring as superintendent of the utilities commission.

Kent Countians have served loyally as elected officials over the years. The P.M. Brooks Jr. Building, which houses Chestertown's Volunteer Fire Company, is named after volunteer fireman and former Chestertown mayor Philip Medford Brooks Jr.; Thomas Gross was the first African American to be elected to Chestertown's governing council; Bartus O. Vickers served as Kent's sheriff for 32 years; Clarence Hawkins was the first African American elected to serve as a Kent County commissioner; Jane Burris Neal was the first woman elected to serve as a Chestertown councilperson; Thomas Edward Robinson and his father both served as mayors of Millington; former mayor Elmer E. Horsey and his council made significant improvements to Chestertown that served as the foundation for the town's modernization; Charles N. Satterfield was the first elected mayor of Chestertown, serving from 1931 to 1935. Philip G. Wilmer was Chestertown's second elected mayor and served from 1935 to 1963—28 years—which is the longest any Chestertown mayor has served. Rosalie Brady Kuechler was the first woman to be elected to Rock Hall's council and the first woman to be elected Rock Hall mayor.

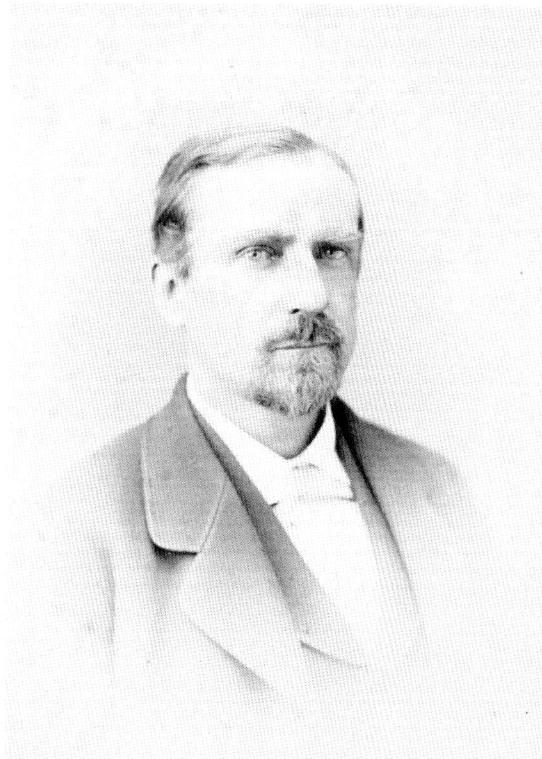

**The Honorable James Alfred Pearce**
A watering trough located in Fountain Park in downtown Chestertown was dedicated to Judge James Alfred Pearce, who was born in Chestertown, practiced law in Chestertown, and served as state's attorney for Kent County. He also served as judge for the Maryland Court of Appeals, chaired the Maryland Public Service Commission, taught at Washington College, served on its board, and was chancellor of the Protestant Episcopal Diocese of Easton. (Courtesy of the Historical Society of Kent County.)

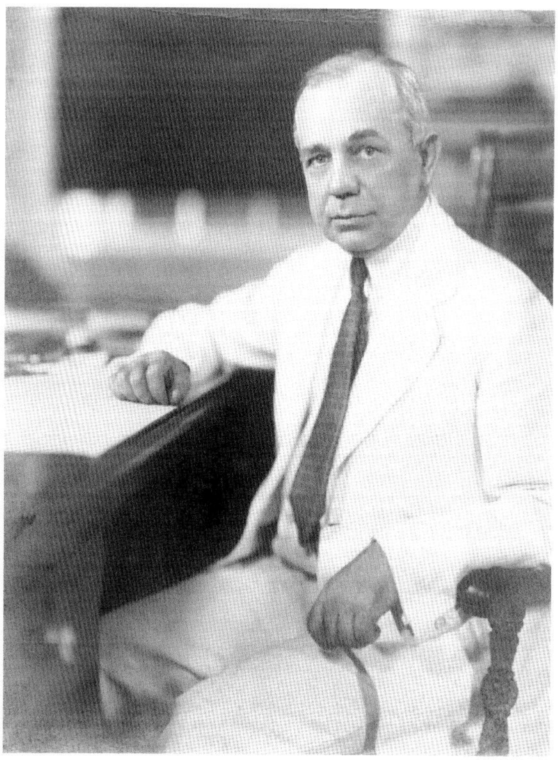

**Harrison Wilson Vickers Jr.**
His office on Court Street in Chestertown had been used by his father and grandfather and was continuously used as a law office for 120 years. Vickers practiced law in Kent County for 46 years. He served as state's attorney for Kent County and served as a Maryland conservation commissioner. It is said he continued his law practice even after going totally blind. (Courtesy of Jeanne A. Knox.)

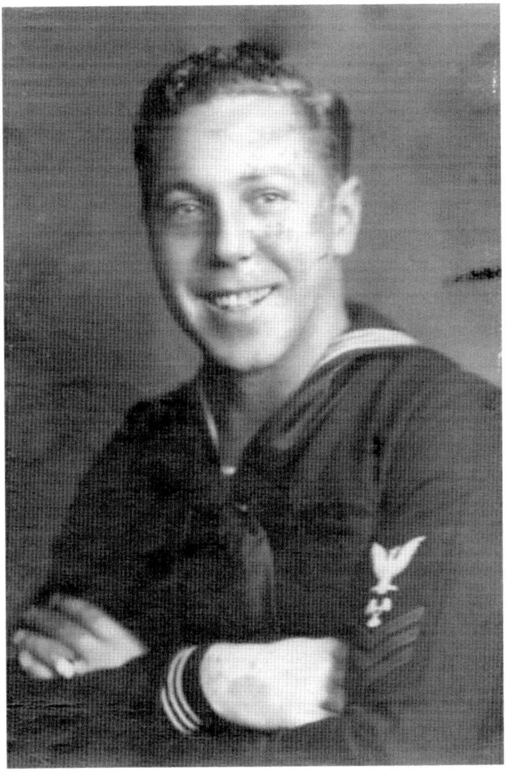

**C. Henry Price**
A native of Betterton, C. Henry Price served as a US Navy machinist mate first class during World War II. He was on the USS *Juneau* when he was killed along with 687 men during the naval battle of Guadalcanal in 1942. The Betterton American Legion Post was founded in 1949 and is named the C. Henry Price Post 246 in his honor. (Courtesy of Charles H. Price.)

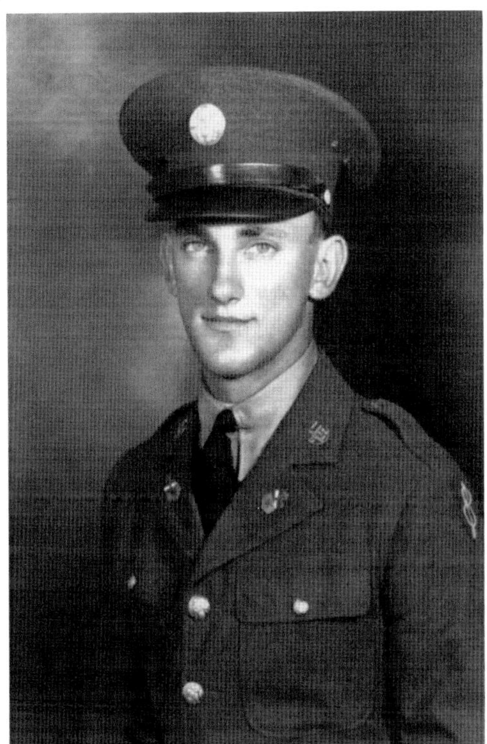

**Sgt. Preston Ashley**
The Rock Hall American Legion Post 228 is named after Sgt. Preston Ashley, who was wounded in battle and died at age 23 in North Africa during World War II. The post home was chartered in 1949 and has an M60 Vietnam-era battle tank donated by the US Army sitting at its entrance. (Courtesy of Rock Hall American Legion Post 228.)

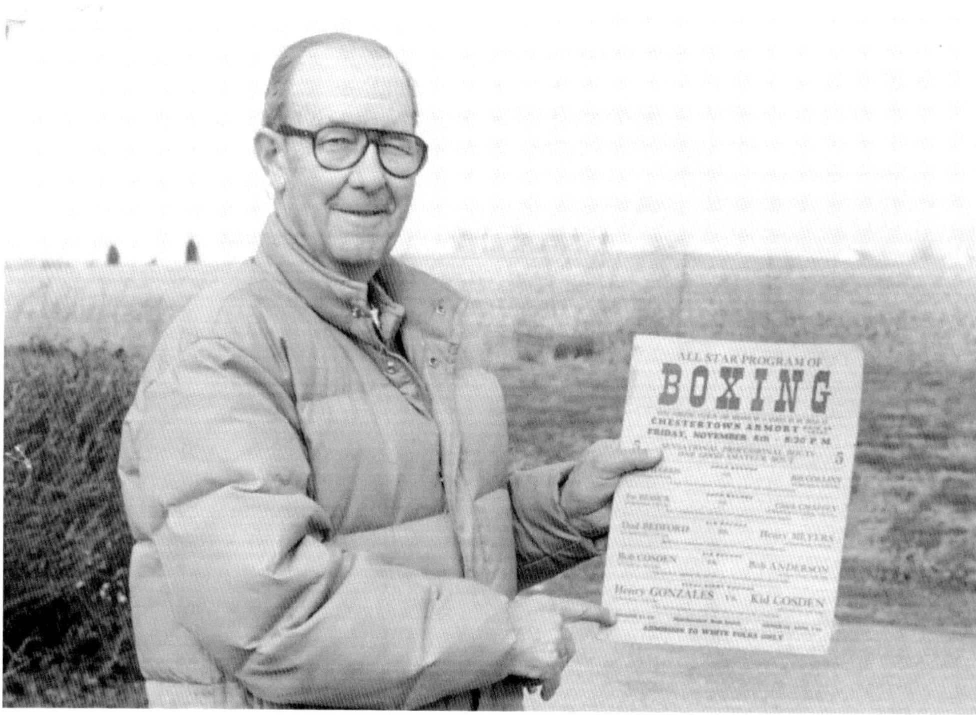


### Henry Gsell

From Kent County deputy sheriff to Kent County sheriff in the early 1940s, Henry Gsell also served 16 years as the Kent County clerk of court before returning to law enforcement as Chestertown's police chief. He was a boxer under the name of Henry "Gonzales" and participated in local boxing events to raise money for the local hospital. He was founder and lifetime member of the Kent County Gun Club. (Courtesy of the Historical Society of Kent County.)

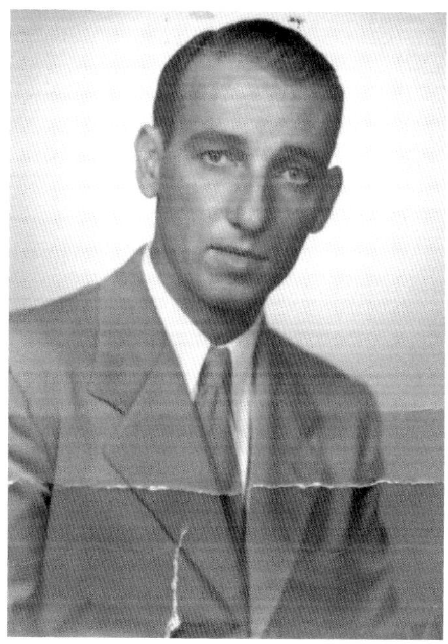

### John Rasin Jewell

Former Kent County state senator John R. Jewell was appointed commissioner of the Maryland Department of Motor Vehicles in 1959. He was appointed the first secretary of a newly created Maryland Department of Licensing and Regulation in 1970 by Gov. Marvin Mandel. The new department combined 32 separate regulatory agencies. (Courtesy of Joyce Jewell Willis.)

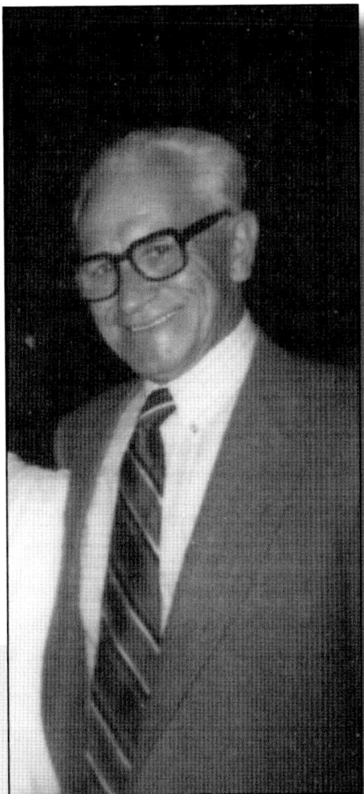

**Charles Samuel "Brother" Jacquette Jr.**
Fireman First Class Jacquette of Rock Hall was assigned to the USS *Reuben James*, an American destroyer, in World War II. The *Reuben James*, on watch in the North Atlantic waters, was the first US Navy ship torpedoed and sunk by German forces in 1941. "Brother" was one of only 44 survivors. He endured by hanging onto lifeboats and tying his shoestrings in his life jacket to keep it secure. Brother returned to Rock Hall, bought a boat, and named her the *Reuben James*, using her to fish and oyster. After Brother died, the *Reuben James* was disassembled, and its bow and stern became part of the facade at 5781 North Main Street in Rock Hall. (Left, courtesy of Teresa Jacquette Jetton; below, author's collection.)

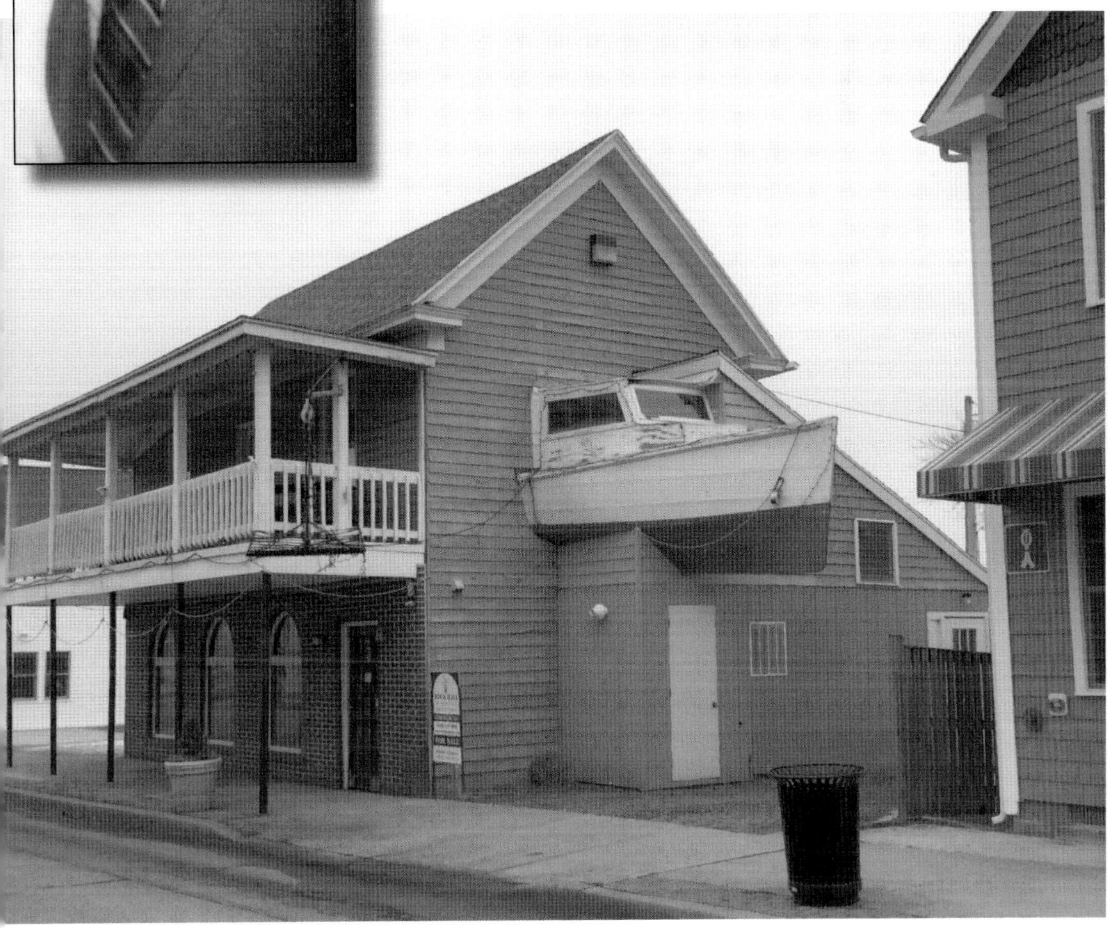

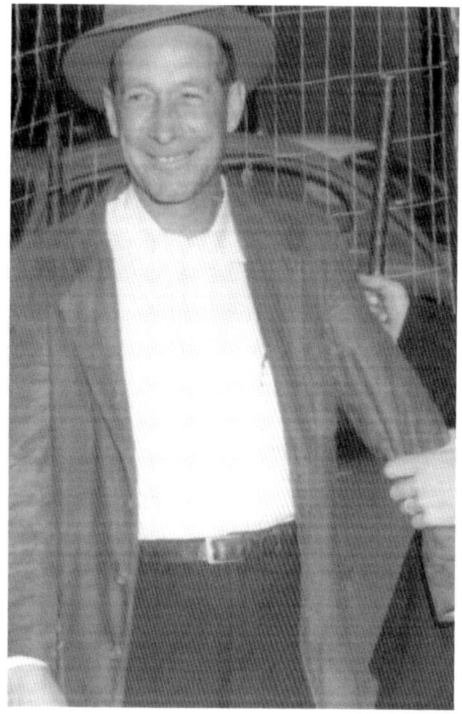

**Bartus O. Vickers**

Lifelong Kent Countian Bartus O. Vickers served in World War II as a member of the Navy SeaBees. His father was Kent County's sheriff in the 1930s. Vickers was elected Kent County sheriff in 1946 and served for 32 years. He died of a heart attack his first full day out of office. He had just been elected and was to be sworn in as Kent County's register of wills. (Courtesy of Pat Vickers Smith.)

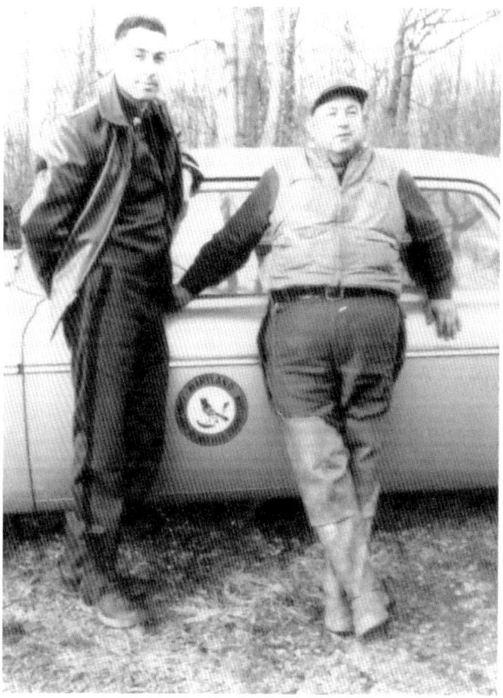

**Robert Lee Robinson Jr.**

He had a reputation as a friend of both the hunter and the hunted. "Bozy" retired as a district game warden after 30 years working for the Maryland Department of Natural Resources. The State of Maryland named the Bozy Robinson Work Center at the Millington Wildlife Management Area in his honor. Game Wardens Bozy (right) and Edward Lee "Sonny" Townsend are pictured here. (Courtesy of Sally Robinson Lane.)

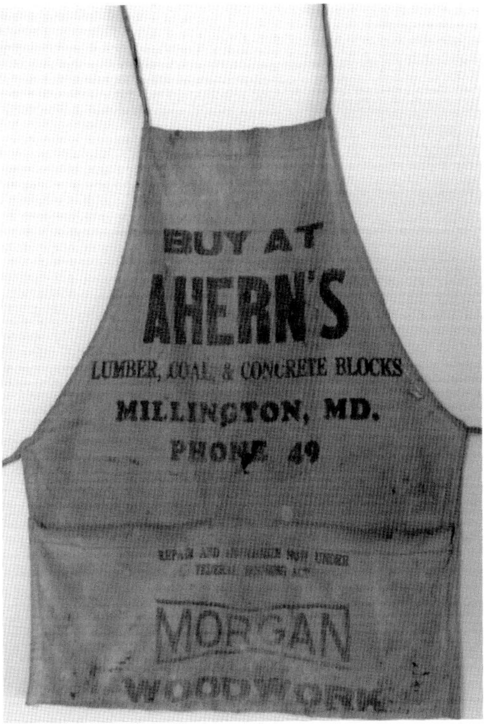


**John Ahern**
Noted as being the second mayor (president of the town commission) of Millington, John Ahern was a dealer in peaches and other fruit. He owned a lumberyard and was a railroad agent and telegrapher. Ahern was president of the Kent County School Board and a driving force for the creation of the modern fire company. He was also a member of the State Library Commission for 15 years. (Courtesy of G. Kevin Hemstock.)

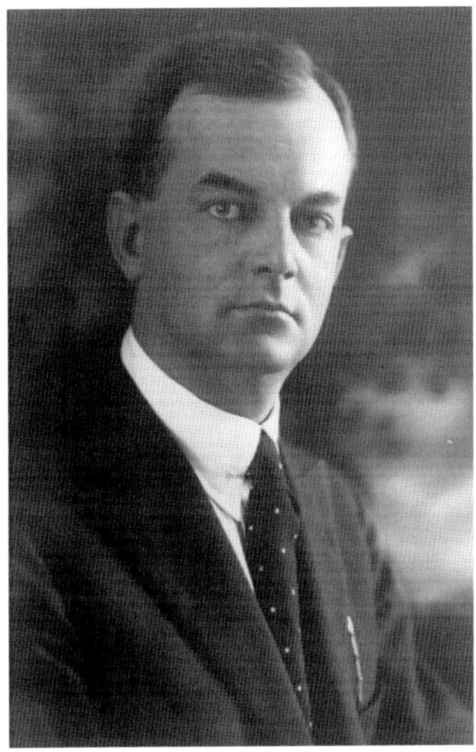

**S. Scott Beck Sr.**
Beck, a Chestertown attorney, served as state's attorney and state senator for Kent County before being appointed comptroller of customs for the Port of Baltimore. He was noted for his involvement in Democratic politics. After suffering from a paralytic stroke that confined him to his home for several months, he recovered sufficiently to practice law again. He served on the Board of Visitors and Governors of Washington College. (Courtesy of the Dick Welton family.)

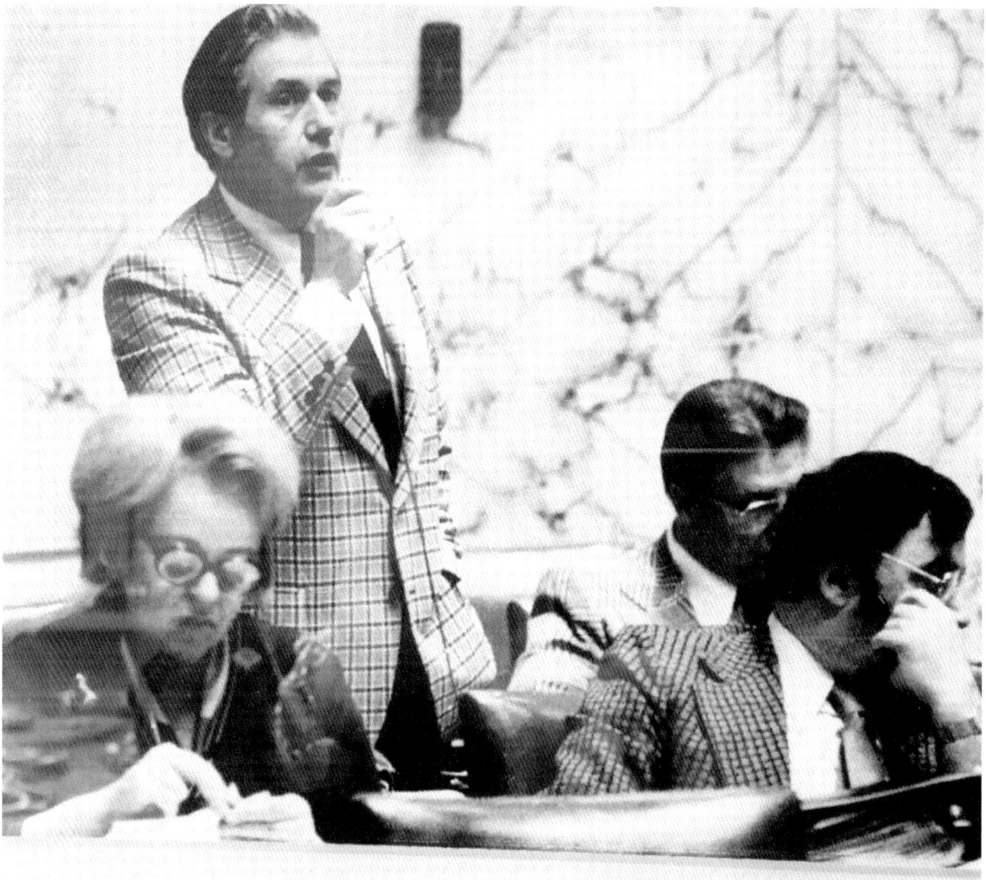

### The Honorable Elroy G. Boyer

Judge Boyer was elected to both the Maryland House of Delegates and later the Maryland Senate. He served in the Senate until he was appointed as circuit court judge for the Second Judicial Circuit of Maryland, which included Kent, Cecil, Queen Anne's, Caroline, and Talbot Counties. He served as attorney for the town of Rock Hall for 33 years and the town of Betterton for 27 years. (Courtesy of E.G. Boyer.)

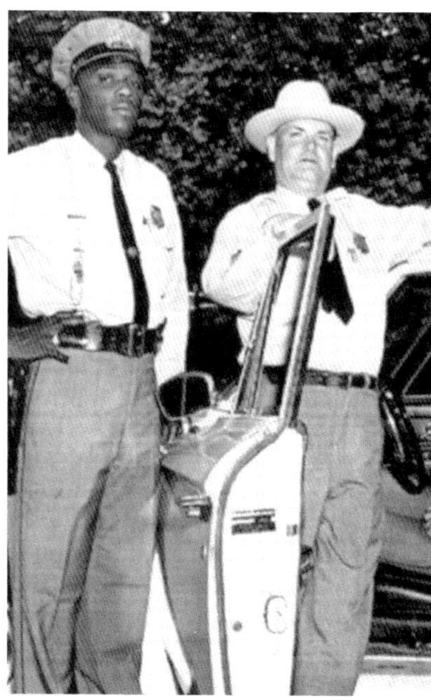

### Howard B. Hadaway

"Babe" (right), pictured here with Chestertown police officer Rudolph Brown, began working for the town of Chestertown in 1945 as a special police officer on weekends. He was appointed assistant chief of police in 1946 and became Chestertown's police chief that same year. Hadaway was chief for 25 years before being appointed Chestertown's supervisor of streets. He worked under four mayors for a total of 39 years. (Courtesy of the Historical Society of Kent County.)

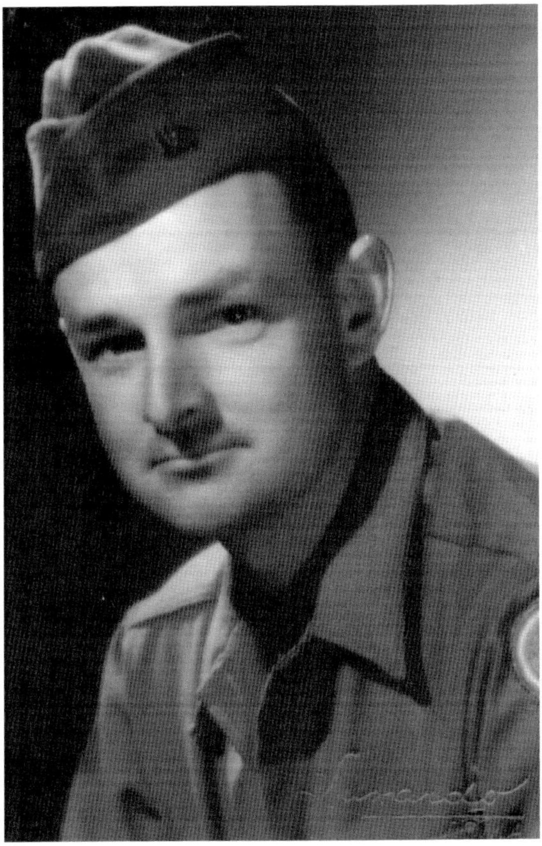

**Alexander Parks Rasin Jr.**
Lifetime Chestertown resident Rasin was a prominent attorney, political leader, and banker admired for his guidance, influence, leadership, and humility. After returning from service in World War II, he practiced law in Chestertown for the rest of his life, during which he also served as state's attorney, president of the Peoples Bank, and chair of the Republican State Central Committee. (Courtesy of Martha F. Rasin.)

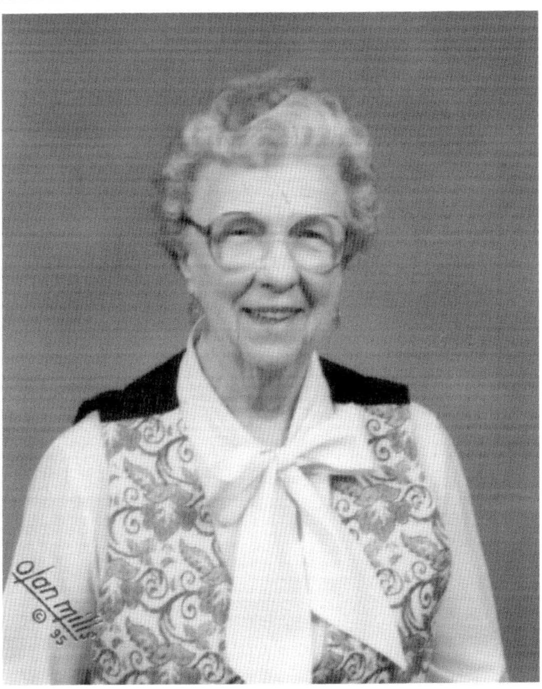


**Margaret E. Mulford**
Both Margaret E. Mulford and her mother, Annie Thornley Mulford, served as postmasters at the Galena Post Office. Margaret began her career assisting her mother as a postal clerk from 1931 to 1945. In 1945, she was appointed postmaster, succeeding her mother. She retired from the US Postal Service after 41 years of service. Margaret was a lifetime resident of Galena. (Courtesy of Joanne G. Mulford.)

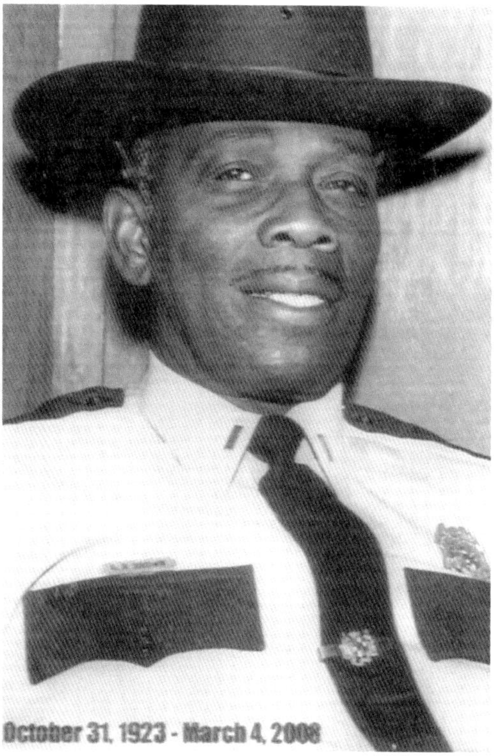


**Lt. Rudolph Brown**

Brown was the first African American to serve on a Kent County police force. He was honored by the town of Chestertown after serving for 21 years, retiring as a lieutenant. Brown was also a Kent County Public School bus contractor for many years and active in the Asbury United Methodist Church near his home in Georgetown, Kent County. (Courtesy of Dorothy Brown.)

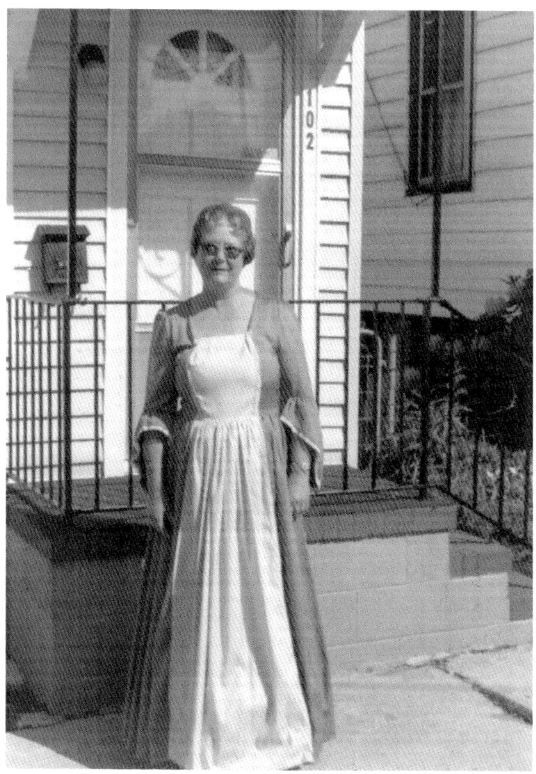

**Jane Burris Neal**

The first woman elected to serve as a Chestertown councilperson, Jane Burris Neal was known for devoting much of her time as a volunteer. She held many offices as a member of the First United Methodist Church in Chestertown and was involved for many years with the Frank M. Jarman American Legion Post No. 36 Auxiliary also in Chestertown. Neal especially enjoyed her work as a hospice volunteer for many years. (Courtesy of Elmer E. Horsey.)

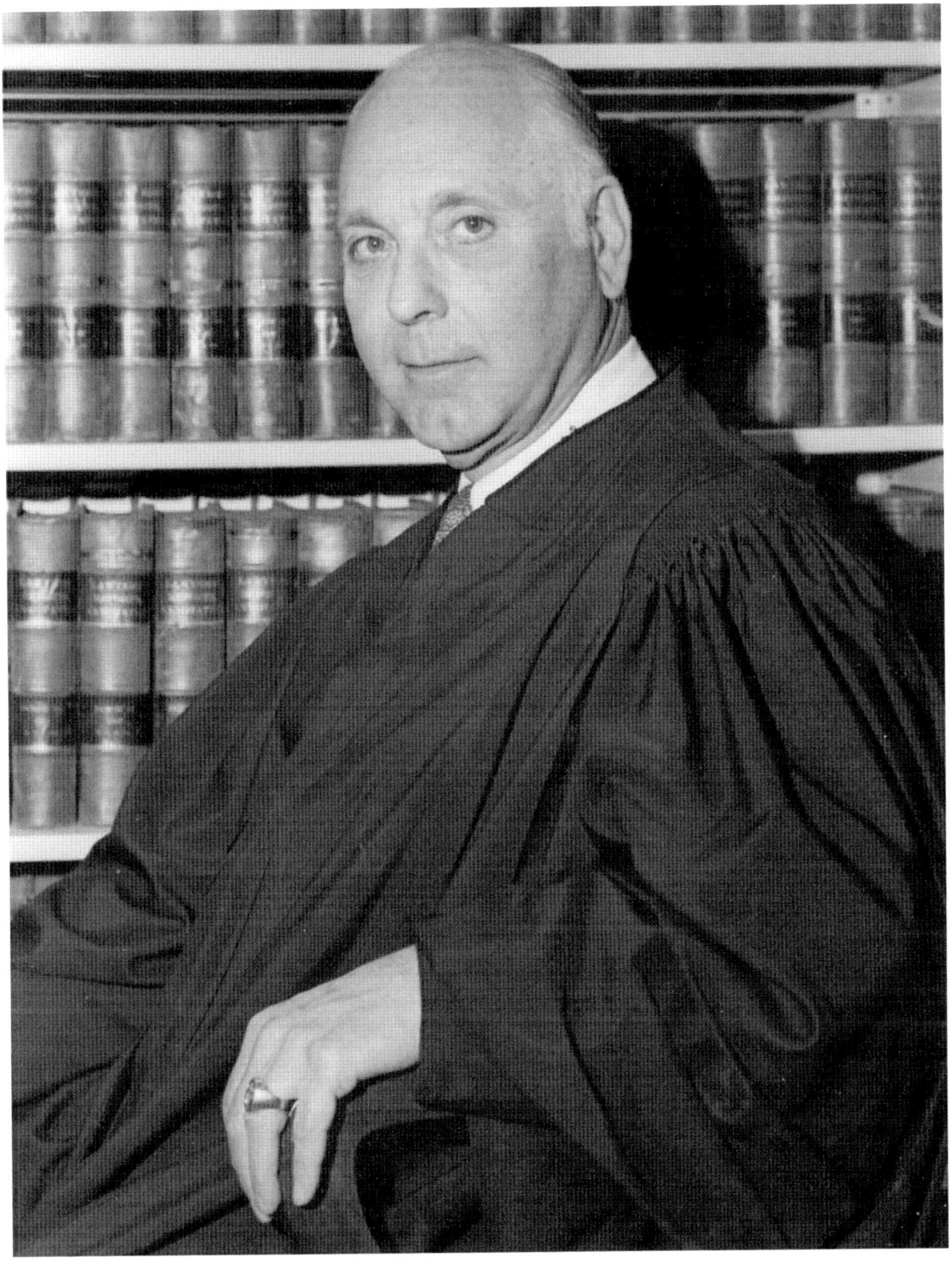

**The Honorable George B. Rasin Jr.**
Rasin led a movement to modernize juvenile justice in Maryland. He was a circuit-court judge for Kent County and became chief judge and administrative judge of the Second Circuit. He served as a member of the Board of Visitors and Governors of Washington College. While in the Army, he was assigned as a special agent to the Counter-Intelligence Corps in the Division of Military Intelligence. He joined the US foreign-aid program and was a security officer in Paris. He retired from the bench in 1987 and served as a settlement judge for the Second Circuit until 2006. Judge Rasin also held national juvenile-justice posts and was a member of the National Council of the Juvenile Court Judges' executive committee. (Courtesy of Gale E. Rasin.)

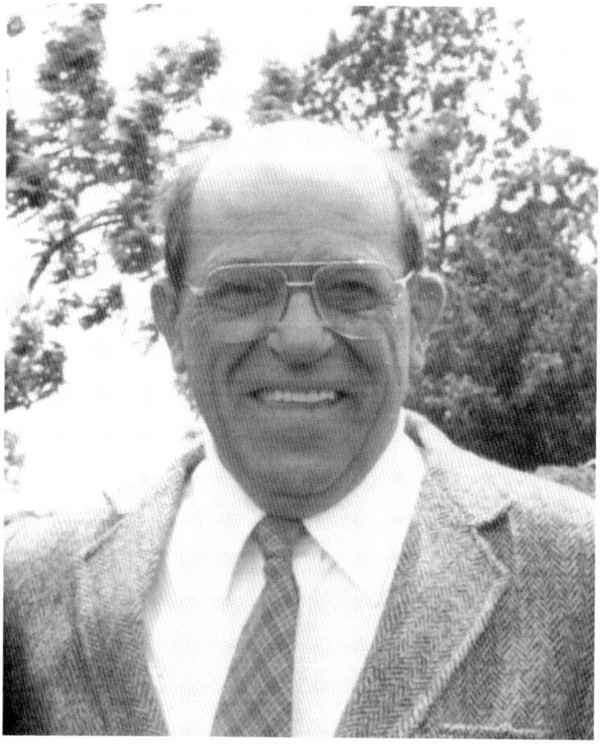

## Samuel F. Sessa

Sam Sessa of Galena was a Kent County businessman interested in serving his community. He was president of the Kent County Parks and Recreation Board, president of the Kent County Board of Zoning Appeals, and president of Kent County Election Supervisors. He was part owner and operator of Valley Green Farms in Chesterville and served in the US Air Force during the Korean War as a flight engineer. (Courtesy of Phyllis Sessa.)

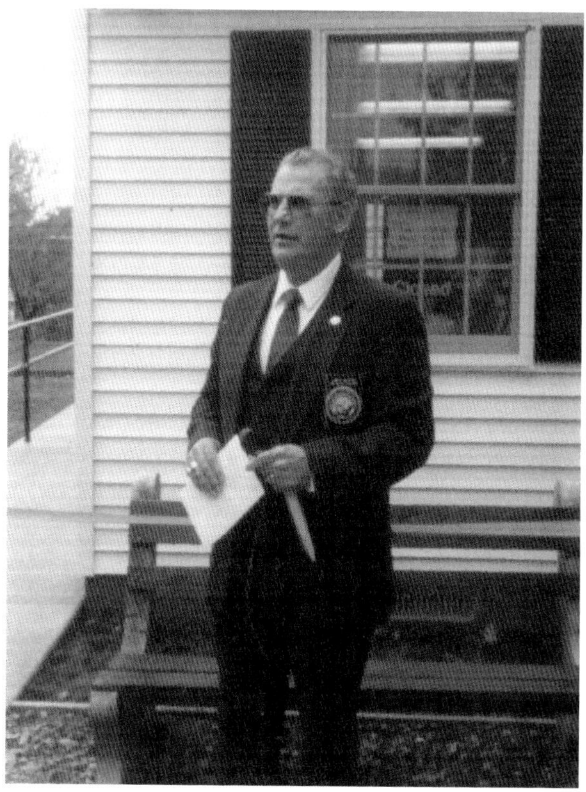

## John R. Mulford Sr.

John R. "Johnny" Mulford originated and developed the town seal for Galena. He served on the Galena Town Council first as a councilman and then as mayor for a number of years. A lifetime resident of Galena, Johnny owned and operated the John R. Mulford and Son Contracting Company for 20 years. He and his wife, Joanne, were legendary for their extraordinary Christmas decorations. (Courtesy of Joanne G. Mulford.)

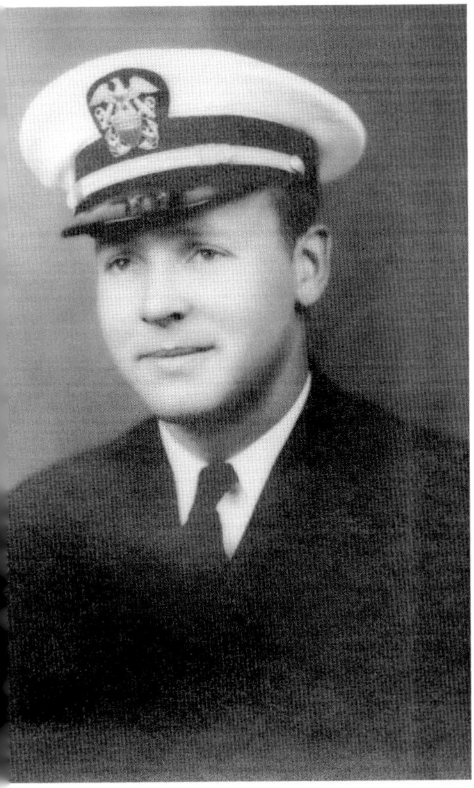

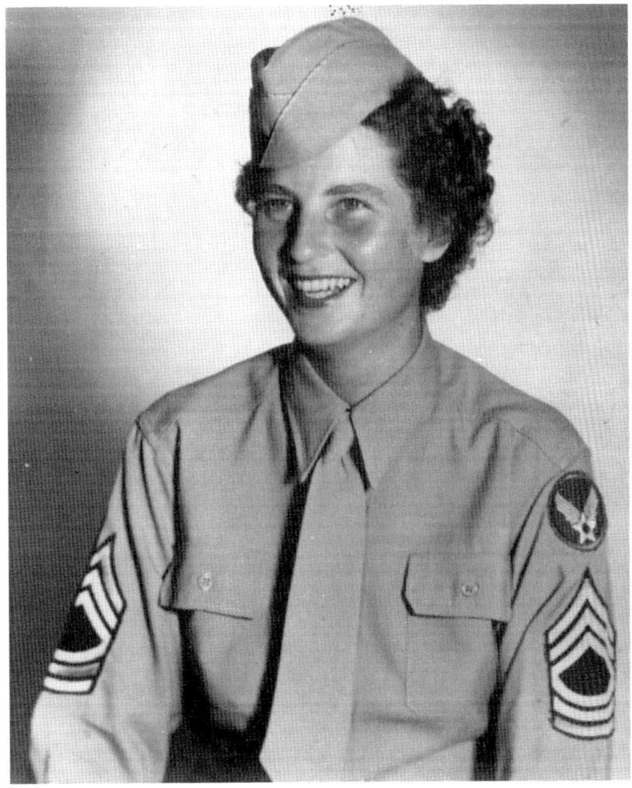

**Philip Medford Brooks Jr. and Josephine Redman Brooks**
Chestertown's mayor and council named the present fire company building, the P.M. Brooks Jr. Building, in honor of Brooks' (left) longtime service with the Chestertown Volunteer Fire Company. He served as mayor of Chestertown for 10 years and was a third-generation grain dealer in Chestertown. He also served with the US Navy in the South Pacific. His wife, Josephine Redman Brooks (right), was a veteran of World War II, having served in the Women's Army Corps. She was active in the local Girl Scouts and involved with the Auxiliary of the Chestertown Volunteer Fire Company. (Both, courtesy of Patricia Brooks.)

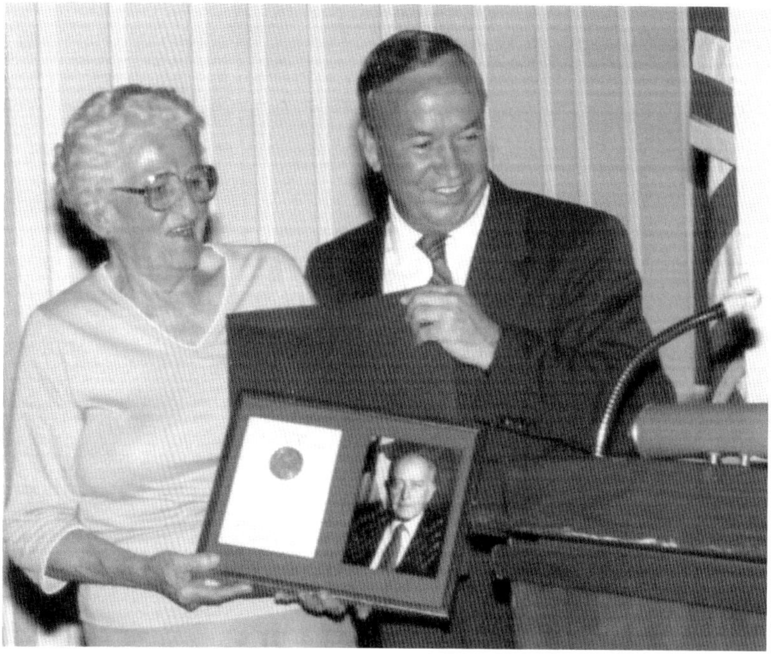

**Kathryn Bringman Ozman**
Appointed the first Maryland District Court commissioner for Kent County in 1971, "Miss Kitty" held the position over 25 years. She is shown receiving recognition from Maryland secretary of state Winfield Kelly on behalf Maryland's governor. The Kent County Commissioners and the Town of Chestertown also recognized her integrity, dedication, and commitment. She and her husband, James T. Ozman, also owned Ozman's Inc. automobile sales and repair in Chestertown for over 25 years. (Author's collection.)

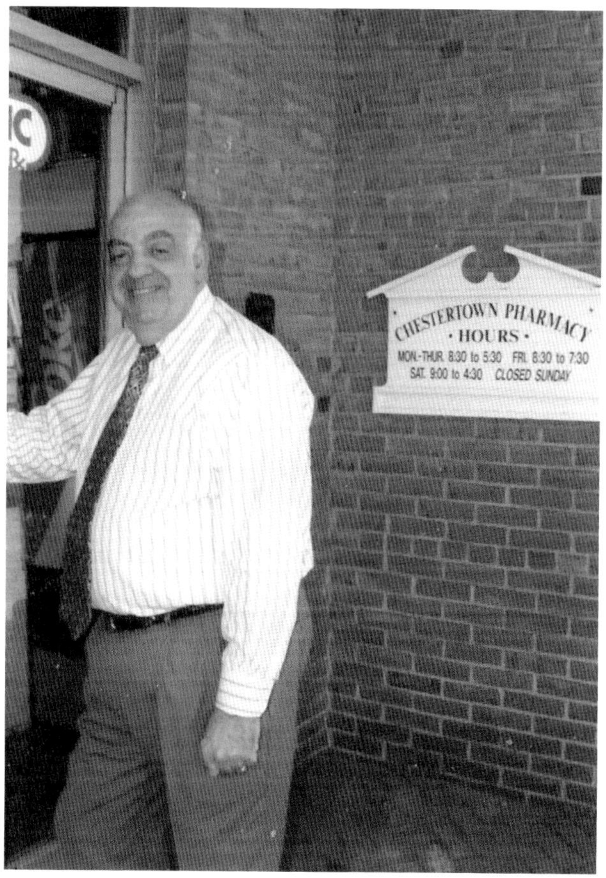


**Vito Tinelli Jr.**
Following graduation from the University of Maryland School of Pharmacy in 1960, "Doc" joined his brother-in-law Alphonse Poklis as a pharmacist at the Chestertown Pharmacy in downtown Chestertown. Doc owned and operated the Chestertown Pharmacy for almost five decades. He served four terms as a Chestertown town councilman from the Fourth Ward. (Courtesy of Shirley Tinelli.)

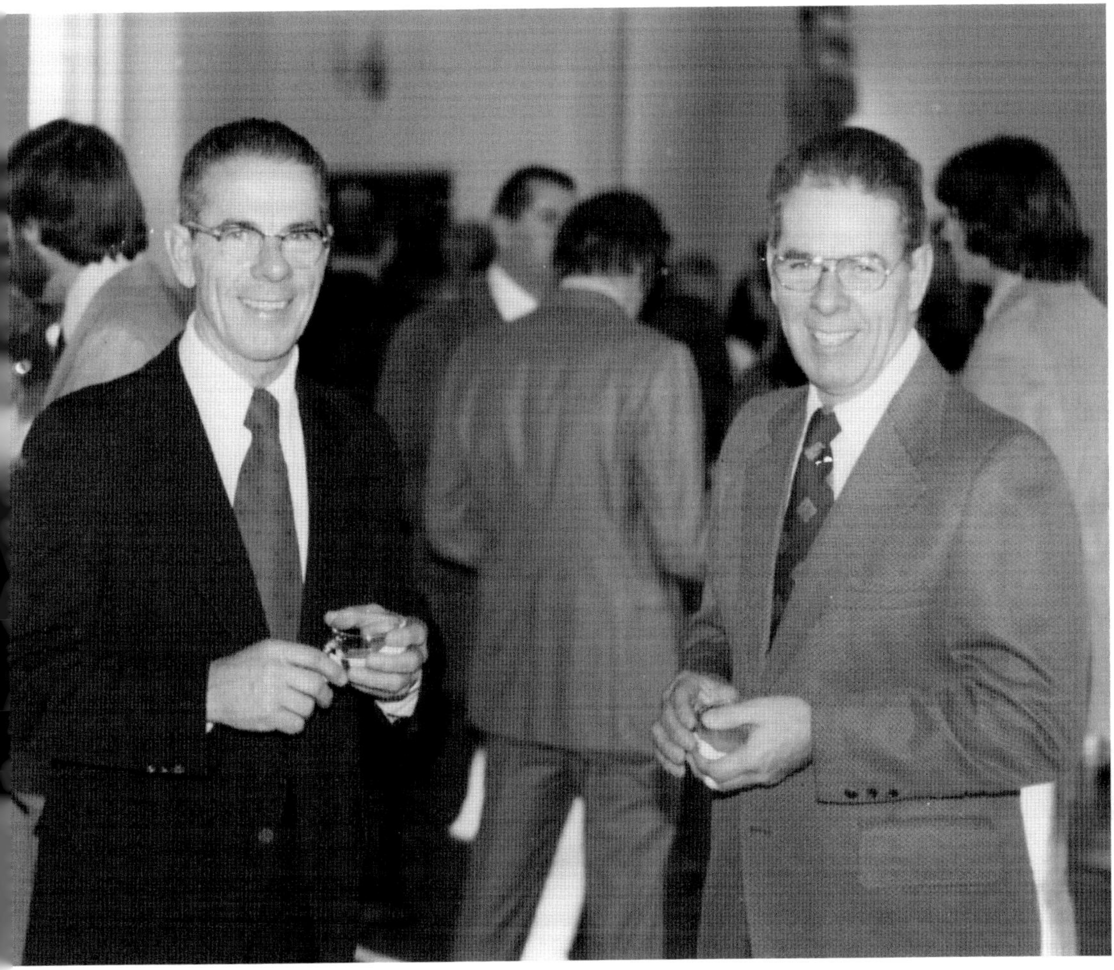

**Strong Brothers**

Twins Bobby (left) and Joe Strong (right) were the first set of twins to sign up in 1942 in the Class V-5 cadet group at the Pensacola Naval Station. They were assigned to submarine patrol duty on the Atlantic coast of the United States.

Joseph Wilbur Strong Sr. of Chestertown served in the US Navy as a pilot during World War II. Following the war, he owned and operated C.W. Kibler and Sons Inc. in Chestertown, a business dealing in grain, fertilizer, lime, seed, and coal. He also owned and operated Kibler's Marina from 1959 until 1995 and the Old Wharf Inn both on Chestertown's waterfront from 1975 until 1985. He retired in 1995. He served as a Kent County commissioner and was a member of the board of directors of Chesapeake Bank and Trust.

Robert H. Strong Sr. of Rock Hall served in the US Navy as a pilot during World War II. Following the war, he owned and operated a produce-distribution company before purchasing the Rock Hall Lumber Company in 1954, Chestertown Lumber Company in 1964, and Kent Island Lumber Company in 1975. In 1961, he purchased Overton farm in Eastern Neck, just outside of Rock Hall, where he raised his family. In 1978, he moved to Trumpington Manor farm, also in Eastern Neck, where he continued farming and managing various hunting clubs. Following his service as chairman of the board of the Maryland National Bank he was elected to serve as chairman of the board for the Chesapeake Bank and Trust. He was an accomplished sailor, winning many races in his Thistle, the *Gail C.* (Courtesy of Mildred Willson Strong.)

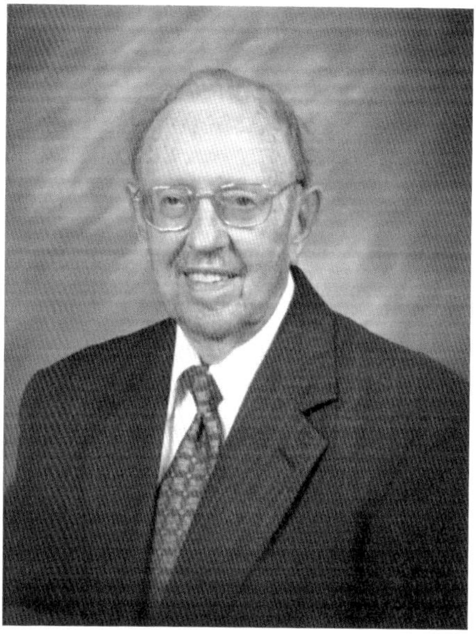

**William Briscoe**
"Bill" served as councilman for Galena for 18 years and then as mayor of Galena for 12 years. He was a life member of the Galena Volunteer Fire Company where he served as president. He was a World War II Army veteran serving in the European theatre with the 109th Infantry, 20th Division. He was a farmer and also worked for Woodall & Stidham, which he later bought and operated. (Courtesy of Robin Flaherty.)

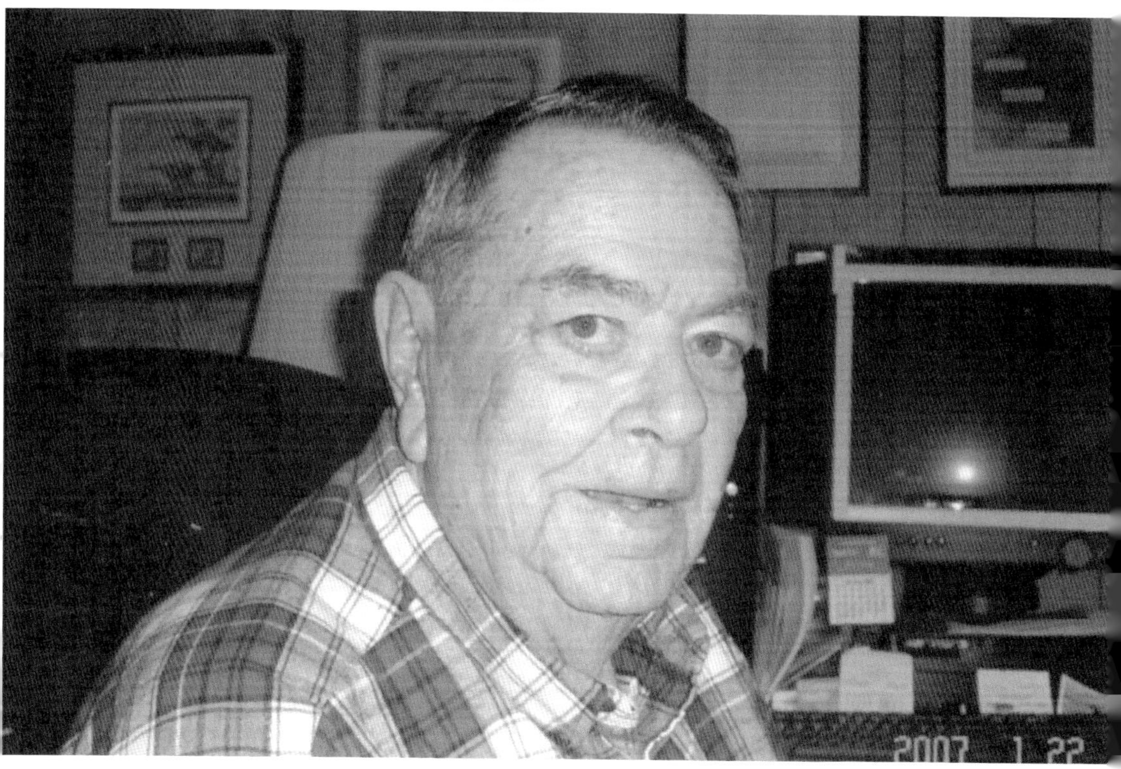


**Medford Capel**
A lifelong Chestertown resident, "Med" began working for the Town of Chestertown in 1950 and retired as superintendent of the Chestertown Utilities Commission after serving 53 years. His expertise guided the town through major lagoon improvements and extension of water and sewer lines to newly annexed areas. The Chestertown lagoon was named Capel Lagoon in his honor. He also served as the chairman of the Kent County Sanitary Commission for several years. (Courtesy of Medford Capel.)

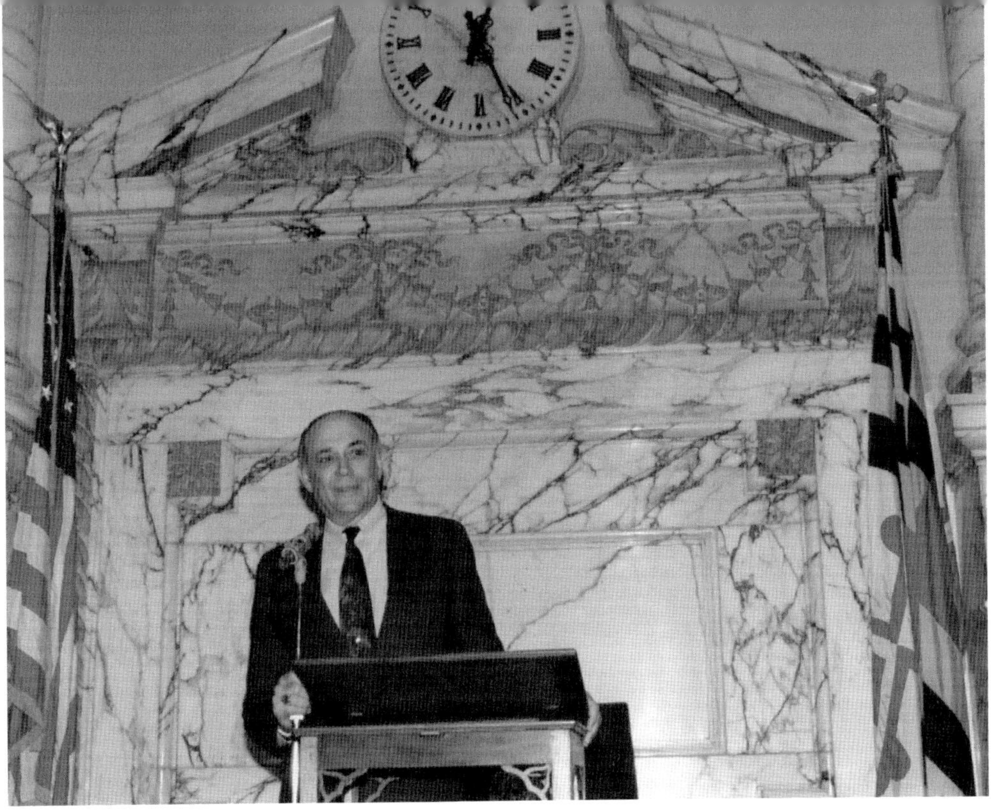

**R. Clayton Mitchell Jr.**
Mitchell was the only Kent Countian as of this writing to ever serve as Speaker of the House for Maryland. Kent Countians honored this achievement by naming the county office building the R. Clayton Mitchell Jr. Kent County Government Center. Mitchell served in the Maryland House of Delegates from 1971 to 1992 and as Speaker of the House from 1987 to 1992. (Courtesy of R. Clayton Mitchell Jr.)

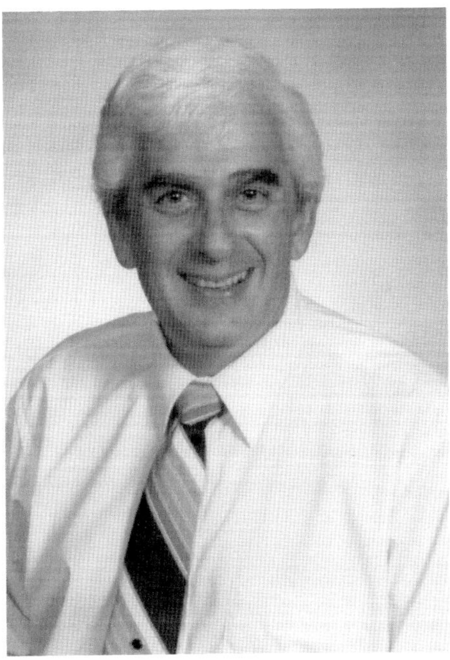

**Harry Pisapia**
Pisapia was the mayor of Galena for 21 years and the longest-serving mayor in Galena's history. He also serves the community as a formidable referee for soccer and other sports games. He was the official announcer for Kent County High School football games for 20 years and elected a member of the Kent County Athletic Hall of Fame. (Courtesy of Harry Pisapia.)

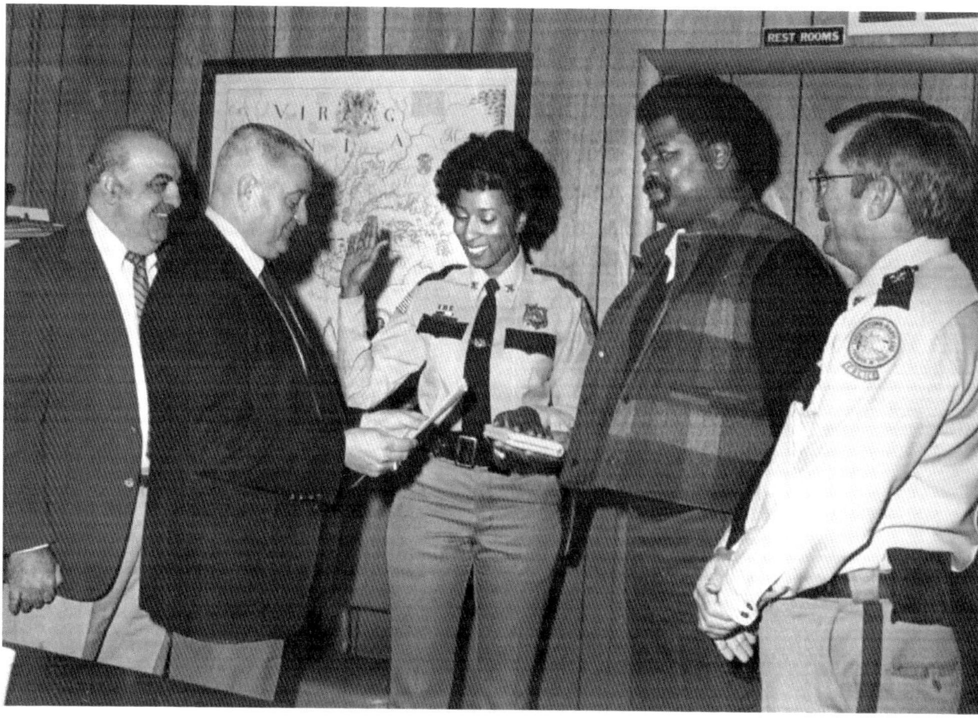


**Marcellene Beck**

The first female police officer in Chestertown and the first female African American police officer in Chestertown and Kent County was Marcellene Beck of Chestertown. She served 13 years with the town of Chestertown and then worked as a deputy sheriff with Kent County for a combined service of 34 years. Pictured here are, from left to right, Chestertown councilman Vito Tinelli, Mayor Elmer Horsey, Beck, Asbury Hunley, and Chief John Warren. (Courtesy of Marcellene Beck.)

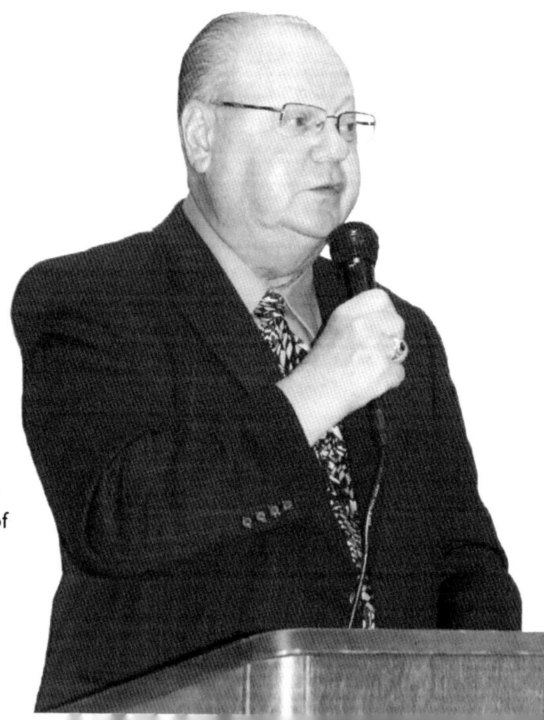

**Thomas Edward Robinson**

Both father and son served as Millington town officials. Thomas Edward "Ed" Robinson served as president of the Millington Town Council before becoming Millington's first elected mayor, a position he held for over 20 years, and his father, William Noland Robinson, also served the town of Millington as president of the town council. Ed served as the president of the Maryland Municipal League and as Kent County administrator. (Courtesy of T. Edward Robinson.)

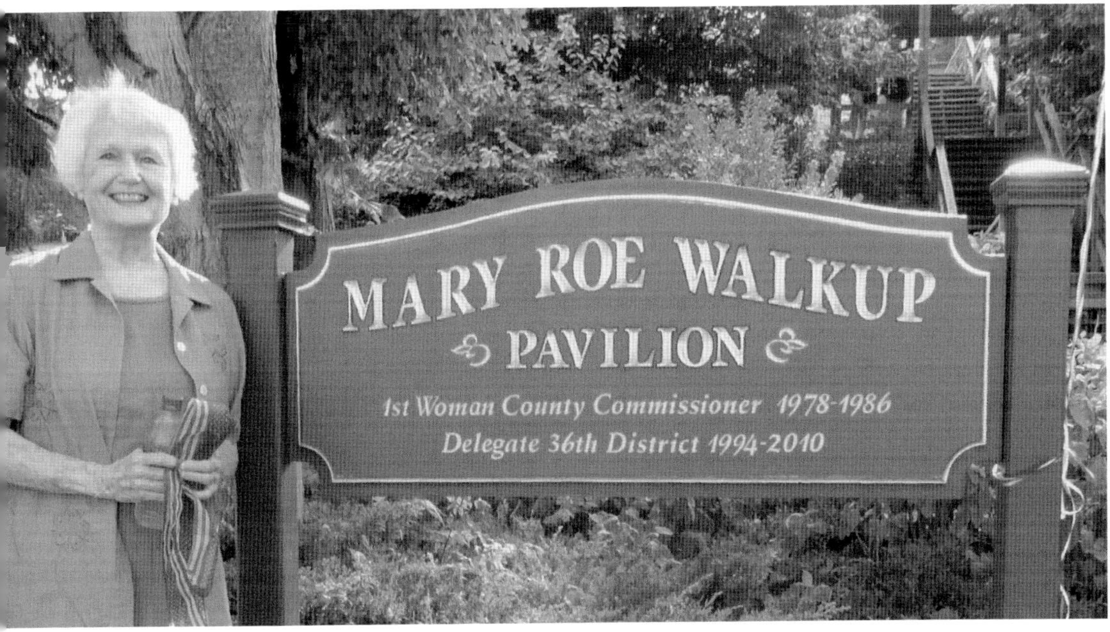


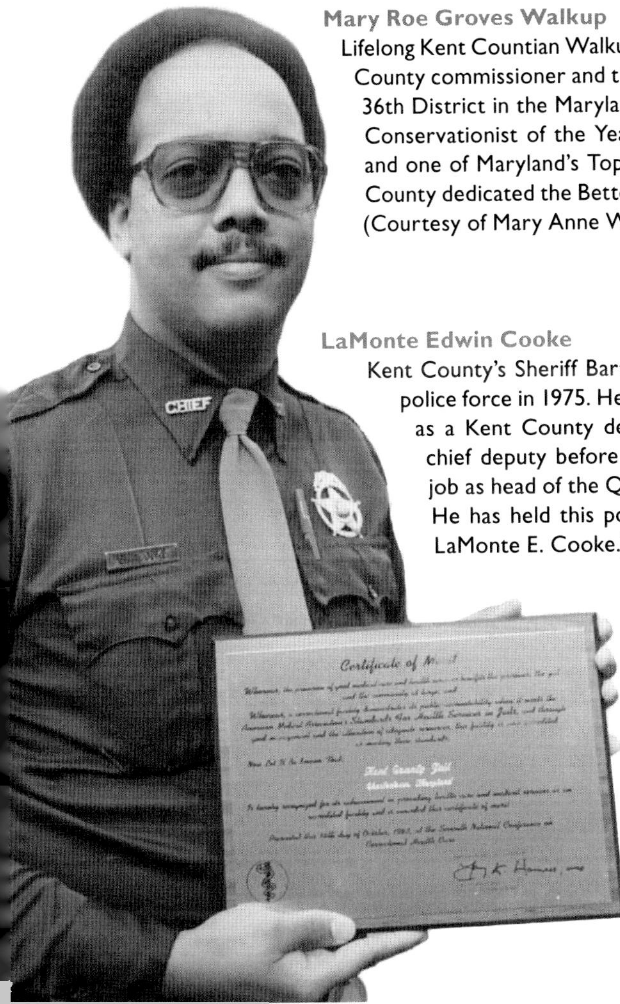

**Mary Roe Groves Walkup**

Lifelong Kent Countian Walkup was the first woman elected as a Kent County commissioner and the first woman elected to represent the 36th District in the Maryland House of Delegates. She was named Conservationist of the Year by the Maryland Wildlife Federation and one of Maryland's Top 100 Women by the *Daily Record.* Kent County dedicated the Betterton Beach picnic pavilion in her honor. (Courtesy of Mary Anne Walkup.)

**LaMonte Edwin Cooke**

Kent County's Sheriff Bartus O. Vickers welcomed Cooke to his police force in 1975. He was the first African American to serve as a Kent County deputy sheriff. Cooke was promoted to chief deputy before leaving Kent's sheriff's office to take a job as head of the Queen Anne's County Detention Center. He has held this position for over 27 years. (Courtesy of LaMonte E. Cooke.)

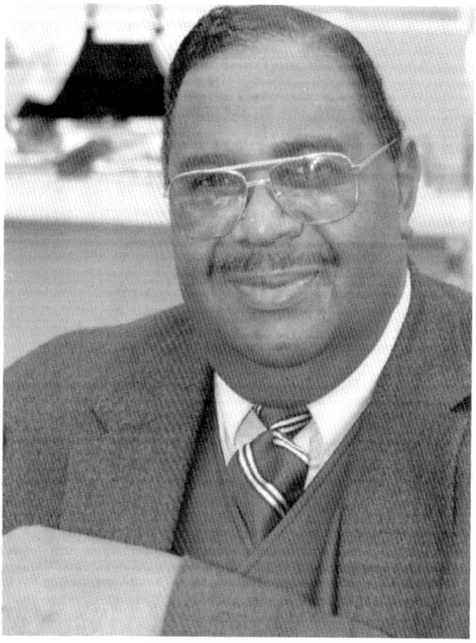

**Clarence Hawkins**

Hawkins was the first African American elected to serve as a Kent County commissioner. He was a delegate to the Democratic National Convention from Maryland in 1996 and a candidate for the Maryland House of Delegates, District 36, in 1998. Hawkins retired as a teacher and administrator in the Kent County Public Schools system. He earned his ministerial degree in the African American Episcopal Church. He is also an artist. (Courtesy of Clarence Hawkins.)

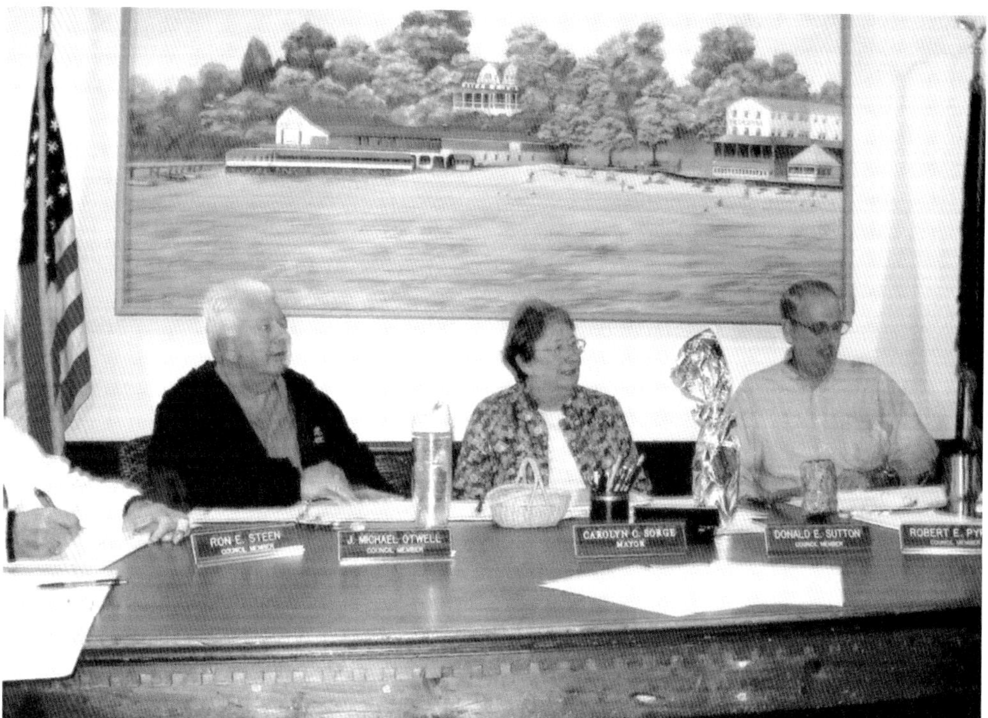


**Carolyn Clark Sorge**

Sorge guided the redevelopment of a historic church in Betterton to its present use as a community center, town office, and Betterton Heritage Museum. "Candi" retired as mayor of Betterton in 2014 after 26 years as mayor and three years as a councilmember. Pictured here are Mayor Sorge (center), Councilman J. Michael Otwell (left), and Councilman Donald Sutton (now mayor). (Courtesy of John Sorge.)

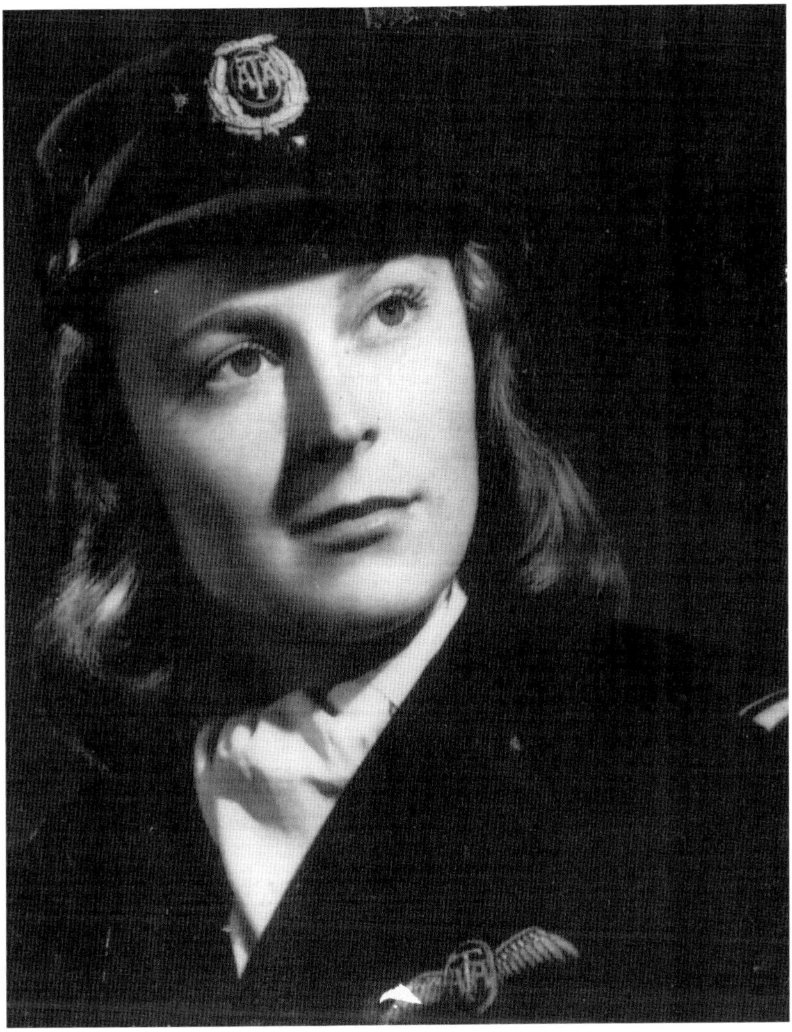

**Betty Lussier**

Lussier's family moved to a farm near Rock Hall when she was four years old. She studied journalism at Washington College in Chestertown and at the University of Maryland in College Park, where she learned to fly in a civilian pilot-training program. Lussier was still a college student when World War II broke out, and she went to England to help the British fight off an impending Nazi invasion. Armed with a private pilot's license, she joined the Air Transport Auxiliary and was soon ferrying planes and pilots for the Royal Air Force (RAF). After the Normandy invasion, when women pilots were barred from delivering planes to the combat zones on the continent, she complained to Sir William S. Stephenson, who was in the RAF with her father in World War I and headed British intelligence in the United States. He steered her to the newly formed American Office of Strategic Services, which was recruiting field agents. She worked with a special liaison unit in Algeria, Sicily, Italy, and France, helping to set up a chain of double agents and transmit misinformation to the enemy. After the war, she set up income-generating projects for women in Africa and elsewhere. Lussier has authored two books: *Amid My Alien Corn,* written in 1957, a story of Lussier's struggle against many odds to produce a successful corn crop and demonstrate to the natives of Spanish Morocco a way of improving both their food supply and their ancient ways of life, and *Intrepid Woman*, written in 2010, a memoir of her wartime experiences in England. (Courtesy of Betty Lussier and Joan Strong Elburn.)

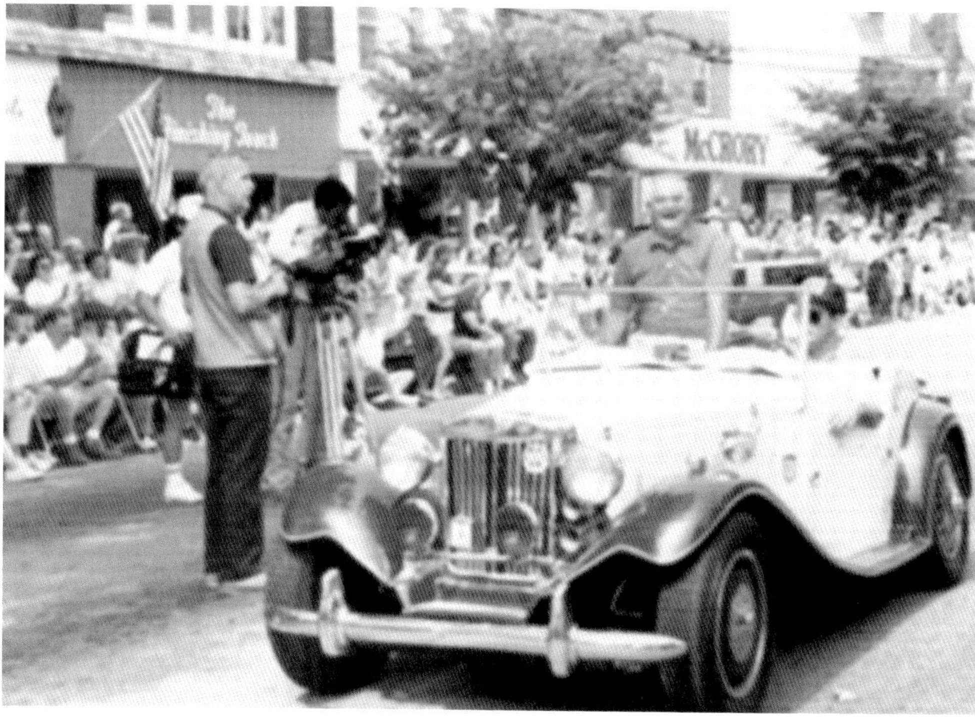


**Elmer Edward Horsey**
Known as "Chief" to his family and friends, he served as Chestertown's mayor for 16 years. Horsey and his council made significant improvements to Chestertown that served as the foundation for the town's modernization, including downtown brick sidewalks, public housing, the development of two industrial parks, and annexations. He has been active on a number of Kent County and State of Maryland boards and commissions. (Courtesy of the Horsey family.)

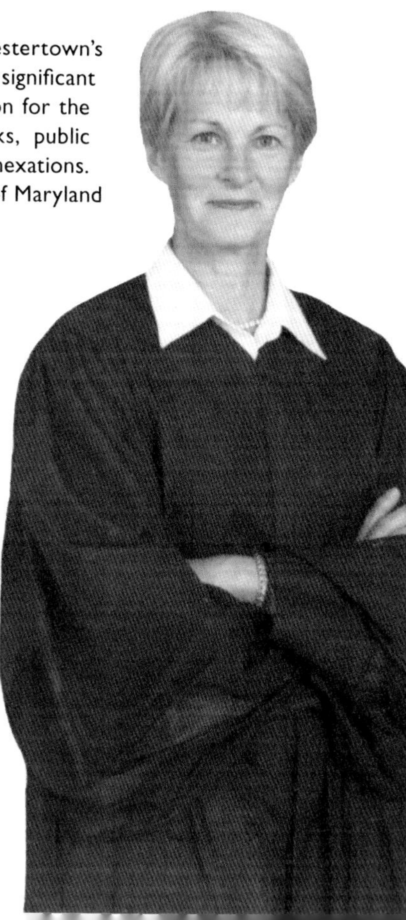

**The Honorable Martha Frisby Rasin**
Born and raised in Chestertown, Rasin made law her career. As a judge on the District Court of Maryland, she was known to be patient and even-tempered. Appointed chief judge of the District Court of Maryland, she became the first woman in Maryland to hold one of the state's three top judicial posts. She oversaw many District Court improvements, and led the expansion of protection for victims of domestic violence. (Courtesy of Martha F. Rasin.)

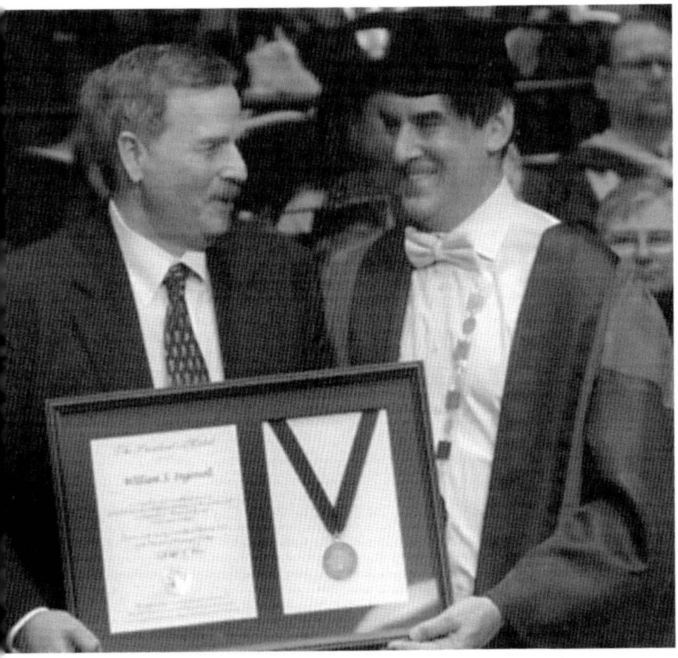

**William Stevens Ingersoll** Born in Chestertown, Ingersoll began working for the town of Chestertown in 1975, first serving as a grants administrator, later adding zoning administrator, and ultimately becoming town manager in 1984. He was awarded the President's Medal by Washington College for his exemplary public service record in 2013. Still on the job in 2015, he has worked with four different mayors. Pictured here are Ingersoll (left) and Washington College president Mitchell B. Reiss. (Courtesy of Washington College.)

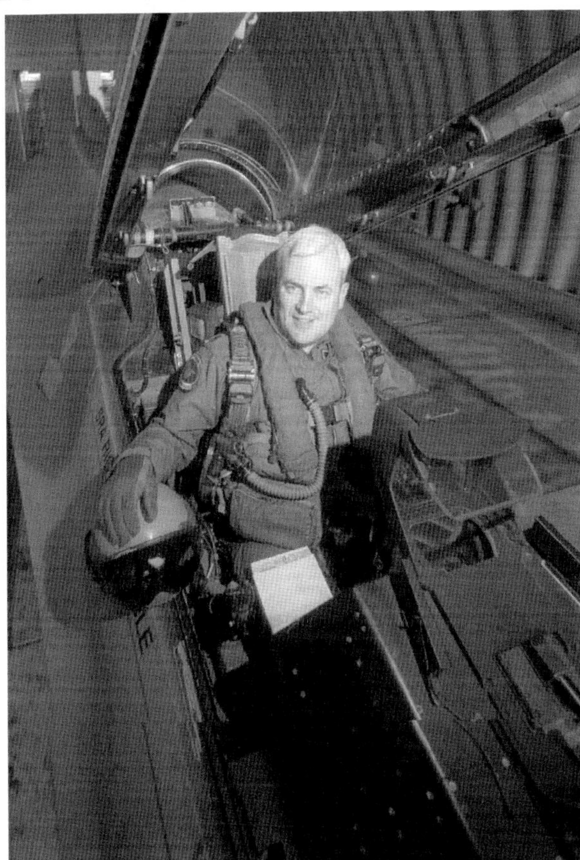

**Lt. Gen. Robert Richard Dierker** A graduate of the US Air Force Academy, Dierker of Chestertown served in the US Air Force in operational and staff positions in the United States, Southeast Asia, Northeast Asia, and Europe and commanded a fighter group and a fighter wing. He was a command pilot and master parachutist. His last tour of duty was as deputy commander, US Pacific Command, Camp H.M. Smith, Hawaii. (Courtesy of 51 Fighter Wing Photo Lab, Osan Air Base, Korea.)

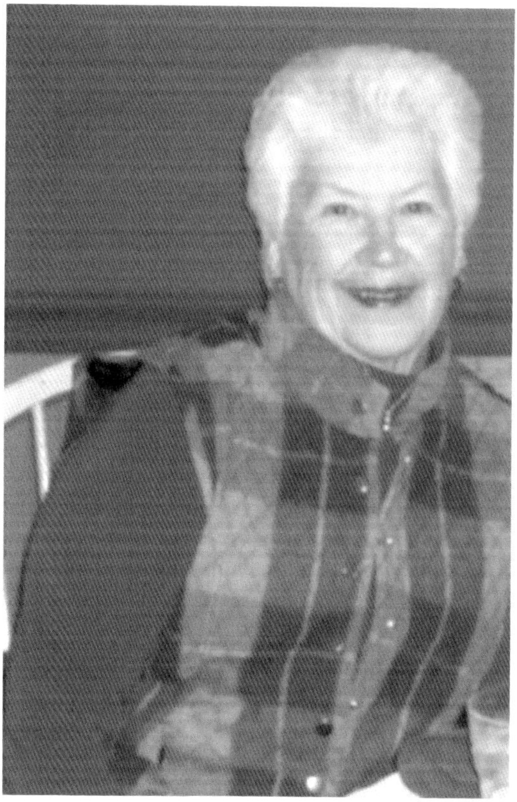

**Rosalie Brady Kuechler**

Kuechler was the first woman to be elected to the Rock Hall Council and the first woman to be elected mayor of Rock Hall. Kuechler spent 30 years as an elected official in Rock Hall. She also served as the president of the Maryland Municipal League. She has been an active volunteer in Rock Hall and Kent County for many years. (Courtesy of Rosalie B. Kuechler.)

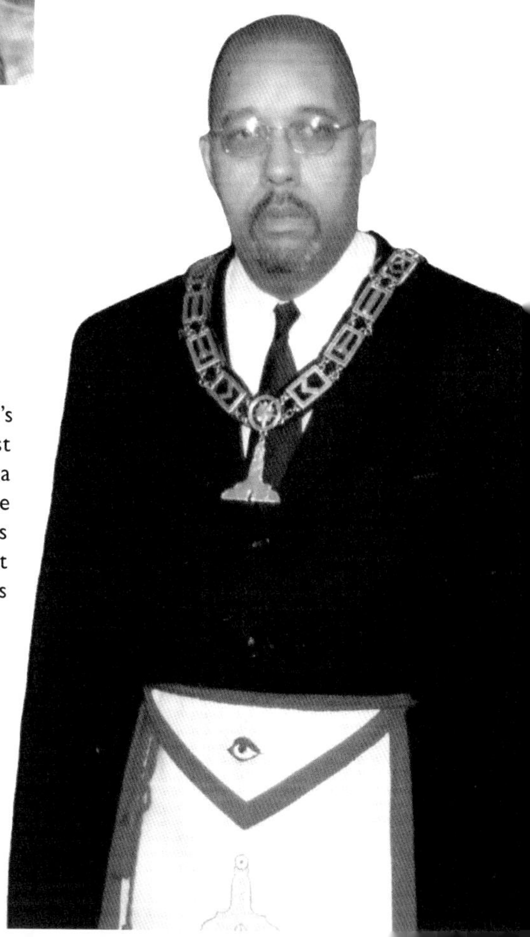

**Thomas Gross**

The first time he ran for a position on Chestertown's town council, "Thom" ran in Ward Two and lost by one vote. Two years later, after the town did a redistricting of the wards, he ran in Ward Three and won a seat as councilperson for Chestertown's Third Ward by a two-to-one margin. He was the first African American to be elected to Chestertown's governing body. (Courtesy of Thomas Gross.)

# CHAPTER TWO

# Talent

Kent County has talent. Artists, musicians, writers, decoy carvers, photographers, and athletes all enrich Kent County's quality of life.

The county has produced artists such as Emma Kipling Hess Ingersoll, who was considered one of the top 10 miniature painters in the country, and Gretchen Wood Call, who helped found the Chestertown Arts League. Kent County musicians include Sylvia Frazier, gospel-music producer and promoter; Randolph Waddell "Jazz" Johnson, who played music throughout his entire life; Rick Larrimore and his interpretation of Rod Stewart; Sue Dunning Matthews, jazz vocalist and favorite local performer; Karen Somerville, who can sing soprano, alto, tenor, or bass; Tom McHugh, who sings, plays the banjo, blues harp, Native American flute and the kazoo; and Marlon Saunders, who sang an Academy Award–nominated song live at the 80th Annual Academy Awards.

Kent County writer Gilbert Byron was often called the "voice of the Chesapeake"; James M. Cain wrote crime novels that inspired highly successful movies; Frank Ruth was often referred to as the poet laureate of Kent County; and Julia Elma Clark spent 67 years as a farmer's wife writing short stories and poetry about her family, land, animals, friends, and the community and later compiled them into eight booklets.

Kent County decoy carver Charles "Speed" Joiner has fashioned the majority of species in the Chesapeake Bay. Other artisans include father and son carvers William and Allan Schauber, and Jesse Urie, who made ducks for Pres. Lyndon B. Johnson, Arthur Godfrey, and Jack Schroeder, two-time winner of the Maryland duck-stamp contest.

Kent County photographer Heather Davidson's photographs and articles have appeared in over 50 different magazines and books.

Kent County athletes include Stanley B. "Jerry" Giraitis, who scored five field goals in 59 seconds while playing basketball, catching the attention of Ripley's Believe or Not, sisters and jousters Dottie LaPlaca and Peggy States-Edwards, Major League Baseball players William Beck "Swish" Nicholson and Ryan Orlando Thompson, and Olympic medal–winner Betsy Beard Stillings.

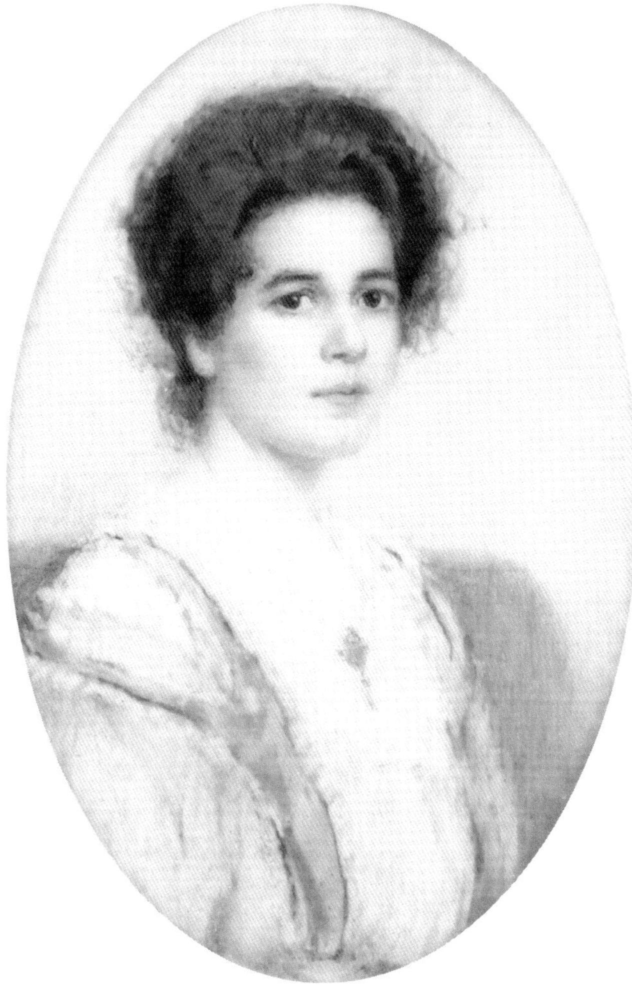

### Emma Kipling Hess Ingersoll

Emma Kipling Hess Ingersoll was born in Chicago in 1878 and trained at the School of the Art Institute of Chicago. At the 1904 Louisiana Purchase World's Fair in St. Louis, she was awarded a medal at the internationally juried art exhibition. Her exquisite miniatures (portraits painted in oil on thin slices of ivory) were sought by Chicago notables. Throughout her life, her work was exhibited in many venues, including the Corcoran Gallery in Washington, DC. In 1911, Emma Kipling Hess Ingersoll and her husband, Daniel Winthrop Ingersoll, moved by train to rural Kent County, where they bought land and built a house on a rise overlooking the Chester River and named it Silver Hill Farm. As novice farmers, Winthrop and Emma found it to be "damn hard work," but somehow in addition to all the chores of farm, home, husband, and children, Emma managed to eke out time for her art. Besides her much-beloved miniature portraits of family members, many miniatures were done on commission, some of people in Kent County, and many more for prominent Chicago families. The Chicago commissions were arranged by her agent in Chicago, and the miniatures were often painted with a single-haired brush. At the peak of her career, Emma was described as one of the top 10 miniature painters in the country. While at home in Kent County, Emma taught local artists and painted oils, pastels, and watercolors of local landscapes. These paintings show pastoral and water scenes of great peace and beauty, charmingly chronicling places and activities long past but with landscapes still discernible and sometimes barely changed, in the present day. (Courtesy of the Ingersoll family.)

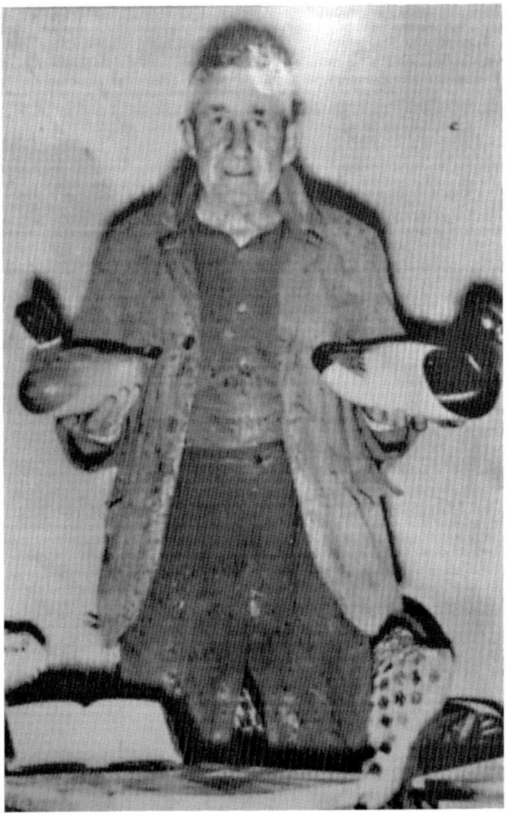

John B. Glen
A waterman and farmer most of his life, "Captain" Glen of Rock Hall is shown with a mallard duck (left) and canvasback duck (right) he carved. He started carving about 1916. All of his decoys were hand-chopped. It is said he designed silhouette goose decoys, the first ever used in the cornfields. He named his farm Decoy Farm. He also carved baldpate, black duck, goose, pintail, redhead, and scaup decoys. (Courtesy of Rock Hall Museum.)

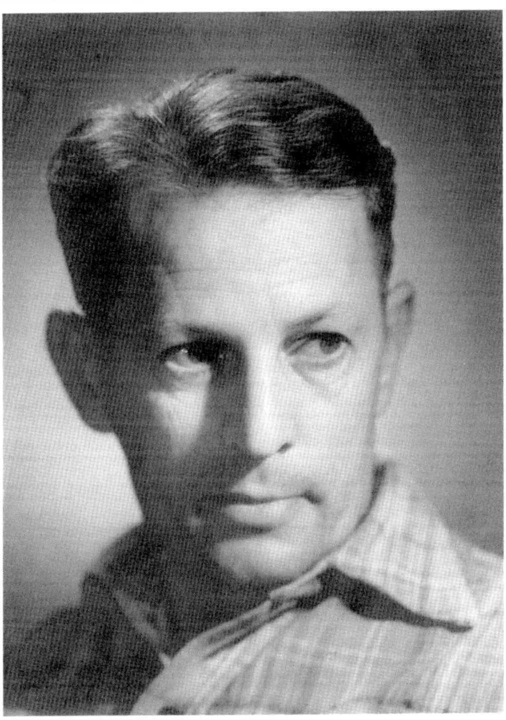

Gilbert Valliant Byron
He was often called the "Voice of the Chesapeake" and the "Chesapeake Thoreau." Byron, an American author, was born in Chestertown. He was best known for his poems, short stories, novels, historical research, and magazine and newspaper columns and articles detailing life on the Chesapeake Bay throughout the 20th century. During his lifetime, he published 14 books, over 70 short stories, and hundreds of poems and articles. (Courtesy of Jacques Baker.)

### Jesse Arthur Urie and Jesse Roger Urie

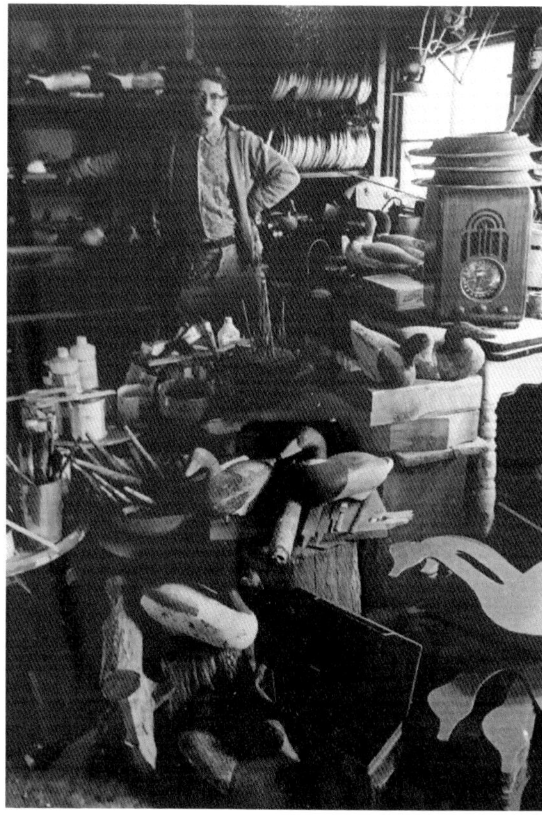

He was a duck decoy and miniature duck craftsman. "Capt." Jesse Urie, pictured on the right, a waterman from Rock Hall for many years, made ducks for Pres. Lyndon B. Johnson, entertainer Arthur Godfrey, and astronaut Walter M. Schirra Jr. Many of his decoys were sent to the Soviet Union and Australia. He also taught decoy-making to children. Urie's work has been displayed at many wildlife shows and was described in books such as *Gunning on the Chesapeake* and *Chesapeake Bay Decoys*. He served as president of the Chesapeake Bay Decoy Makers in Havre de Grace, Maryland. His son Jesse, pictured below, worked with his father as a decoy carver most of his life. He was born in Rock Hall, and hunting and fishing were his favorite pastimes. Jesse served in the US Army during the Korean War and was also president of the Chesapeake Bay Decoy Makers. (Right, courtesy of Rock Hall Museum; below, courtesy of William A. Schauber.)

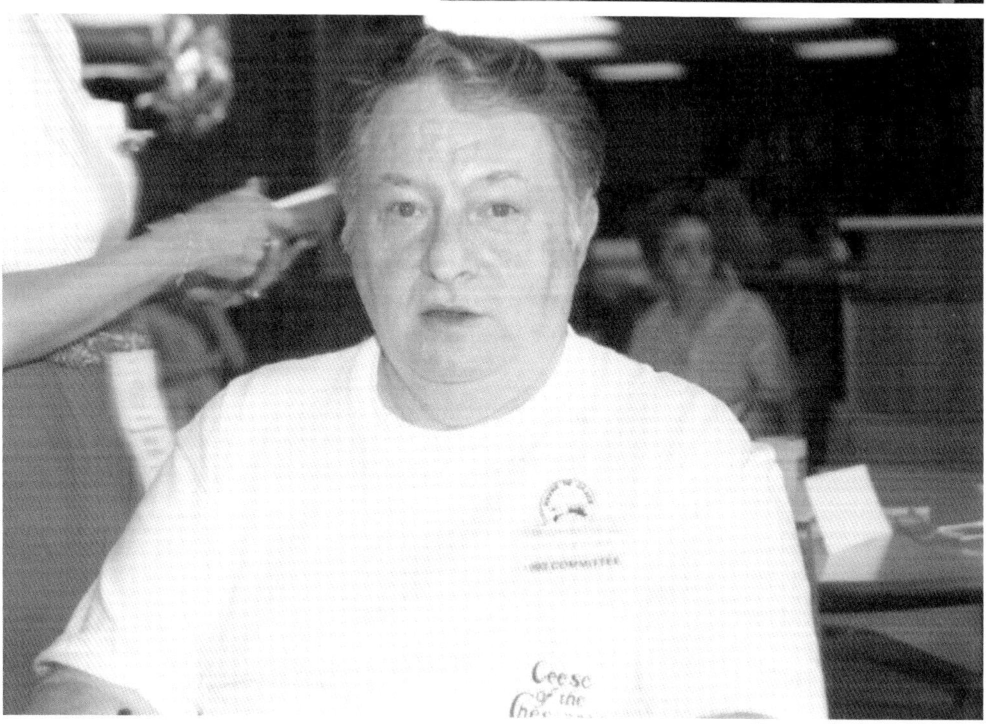

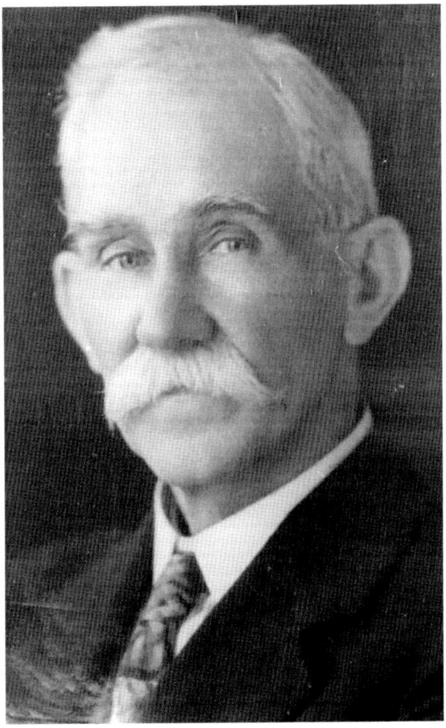

**Frank H. Ruth**
Often referred to as the poet laureate of Kent County, Frank Ruth of Galena contributed many poems of interest to the local newspaper throughout his lifetime. He was deemed one of Kent County's oldest citizens in 1948. He was also an expert with a pen and displayed many of his artistic drawings in his home. (Courtesy of the Historical Society of Kent County.)

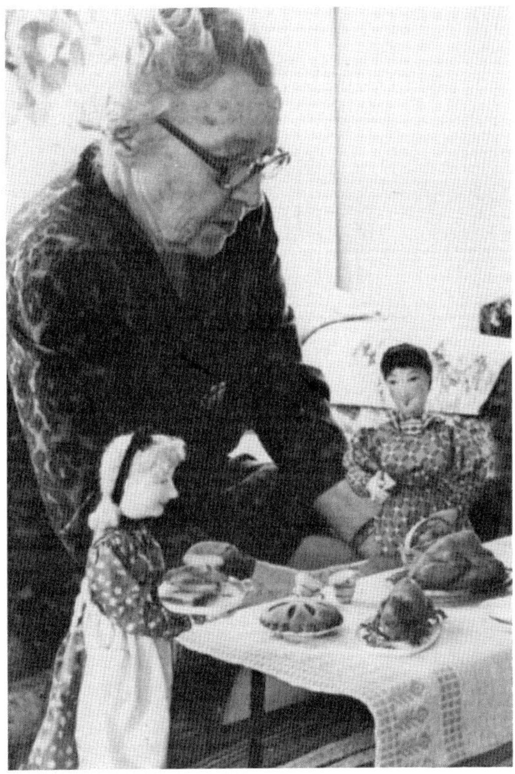

**Elizabeth Christian Stirling**
A Still Pond resident for many years, "Betty" constructed small figures and animals into storybooks. Her legendary and historical displays became popular when an exhibit representing fairy tale and historical characters was displayed by Baltimore's Enoch Pratt Library. She began creating her figures in the late 1940s and published a book about them called *Fact and Fantasy* in 1974. (Courtesy of the Historical Society of Kent County.)

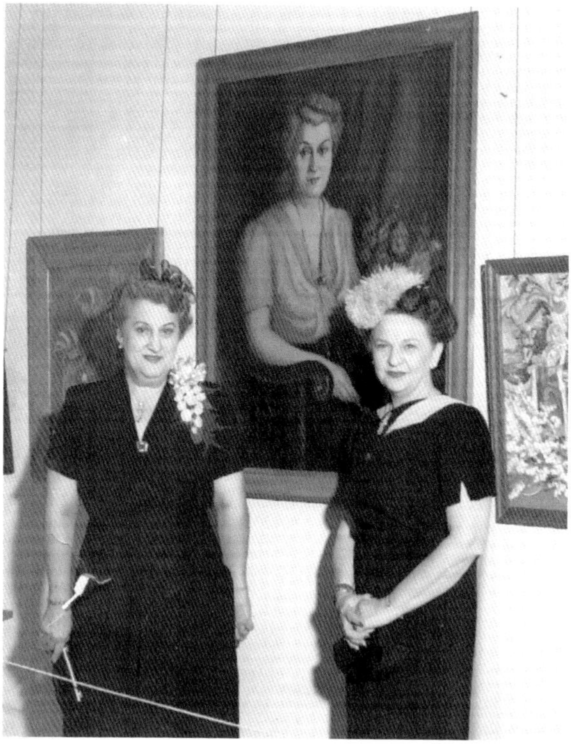

**Gretchen Wood Call**
Chestertown artist Call, pictured on the right with her unidentified subject, founded the Puerto Rico chapter of the American Artists Professional League and its Maryland Eastern Shore chapter and also helped found the Chestertown Arts League. The Chestertown Arts League held a reception in her honor at her home in 1984 to celebrate her 90th birthday and her art. More than 150 paintings were on display. (Courtesy of Trudy Kratzer Anderson.)

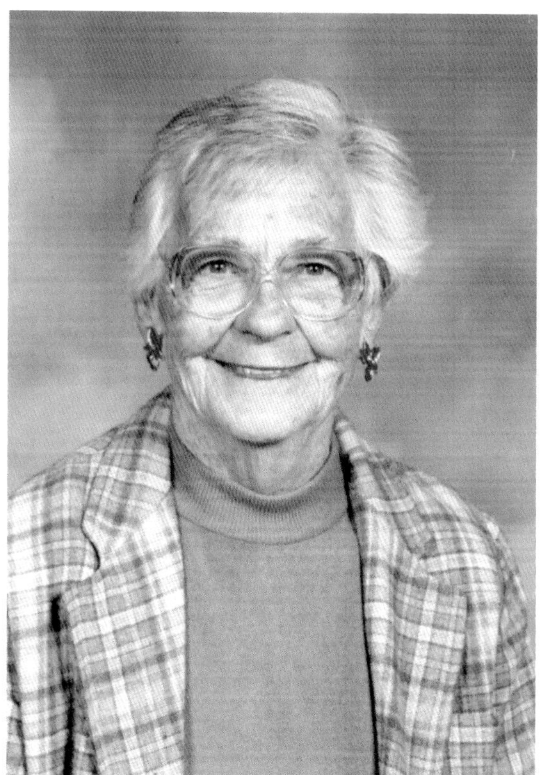

**Julia Elma Clark**
Clark spent 67 years as a farmer's wife, and she wrote short stories and poetry about her family, land, animals, friends, and the community and later compiled them into eight booklets. She was honored as the Kent County representative in the Why Maryland Is Beautiful to Me contest. She had an exceptional ability to recite her stories and poems from memory. (Courtesy of Tom Clark.)

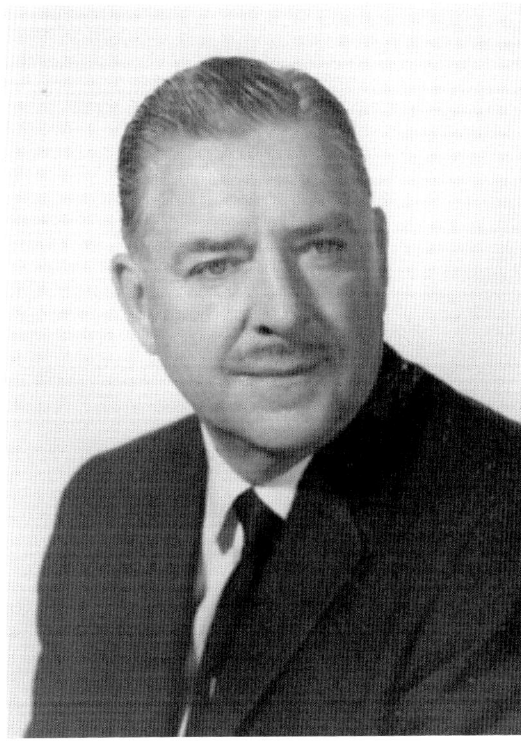

**Stanley Brennan Giraitis**
A first in basketball at Washington College was achieved by Giraitis of Chestertown. His feat of soaring five field goals in 59 seconds got nationwide attention when Robert L. Ripley featured the achievement in his *Believe It Or Not*. The *Baltimore Sun* selected him for its All Maryland basketball team for three successive years. "Jerry" was inducted into Washington College's Athletic Hall of Fame in 1982. (Courtesy of Kathryn Cumiskey Schaefer.)

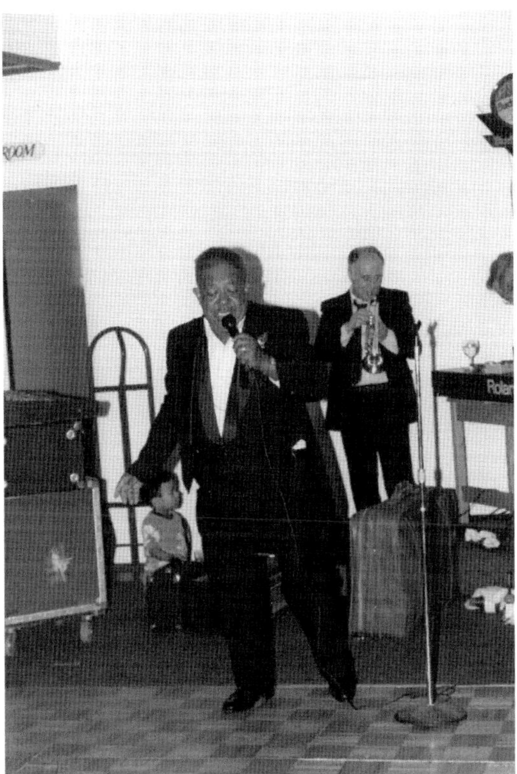

**Randolph Waddell Johnson**
Johnson was born in Kent County. He worked as a supervisor of maintenance at the Tri-State Mall in Delaware for 30 years. He began playing the horn when he was in high school and played music with his band throughout his life, earning the nickname "Jazz." He entertained at private parties, weddings, and local music venues. Jazz also worked diligently for Jane's Church in Chestertown. (Courtesy of Eloise Johnson.)

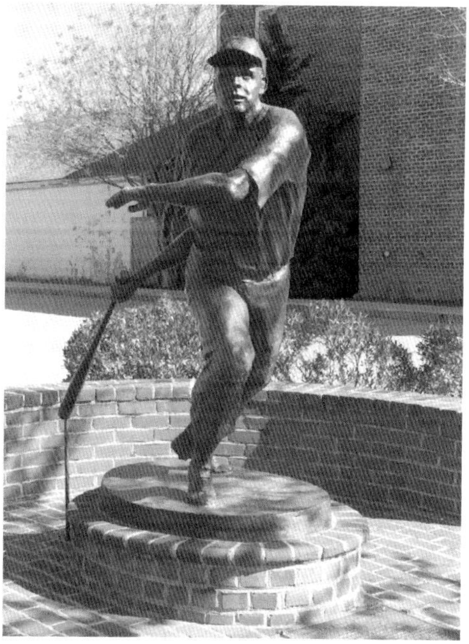

## William Beck Nicholson

Nicknamed "Swish" because of his mighty swing, Nicholson twice led the National League in home runs and RBIs. He was a right fielder in Major League Baseball who played for the Chicago Cubs until 1948 and the Philadelphia Phillies through 1953. The Kent County native attended Washington College. He batted left-handed and threw right-handed. This bronze likeness of Swish was created by Ken Herlihy and is located next to Chestertown's town hall. (Author's collection.)

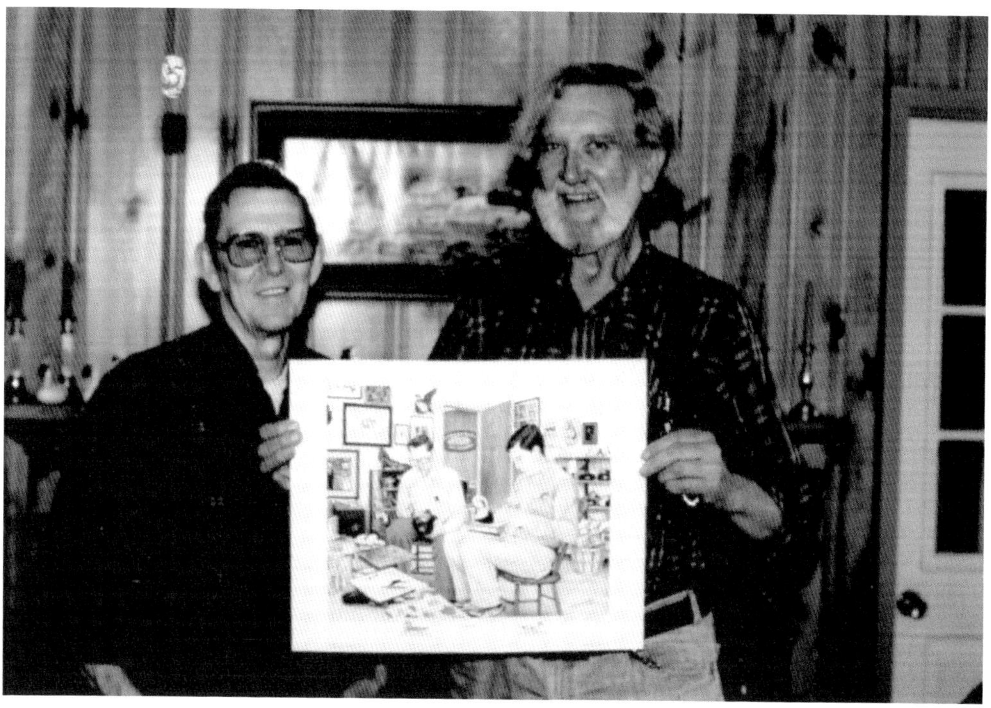

## Jack Rankin Schroeder

A resident of Still Pond, Maryland, for many years, Schroeder was a nationally known illustrator and painter of birds, animals, and rural scenes. He was a two-time winner of the Maryland duck-stamp contest. He had two new species (fish and microscopic crustaceans) named for him by the Smithsonian Institution. Schroeder (right) is pictured here with William A. Schauber. (Courtesy of William A. Schauber.)

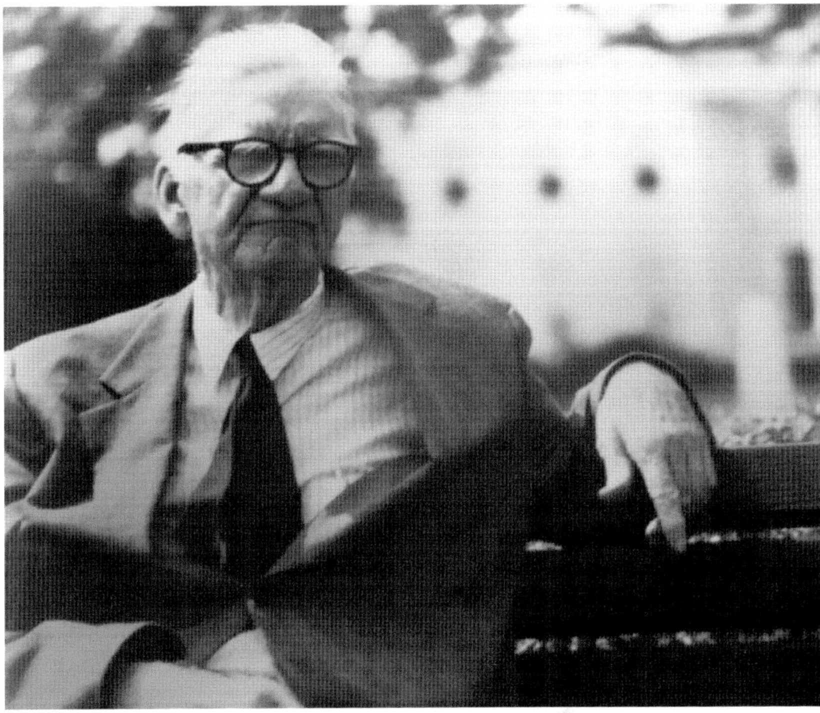

**James M. Cain**
An author and journalist, Cain lived in Chestertown and taught at Washington College. He published his first novel, *The Postman Always Rings Twice*, in 1934. It became a movie in 1946. *Double Indemnity* was filmed in 1944. In 1945 *Mildred Pierce* was released on film starring Joan Crawford, who won the Academy Award for Best Actress for her role. Cain continued to write until his death in 1977. (Courtesy of the Historical Society of Kent County.)

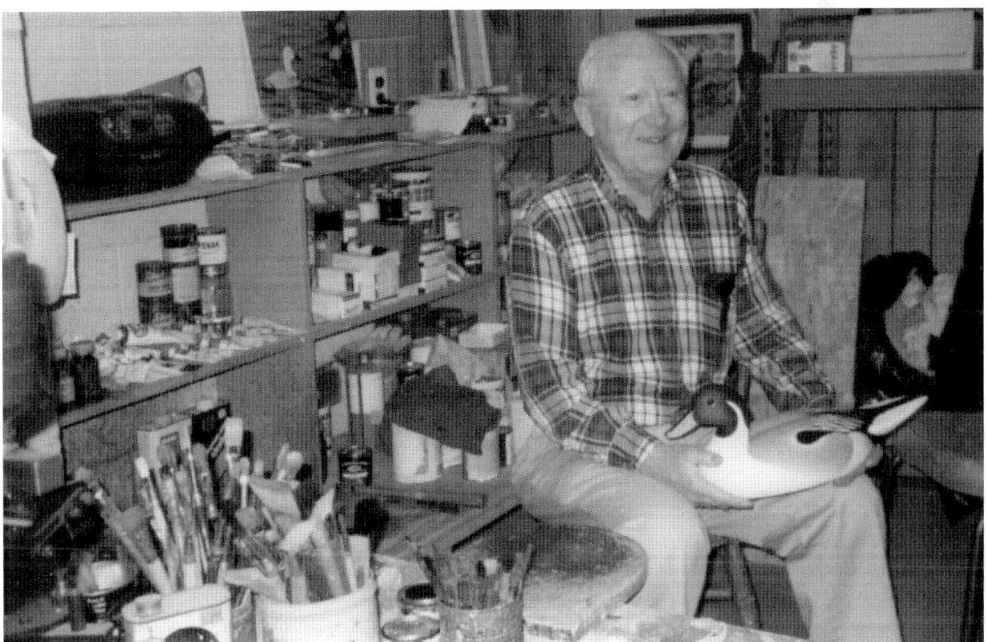

**Charles Joiner**
Known for his speed at carving and painting, "Speed" Joiner of Betterton has been interested in carving since his teenage years. Since then he has carved the majority of species in the Chesapeake Bay area. His canvasback, black duck, and redhead decoys are considered among his best works. He managed the local electric company for many years. (Courtesy of Janet S. Joiner.)

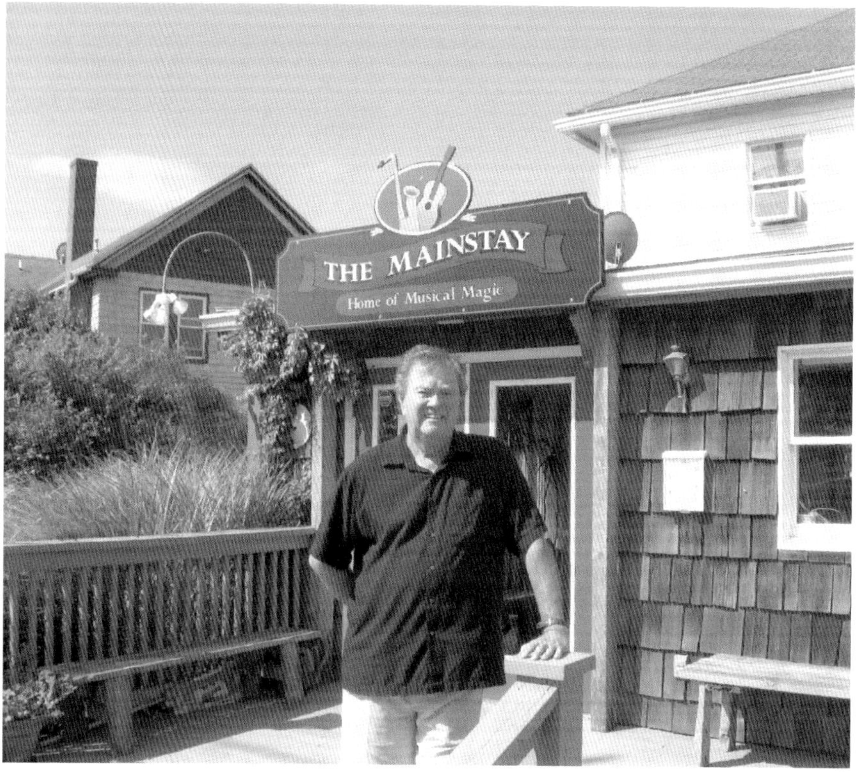


**Tom McHugh**
Rock Hall resident McHugh retired from his college-teaching career and moved to Rock Hall, where he founded the Mainstay as a community center for the arts. The Mainstay has hosted concerts, art shows, community gatherings, and national-level performers and is a venue for local talent. McHugh is also a musician. He sings and plays the banjo, blues harp, Native American flute, and the kazoo. (Courtesy of Mary Lou Troy.)

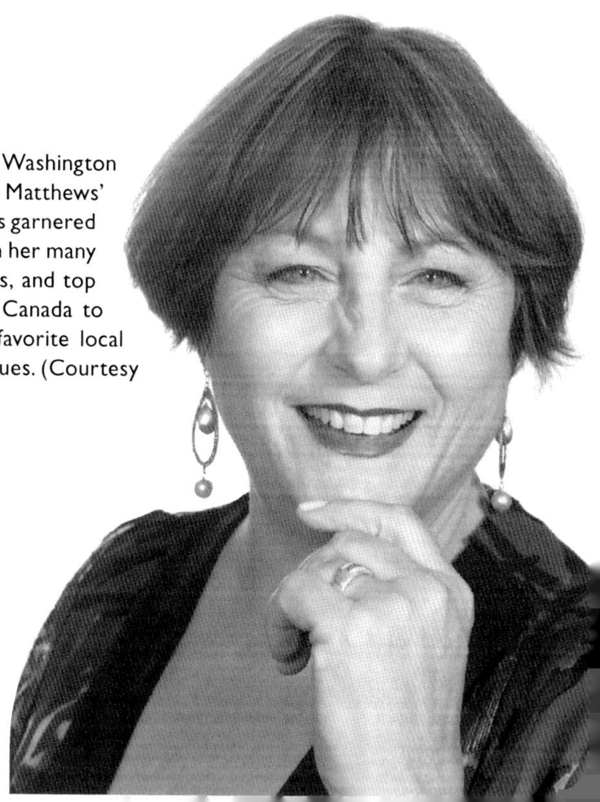

**Sue Dunning Matthews**
She came to Kent County as a student at Washington College and now calls Kent County home. Matthews' highly successful career as a jazz vocalist has garnered her national and international acclaim from her many recordings to concert halls, music festivals, and top jazz club performances, taking her from Canada to Argentina, Ireland to Hungary. She is a favorite local performer with sold-out shows at local venues. (Courtesy of Michael G. Stewart Photography.)

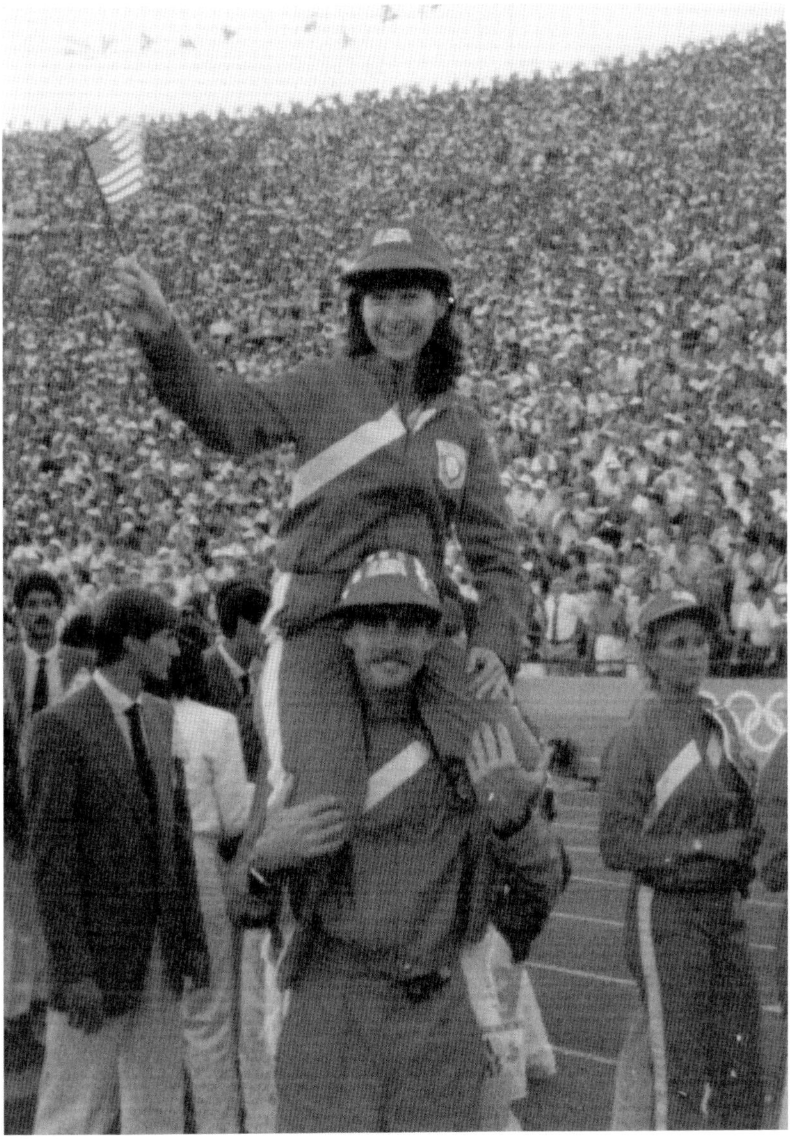

**Betsy Beard Stillings**
The community is proud of the accomplishments of Stillings, formerly of Chestertown. She was the coxswain for the 1984 and the 1988 Olympic rowing teams. She received an Olympic gold medal in 1984 when the team representing the United States finished in first place. She later served as the coxswain for the 1988 team, which finished sixth. In 1979, she was the coxswain for the US Junior National Team girls' eight, which competed in Europe. Stillings's rowing experiences at Washington College and the University of Washington in Seattle helped prepare her for her Olympic performances. She was inducted into the US Rowing Hall of Fame in 1984, received the 1985 Olympia Award, was nominated Sportstar of the Year by the *Seattle Post-Intelligencer* newspaper, and served as an Olympic torchbearer in 1996. Chestertown honored Stillings's accomplishments by declaring August 23, 1984, Betsy Beard Day, and in February 1985 the female legislators of the Maryland General Assembly named her the Exceptional Woman in Maryland. She was inducted into the Washington College Hall of Fame in 2001. (Courtesy of Margaret G. Albertsen.)

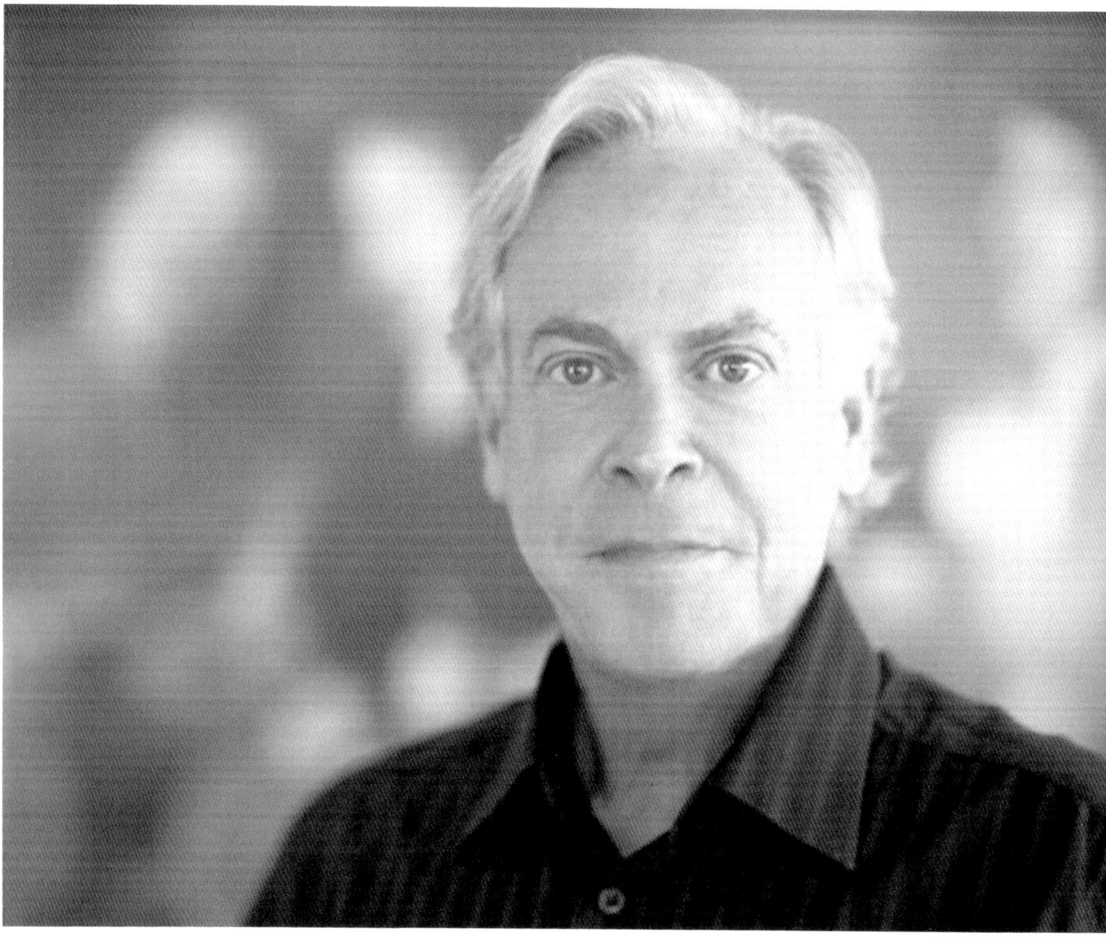

**Mark Bramble**

Born in Kent County, Bramble is the author and director of many Broadway musicals, including *Barnum* (Outer Critics Circle Award for Best Musical) and *42nd Street* (Tony Award for Best Musical in 1981, Laurence Olivier Award for Musical of the Year in 1984, and Tony Award for Best Musical Revival in 2001). He has worked on musical productions all over the world and has been nominated for the Tony Award three times: in 1980 for Best Book of a Musical (*Barnum*), in 1981 for Best Book of a Musical (*42nd Street*), and in 2001 for Best Direction of a Musical (*42nd Street* revival). (Courtesy of Mark Bramble.)

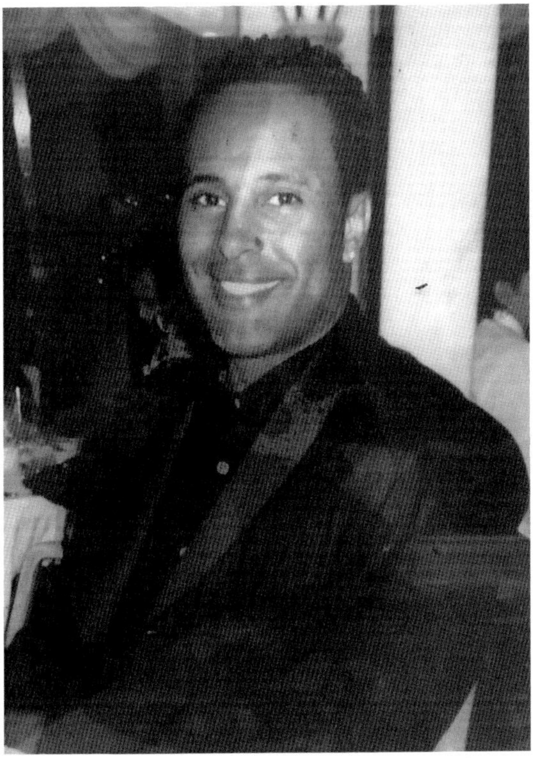

**Ryan Orlando Thompson**
Thompson won a World Series ring with the New York Yankees in 2000. Ryan Orlando Thompson of Edesville was drafted as an outfielder by the Toronto Blue Jays right out of Kent County High School in 1987. He played nine years in the big leagues and was inducted into the Eastern Shore Baseball Hall of Fame. (Courtesy of Arrie Lee Carter.)

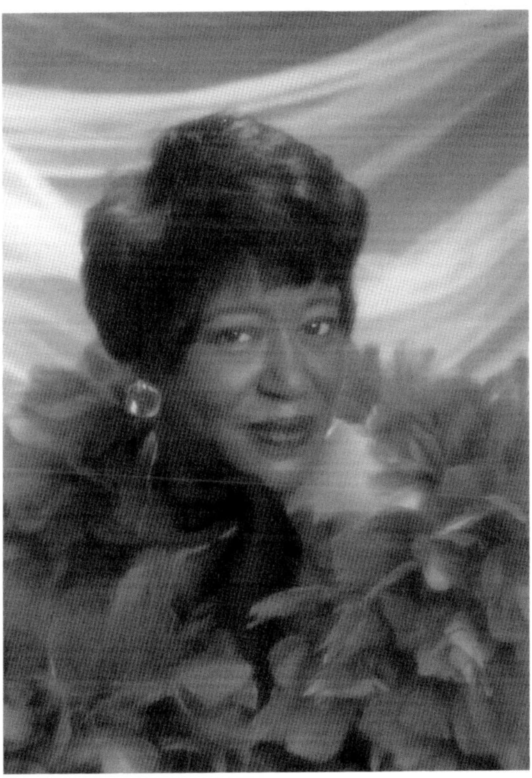

**Sylvia Frazier**
The Martin Luther King Humanitarian Award for significant contributions to the quality of life in Kent County was awarded to Sylvia Frazier of Chestertown in 2013. She was recognized for her work with the 100 Voice Choir and her many other musical contributions to church and community events. Frazier is a gospel-music producer and promoter, and she operates S&B Productions. (Courtesy of Sylvia Frazier.)

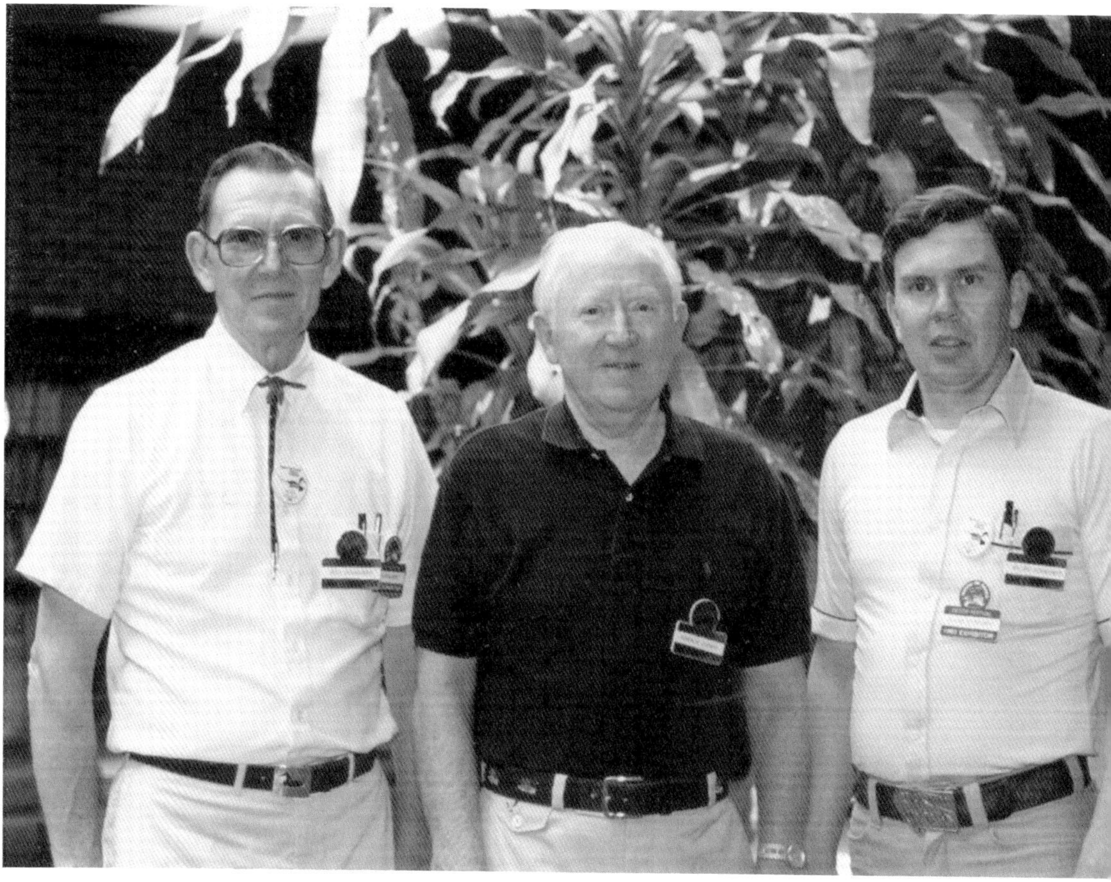

### William A. Schauber and Allan Schauber

A father-son carving duo, "Bill" and Allan both live near Chestertown. One of 16 children, Bill grew up on a farm near Still Pond. He began carving and painting decoys for the mantel in 1965 under the direction of his friend and mentor and well-known decoy carver and painter Charles "Speed" Joiner. Schauber has been making decoys for the Sudlersville Skeet Club since 1968. Wood ducks are his favorite to paint. His son Allan, who also considers Charlie Joiner his friend and mentor, began carving and painting decoys when he was 15. Bill and Allan were honorary chairmen of the 1993 Havre de Grace Decoy Show. Decoys painted by Bill and Allan are highly sought after today. Pictured from left to right are Bill Schauber, Speed Joiner and Allan Schauber. (Courtesy of William A. Schauber.)

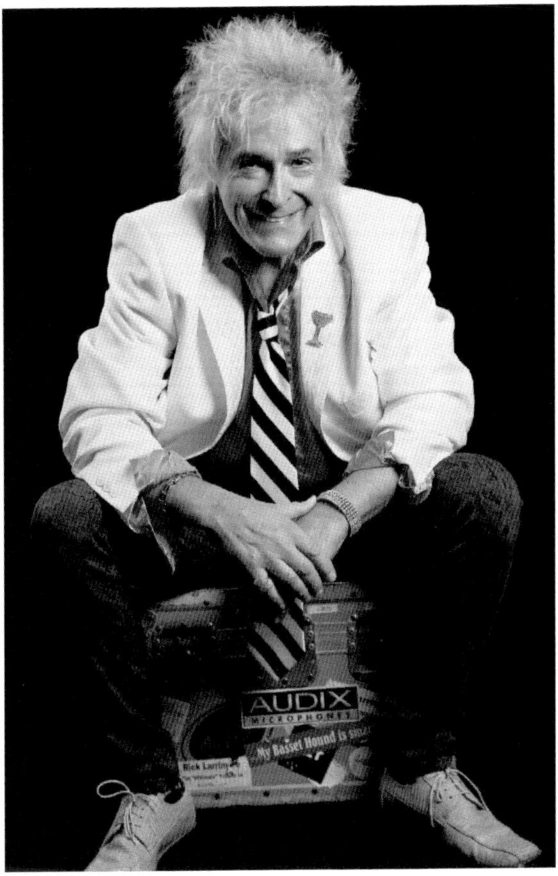


**Rick Larrimore**
Rick Larrimore grew up in Rock Hall and attended Berklee College of Music in Boston. He has been playing drums and singing since he was 14 years old, and his uncanny interpretation of Rod Stewart has mesmerized and fooled many audiences. The ultimate tribute to Rod Stewart featuring Blondes Have More Fun, Larrimore's six piece backup band, has performed countless corporate, casino, and festival events. Larrimore raises funds to purchase service dogs for wounded veterans. (Courtesy of Rick Larrimore.)

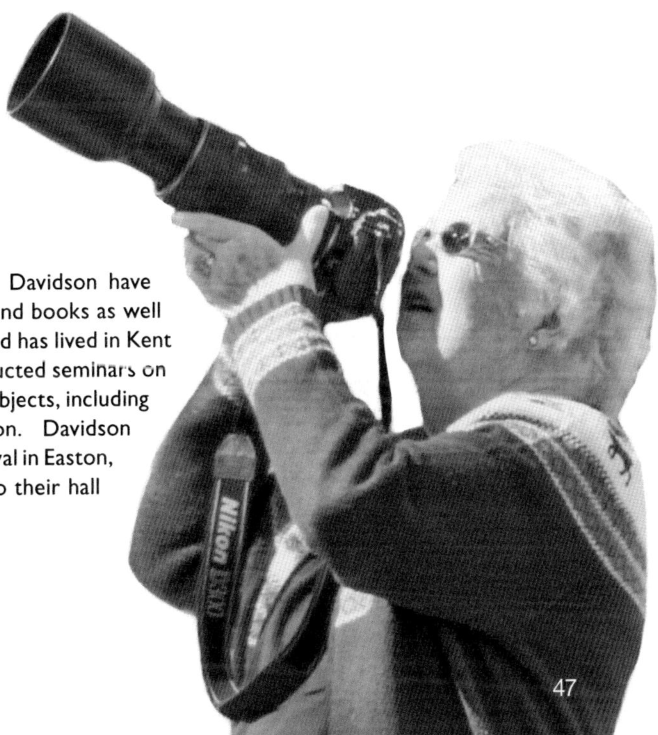


**Heather R. Davidson**
Photographs and articles by Heather R. Davidson have appeared in over 50 different magazines and books as well as 16 calendars. She is a photojournalist and has lived in Kent County for many years. She has also conducted seminars on wildlife photography and other outdoor subjects, including several for the Smithsonian Institution. Davidson exhibited her work at the Waterfowl Festival in Easton, Maryland, for 27 years and was elected to their hall of fame. (Courtesy of Joseph M. Lupsha.)

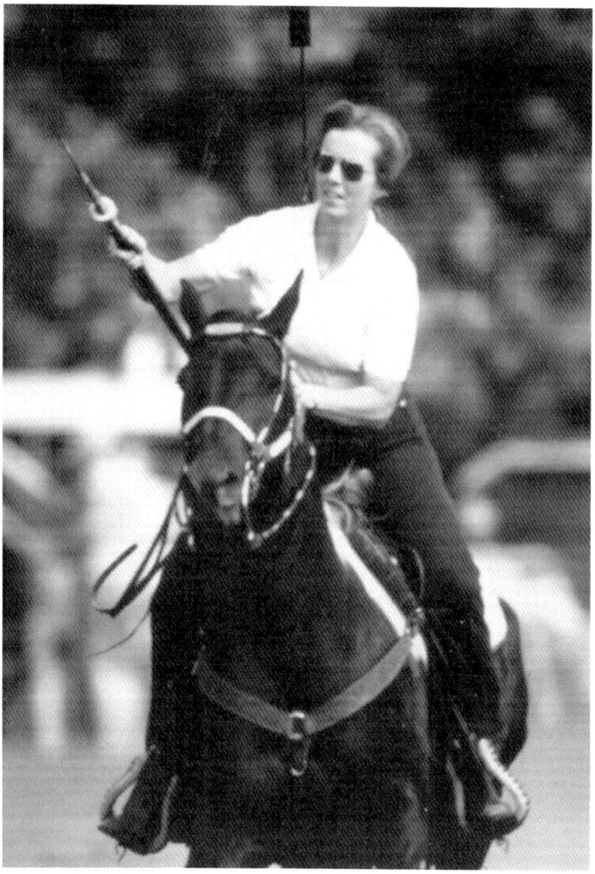

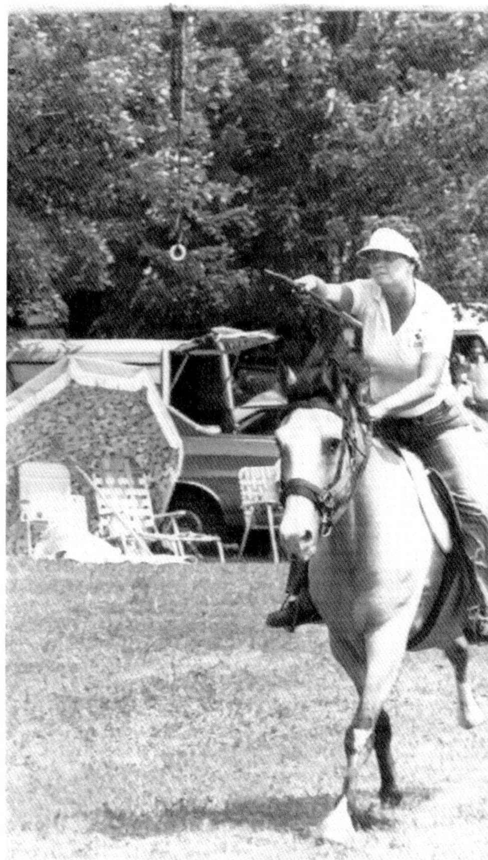

**Dottie States LaPlaca and Peggy States-Edwards**

Jousting is the official sport of Maryland. Sisters Dottie and Peggy are longtime residents of Kent County. Dottie has been riding horses since she was three years old and jousting since she was 16. She was installed into the National Jousting Hall of Fame in 1985 as Maid of Chestertown and has served as secretary and president of the Eastern Shore Jousting Association. Peggy started riding when she was eight and had her own pony by age 10. She began jousting in the 1970s and has won a number of first-page jousting awards. Peggy has served as secretary-treasurer of the Eastern Shore Jousting League. Both Dottie and Peggy were also members of the Maryland State Jousting Association and the National Jousting Association. They have volunteered many hours teaching jousting and have been active supporters to keep jousting the Maryland State sport. Their father was also a jouster. (Courtesy of Dottie LaPlaca and Peggy States-Edwards.)

### Karen Somerville

Karen Somerville's love for music began at home. Both of her parents played instruments and sang. She grew up in an area of Kent County called Worton Point. Karen was the second oldest of four children. Her grandfather played the accordion and harmonica and often played the instruments at the same time. She can sing soprano, alto, tenor, and bass. Somerville has a natural talent, and her performances are gaining recognition across the Mid-Atlantic. She is one of the founders of the African American Heritage Council in Kent County and has a dedicated interest in the preservation of photographs, oral histories, and the documentation of the contribution of African Americans in early Kent County. This includes the restoration of the Grand Army of the Republic lodge hall in Chestertown that served as a focal point for African Americans in rural Kent County for more than 40 years. She is also committed to the preservation of the African American Schoolhouse and Museum located near Worton Point. Somerville was a nominee for the Kent County Dr. Martin Luther King Jr. Humanitarian Award in 2000. (Courtesy of Karen Somerville.)

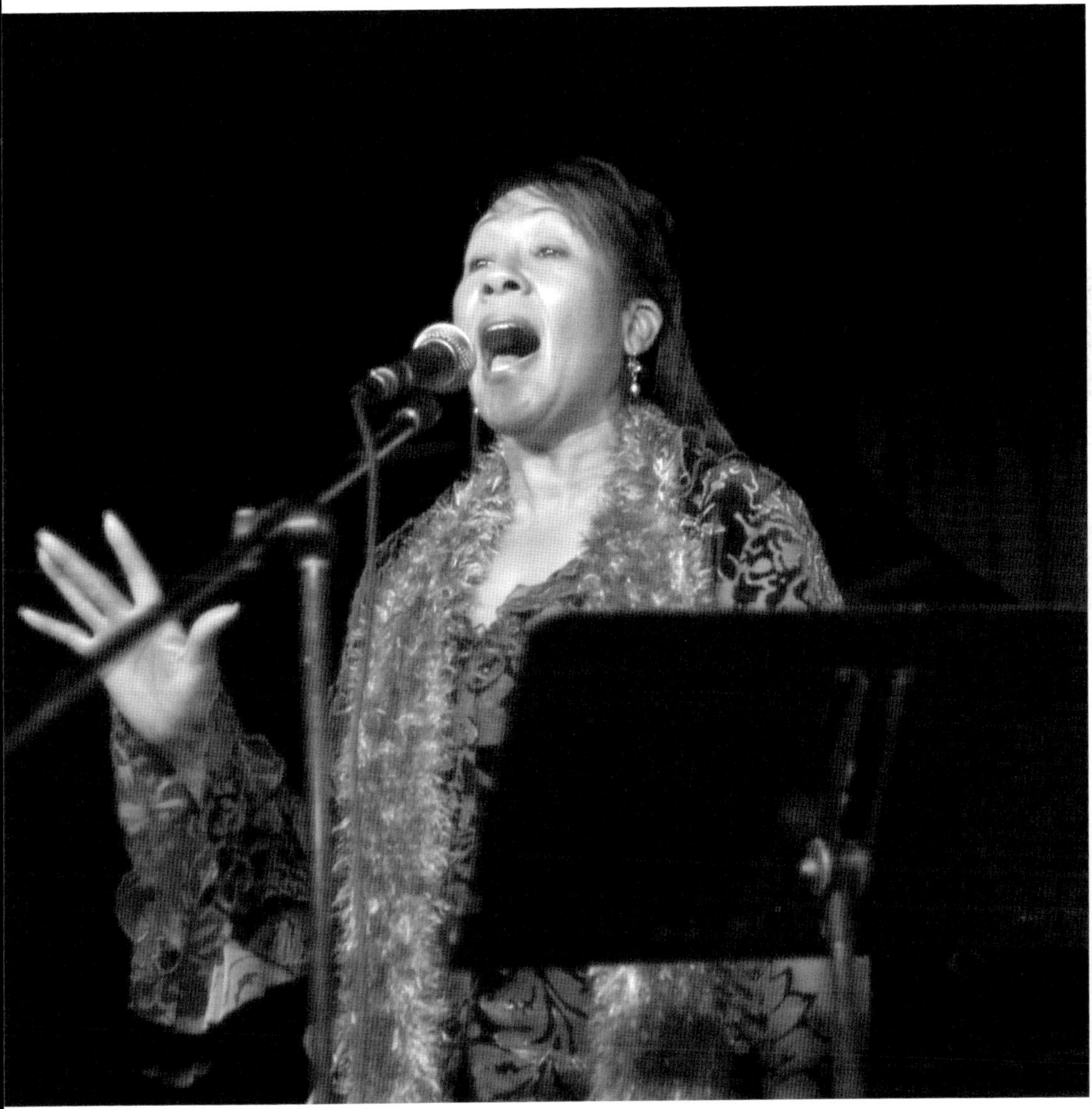

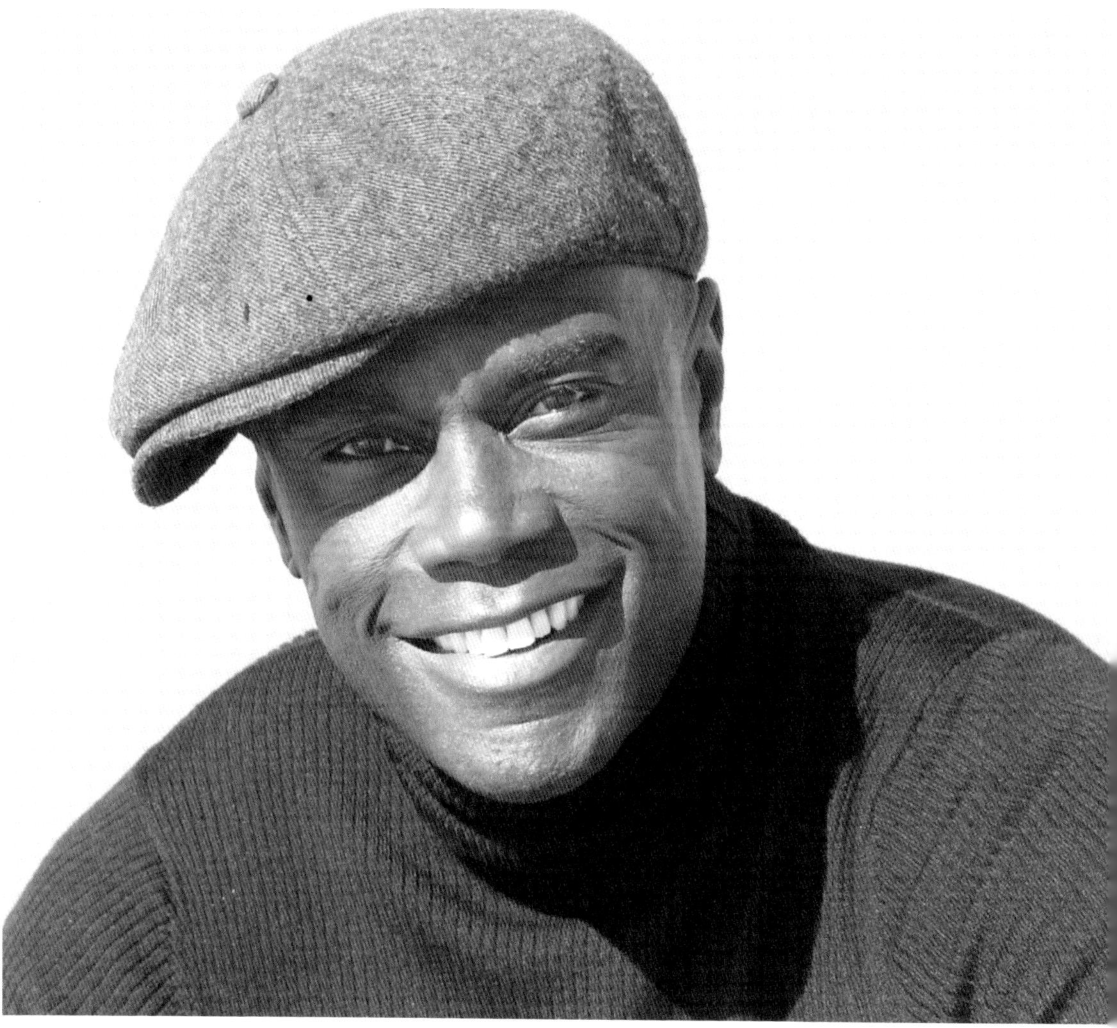

**Marlon Saunders**

Professional singer, songwriter, and record producer Marlon Saunders grew up in Kent County, Maryland. He began singing and playing piano at an early age at the Mount Olive AME Church in Butlertown. He studied at the Peabody Institute of Music of Johns Hopkins University in Baltimore, where he specialized in saxophone studies, and at Berklee College of Music in Boston, Massachusetts. He served as a part-time assistant professor in the voice department at the Berklee College of Music. Marlon has worked with Stevie Wonder, Sam Smith, Bastille, Billy Joel, Sting, Bobby McFerrin, and Michael Jackson, to name a few. Marlon appears as the calypso singer in the Disney film *Enchanted.* He sang the Academy Award–nominated song "That's How You Know" with Amy Adams, who appears in the role of Giselle. The song received Best Song nominations at the Academy Awards, the Golden Globe Awards, and the Critics' Choice Awards. Saunders also performed "That's How You Know" live at the 80th Annual Academy Awards with Tony award–winner Kristin Chenoweth. He has appeared on NBC's *Today Show,* made numerous singing appearances on NBC's comedy *30 Rock,* and appears as a businessman (background actor) in the film *Sex and the City 2.* Marlon has contributed to the video game scene as well, particularly games made by Sega. (Courtesy of Arif St. Michael, Egyptian Prince Photography.)

# CHAPTER THREE

# Community

Kent County's people are memorable for many reasons. Edward L. Athey was a professor and athletic director at Washington College for 38 years; DuPont heiress and philanthropist Louisa d'Andelot Carpenter donated a farm for an Easter Seals Camp that continues in operation today; W.J. Stenger, Helen Wagner, Skirven Startt, Marietta Loud, Miriam Kieffer, Hilda Hill, Helen T. Russell, and Thelma Vansant are among the many who are remembered as beloved Kent County educators. Curtis and Anna Mae Dorsey operated a bus service for over 60 years; brothers Arthur Livingston 'Mike" and John Baynard "Blackie" Harris introduced many Kent Countians to the age of flight; Mary Evelyn Bockmiller Harris made a living by resorting to bartering; public-health nurse Marjorie Hawkins worked to promote the wellbeing of children and infants for 38 years; Joseph P. Linduska exposed the fatal link between pesticides and wildlife reproduction; Dr. Joseph H. McLain helped develop rocket-propellant formulas and devices used for stage separation in space flights; Mary Jane Clark Howard, Anne Baker Maxwell, and Lillie Deringer Kelley cast their ballots in the Still Pond municipal election of 1908—12 years before the 19th Amendment established women's suffrage; Ned Elburn shod some 114,000 horses during his career; L. Bates Russell brought the movies to Chestertown and Kent County; Lillian Shockney, a two-time breast-cancer survivor, was selected by Johnson & Johnson as the Most Amazing Nurse in America; George Wallace was inducted as an umpire into Maryland's American Softball Association Hall of Fame; James Chambers delivered prescriptions to Chestertown residents on his bicycle; Larry William Simns established and became president of the Maryland Watermen's Association in 1973; Lillie Mae Capel Flowers Meredith was 22 and the youngest female sea captain to navigate in rivers, bays, and oceanic waters; and members of the Sutton family have been designated master farmers by *Pennsylvania Farm Magazine*, and they were also named Maryland Farm Family of the Year in 1996.

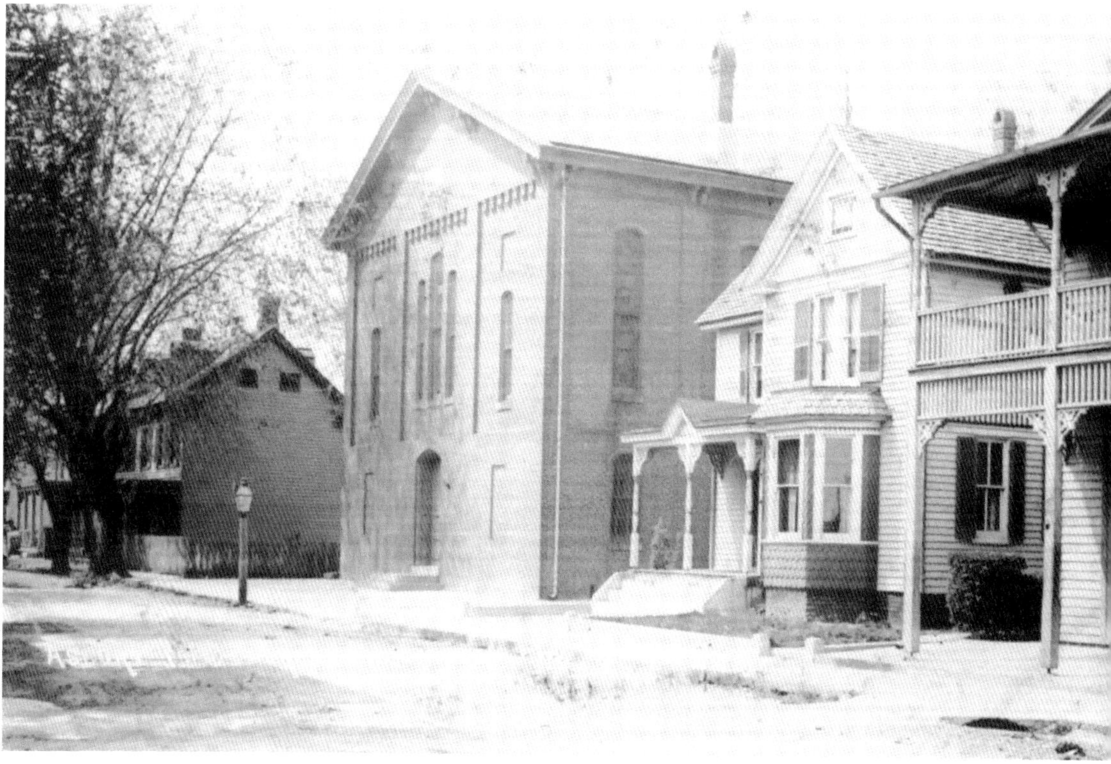

### H. Montgomery Stuart

H. Montgomery Stuart was born in Millington, where he learned the craft of house carpentry and built his first buildings, including the Asbury M.E. Church in 1871 (shown). He was for many years one of the prominent contractors and builders in Chestertown, and many of the most substantial residences and public buildings there stand as memorials to his industry and skill. Stam's Hall, the Chestertown Emmanuel Episcopal Church, Sacred Heart Catholic Church, and the former county jail building were among them. Many of the houses along Queen Street were built by his company, including his own home. He was also often chosen as the contractor for repair and upkeep of the Chester River Bridge and other bridges in the county. (Courtesy of G. Kevin Hemstock.)

**William Medders**

Medders lived in Still Pond for many years, and he owned the William Medders Co. store. The general store (shown below) was originally built about 1875 by George Washington Harper, Medders's father-in-law. Medders purchased the business in 1894 and the building in 1908 when the name was changed to William Medders Co. It is said that during the Christmas season, Medders' store remained opened late in the evening and provided free ham sandwiches and coffee to its customers. Drawings for sleds and dolls were held annually along with visits from Santa. Medders Store building was sold in 1964 when it ceased operation as a general store. Medders is remembered in Still Pond as a great merchant and has been described as "a creator of a country department store." According to the nomination form for the National Register of Historic Places, during the mid-1930s his business was so successful that on a number of occasions men from Woolworth's main office in New York and from Sears, Roebuck & Co. were sent to study his methods. (Courtesy of Holly Harris and Walter Bowie.)

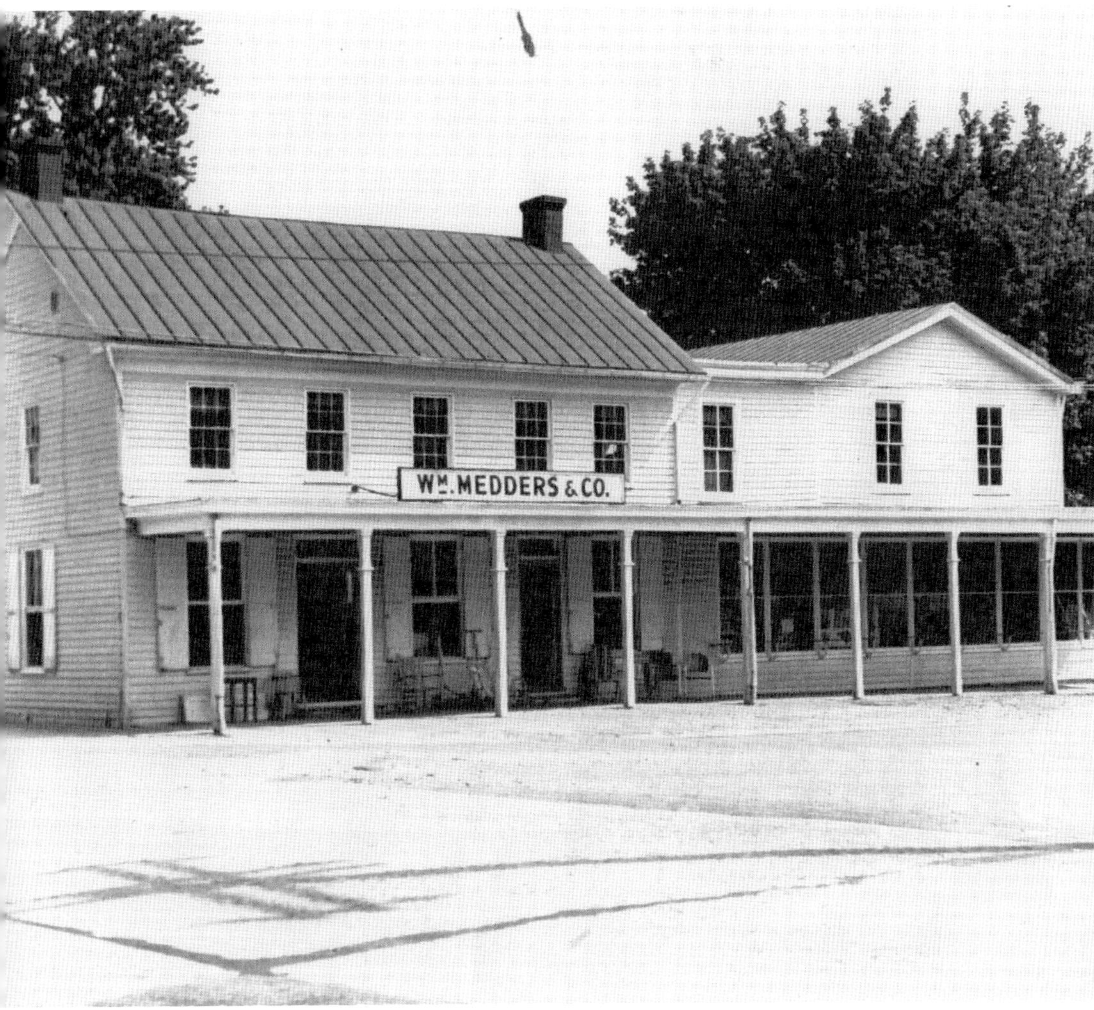

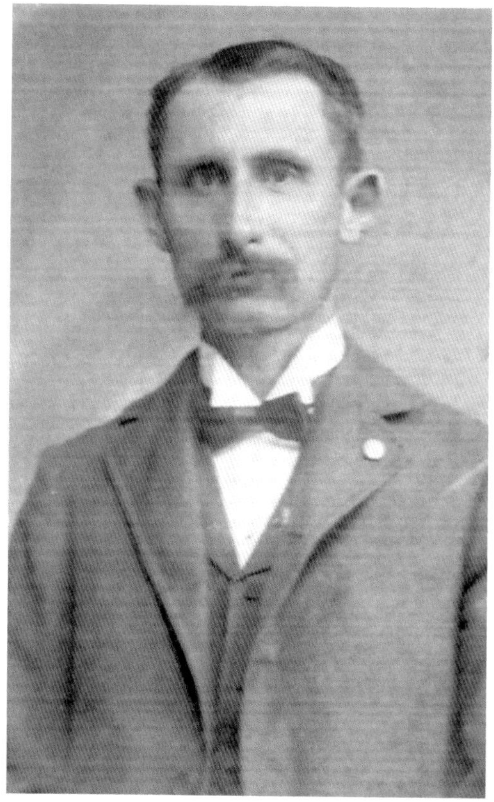

**William Edward Ringgold**

The exact location of Ringgold's blacksmith shop in Chestertown is believed to have been at the end of Court Street, where the law offices of Rasin, Wootten and Hurd are now located (see drawing). "Ned" and his wife, Annie Arters Ringgold, moved to Chestertown in 1893, and he began working with Henry S. Deford at the G.E. Lambert Carriage Building on Cannon Street. Sometime after 1923, Ringgold purchased the property on Court Street that was formerly a wheelwright and blacksmith shop and opened Ringgold Blacksmith Shop. He retired in 1938 after having spent 57 years as a blacksmith. It was said that Ringgold shod some 114,000 horses during his career, averaging 2,000 horses a year and sent 3.5 million nails (about 16 tons) into horses' hoofs. (Both, courtesy of Joan Elburn Farley.)

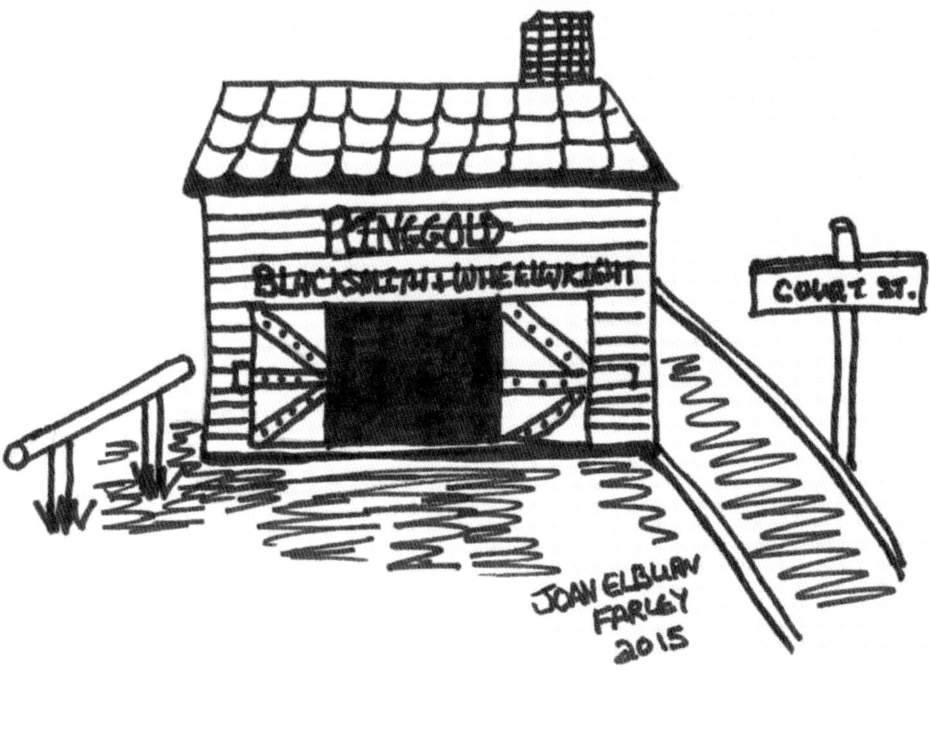

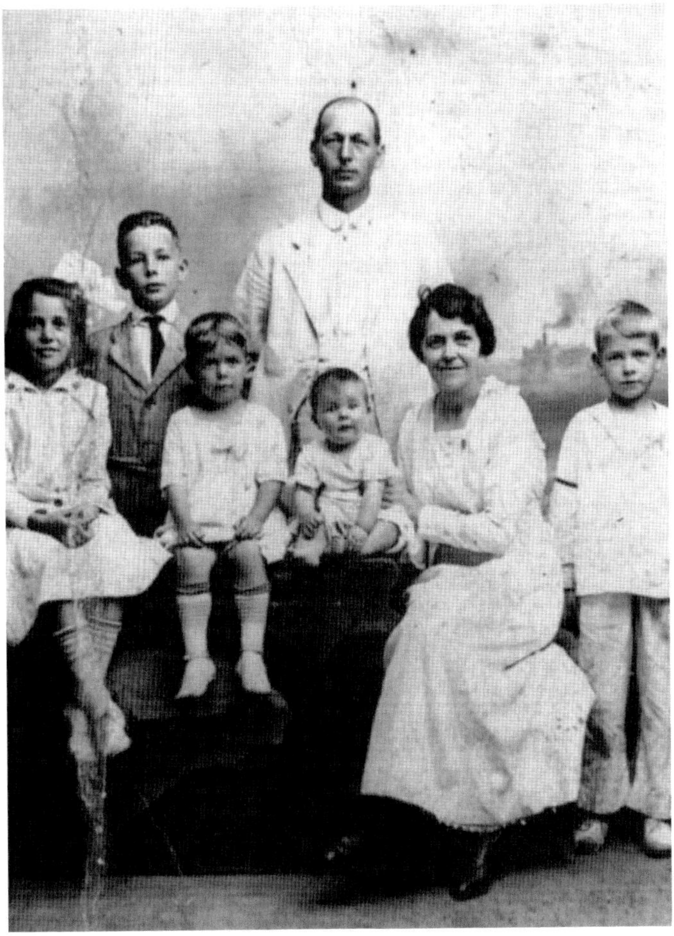

**Mary Evelyn Bockmiller Harris**

Evelyn Harris of Howell's Point, near Betterton, became the sole proprietor of her farm when he husband unexpectedly died during the Depression. She made her living by resorting to bartering, eventually writing her memoirs, which were first published in the *Saturday Evening Post* and later into a book called the *Barter Lady*. Harris gained more than local fame during the Depression years with her book when she proposed a system of swapping to overcome the shortage of money in the faltering economy. She brought peaches and other farm products to town to bargain for other necessities of her family. She was sympathetic to farmers all her life and became an advocate for fair pricing practices for farmers. She was a leader among farmers and farm women and she used her many talents to promote agriculture. As a young girl, Evelyn attended the Peabody Institute of Music in Baltimore, but before she completed her studies she married farmer Arthur L. Harris and moved to the Eastern Shore. Later in life, she returned to Peabody and completed her course of study as a concert accompanist. As a musician, she was organist for many years at the Betterton Methodist Church and on occasion played for community and farm meetings. She also wrote a series of articles in the 1920s for the *Baltimore Sun* titled *The Farmer and His Wife* that were eventually published in book form. This accomplishment led Maryland governor Albert Ritchie to appoint her to an agricultural committee organized to study the farmers' plight. She is remembered as controversial and colorful. Pictured here are, from left to right, (first row) Sara Harris (Fallowfield), Helen Harris (Lasahn), Ruth Harris (Bartlett), Mary Evelyn Bockmiller Harris, and John Baynard Harris; (second row) Arthur Livingston Harris Jr., and Arthur Livingston Harris. (Courtesy of Anne Livingston Harris.)

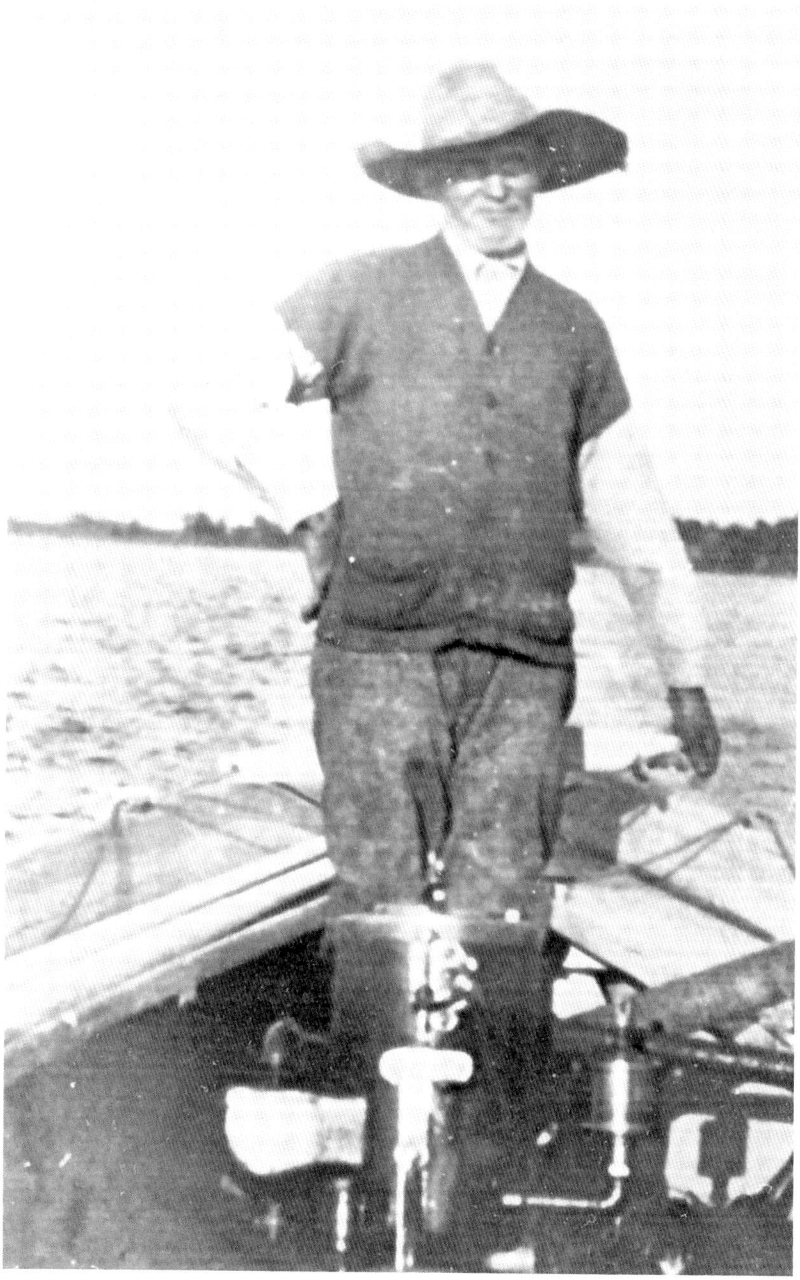

## John Wesley Dickerson

John Wesley Dickerson was born in Cliff City near Chestertown. In 1896, he was appointed commander of the oyster police boat on the Chester River. Like many watermen he built an ark, a 10-foot by 8-foot floating home that was towed to area fishing grounds by his log canoes *C. Russel* and the *Silver Heel*. He could be found in Durding Creek for the oyster season and Miller's Island for spring fishing. With family, "Captain Johnny" worked the water, and on foul days the cards came out. Known as a man of few words and many children, he followed the water all his life. The *Silver Heel* is one of 22 log canoes that still race on the Chester River. (Courtesy of Stephanie Gosman.)

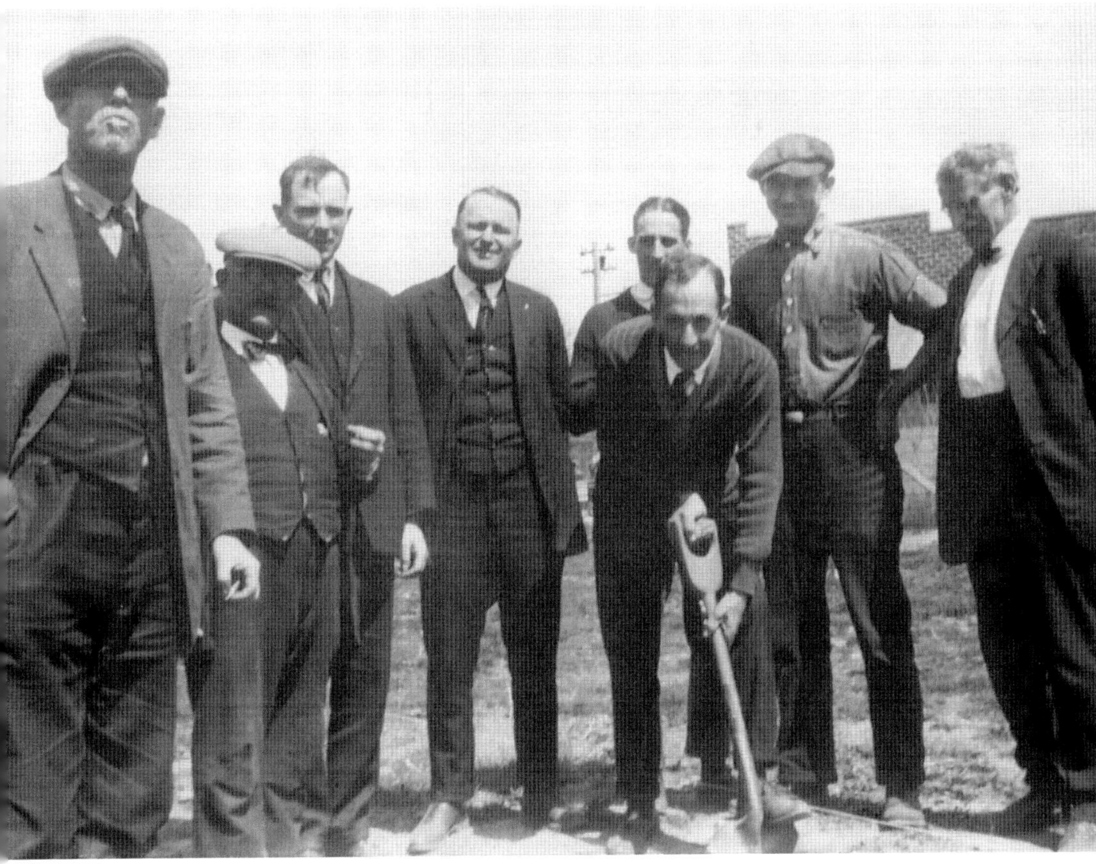

**Benjamin Duling**

An architect and builder, Duling was responsible for construction of numerous homes and businesses in Millington, including the 1915 Millington school, Millington Farmers Bank, 1924 fire hall, and the Bailey Hotel. He served several terms as the president of the Millington's town commission, a position comparable to a mayor. He was a member of the Millington Community Fire Company and several fraternal organizations. Under his leadership, the town's roads were paved and concrete sidewalks poured. He was the lead developer of many of the homes on Comegys Street and Hurtt Avenue, and his efforts led to the laying out of Hurtt Avenue, School Street, and Comegys Street, all in Millington. Pictured here are, from left to right, Edgar "Spud" Stevens, Benjamin Duling, Spencer Stevens, Clarence Melvin Sr., John Tobin Sr. (with shovel), John Tobin Jr., Robert M. Logan, and Doc Hynson. (Courtesy of G. Kevin Hemstock.)

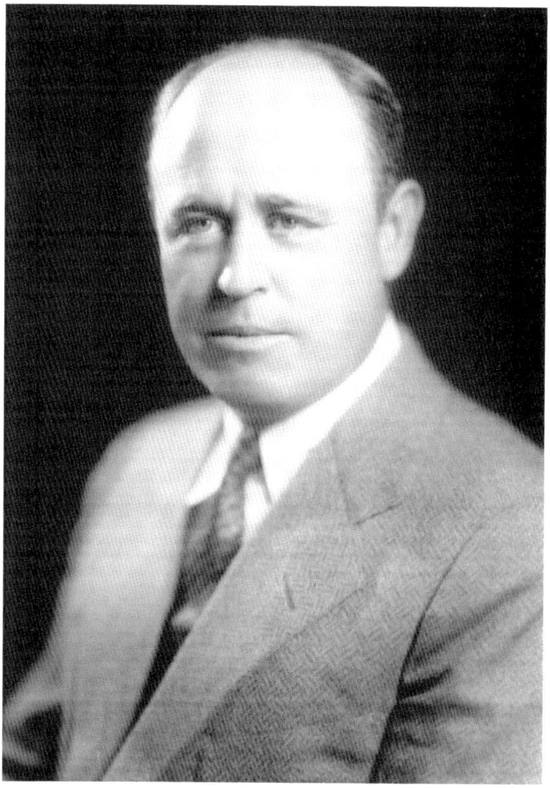

### Col. Hiram Staunton Brown

Brown served as the chairman of the Board of Visitors and Governors of Washington College for 28 years. Colonel Brown also served as chief of finance of the Air Corps during World War I and became president of Radio-Keith-Orpheum Corp. (RKO). Brown was behind the legendary pairing of Fred Astaire and Ginger Rogers. (Courtesy of Heidi Brown Hollomon.)

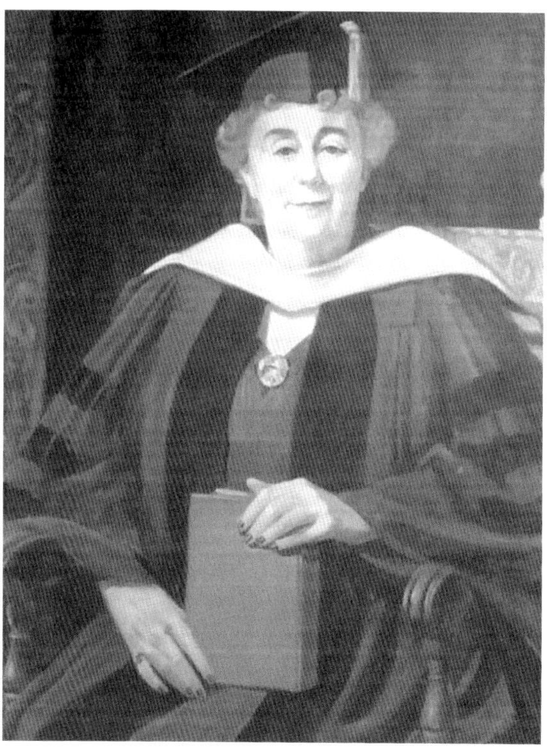

### Mary Adele France

France was the fifth female to graduate from Washington College, and she was born in Chestertown. She served as principal of St. Mary's Female Seminary in St. Mary's City, Maryland, from 1923 to 1927. She founded St. Mary's Junior College and became president of St. Mary's Seminary Junior College (now St. Mary's College of Maryland) from 1927 to 1954. (Courtesy of St. Mary's College.)

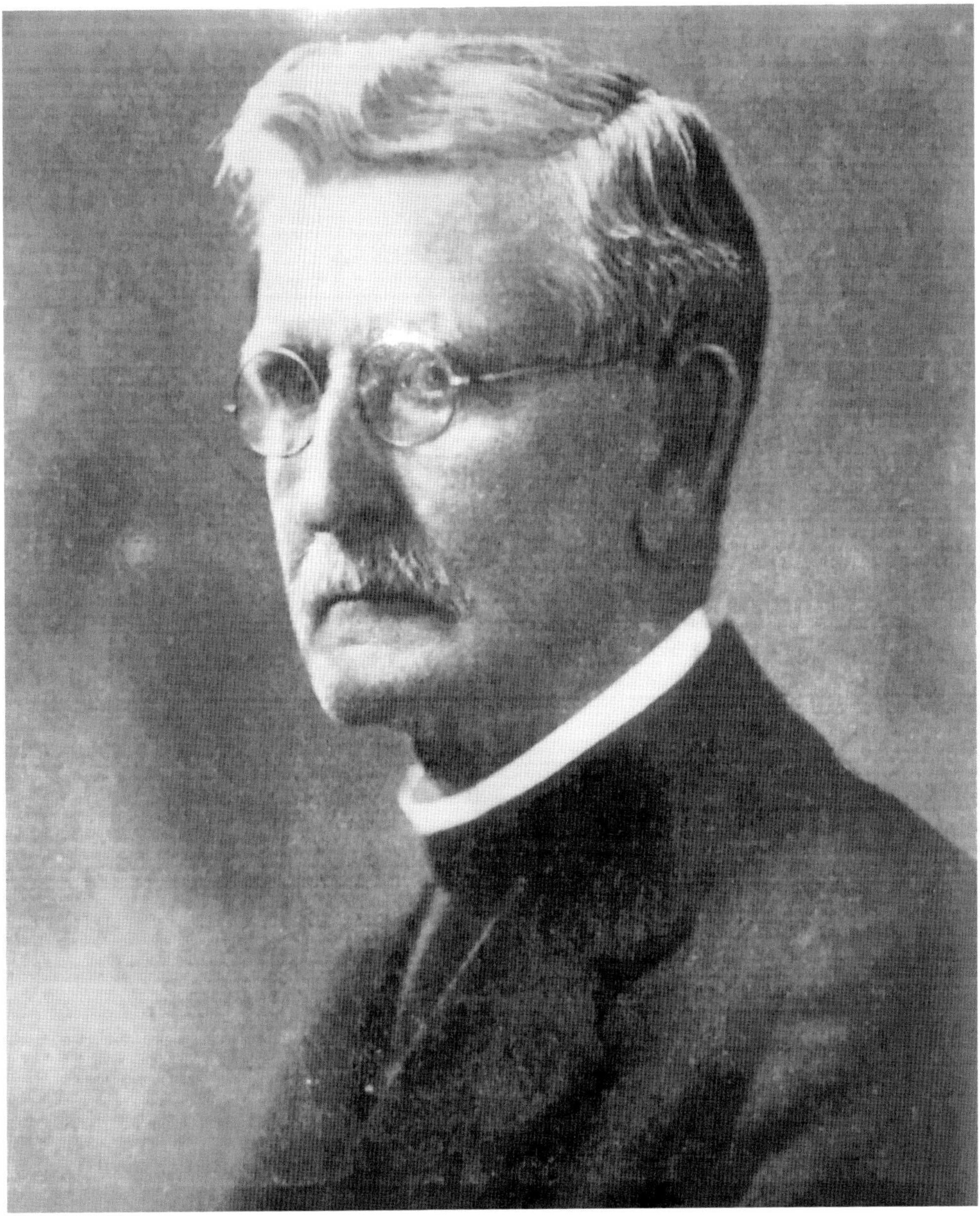

**Rev. Sewell Stavely Hepburn**

A marble plaque at Christ Church I.U. just outside of Worton was placed as a memorial to the Rev. Sewell Stavely Hepburn, who served as rector at the Episcopal church. It reads, "In memoriam, Sewell Stavely Hepburn D.D., priest, 22 years the beloved rector of I.U. Parish, He fed them with a faithful and true heart." After Reverend Hepburn's death in 1932, it was four-year-old Eleanor Noble, his great-granddaughter, who now lives in Kent County and attends I.U. Church, who unveiled the plaque at a church service two years later. Reverend Hepburn was the grandfather of Academy Award–winner Katherine Hepburn. Katherine Hepburn visited Christ Church during her stays at Shepherd's Delight, her grandparents' 250-acre wheat, corn, and soybean farm in Kent County. When the actress died in 2003 at the age of 96, she left $10,000 to Christ Church I.U. (Courtesy of Christ Church I.U.)

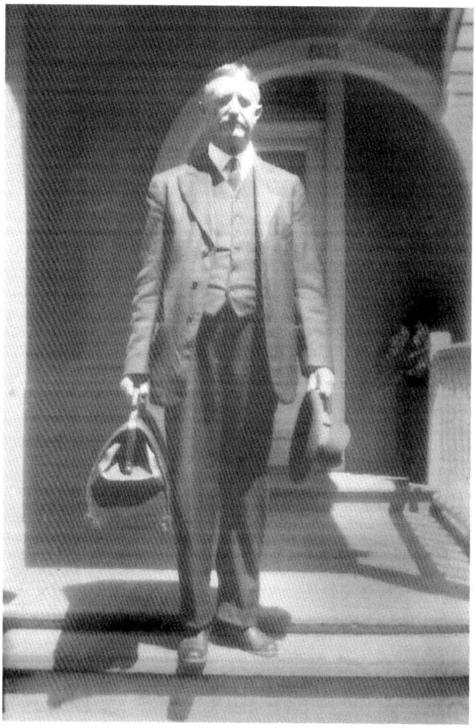

### Walter Tomlinson Pippin

Born in Chestertown, Pippin was a prolific contractor and builder, practicing during a period of great growth in Kent County. Walter began his career at a young age, assisting his father, Robert Kemp Pippin, as a carpenter. After graduating from Maryland Institute in 1886, he returned to Chestertown and formed a partnership with his father, R.K. Pippin & Son. Upon his father's death, Walter continued as Walter T. Pippin. His scope of work varied widely, from remodeling to design and construction. He was responsible for numerous houses and public buildings in Chestertown and the vicinity, including Rock Hall, Kennedyville, Betterton, and Galena. At least 12 buildings along Washington Avenue in Chestertown were the work of Pippin, who became known as the "Builder of the Avenue." He designed and built the Clifton Jarrell house in Chestertown in 1907 (below), said to be one of the finest of his designs. It was destroyed by fire in 1915. (Both, courtesy of the Pippin family.)

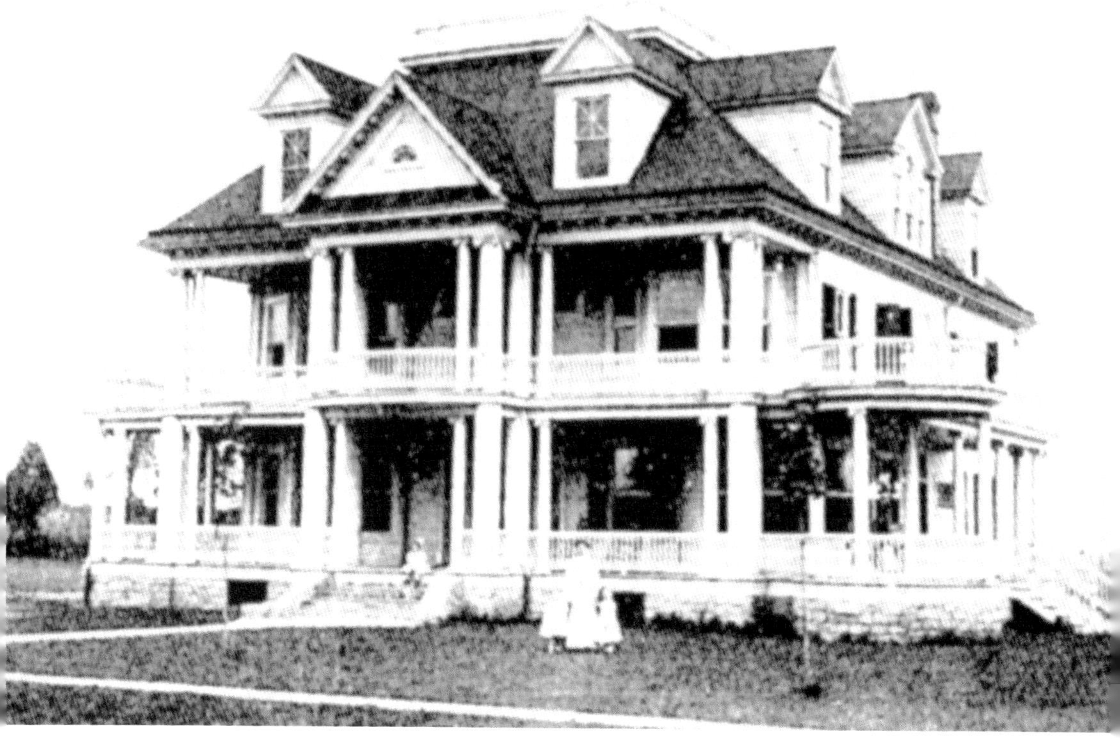

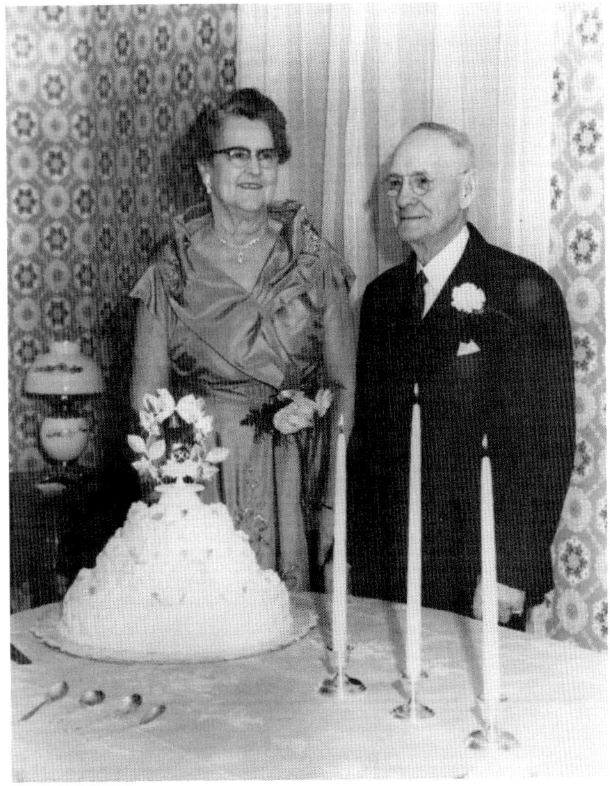

**Clara Jones Williams**
Kent County native "Miss Caddie" was a Kent County public schoolteacher, active in farm-organization work and in the Granges, where she acted as lecturer of the State Grange. She served as chairman for Kent of the Woman's Work of the Farm Bureau and it was through her efforts that women were given a definite place in farm-bureau work. Williams is pictured with her husband, Harry T. Williams. (Courtesy of Elizabeth "Sis" Williams.)

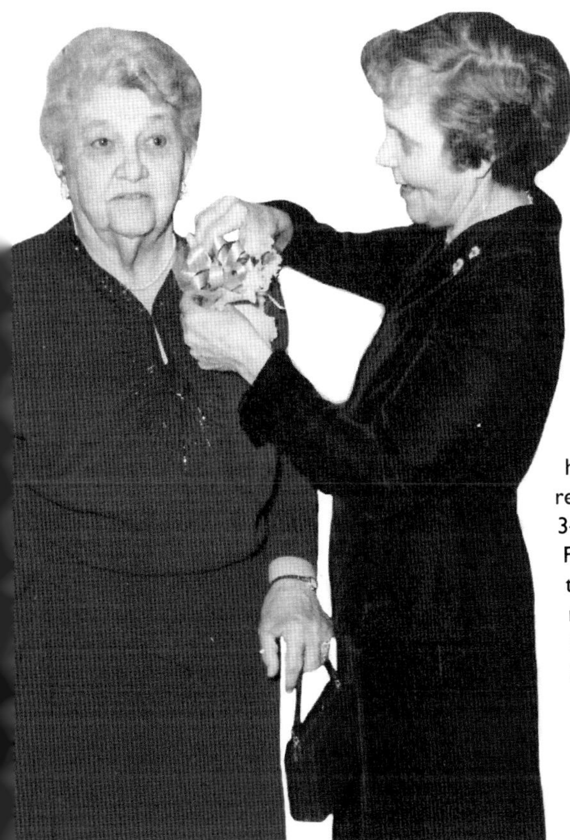

**Nora Maxwell**
In 1928, Nora Maxwell (left) of Worton Point, president of the Kent County Health Association, recognized the need for a hospital in the community. The association rented four rooms on the second floor at 347 High Street in Chestertown, where Dr. F.A. Holden performed tonsillectomies. At the same time, Maxwell launched a drive to raise money for a larger and more permanent hospital building. (Courtesy of the Historical Society of Kent County.)

### Howard W. Goodall

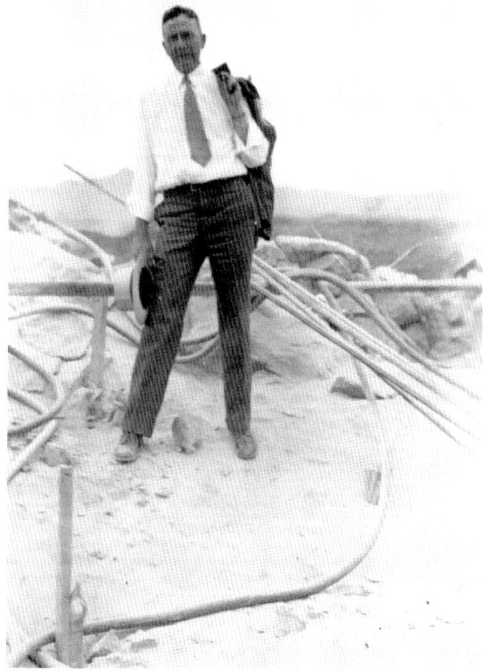

Howard W. "HW" Goodall (right) founded Dixon Valve & Coupling Company in Philadelphia in 1916 in order to design and manufacture hose couplings for the country's thriving growth in the mining, oil, construction, and railroad industries. HW's son, Richard B. "RB" Goodall, began working for the company in 1929 and became president in 1951. RB's sons Richard L. Goodall and Douglas K. Goodall led a team that moved Dixon from Philadelphia to their site in Chestertown. Dixon Valve & Coupling is now a global company and a major employer in Kent County. The company and its over 350 Chestertown employees contribute to the Kent County community in many ways. Dixon is proud to support the Character Counts program with 30 coaches teaching the six pillars of character: respect, responsibility, caring, trustworthiness, citizenship, and fairness to students in preschool through ninth grade. (Both, courtesy of Richard L. Goodall.)

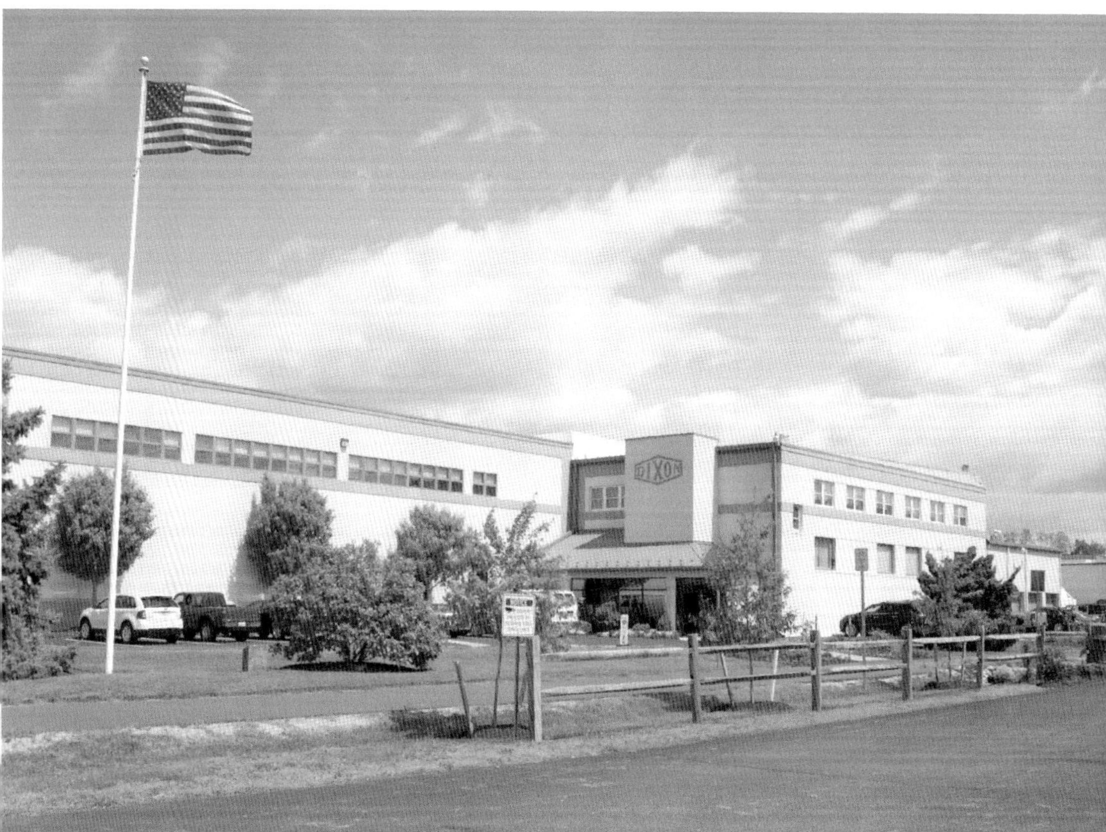

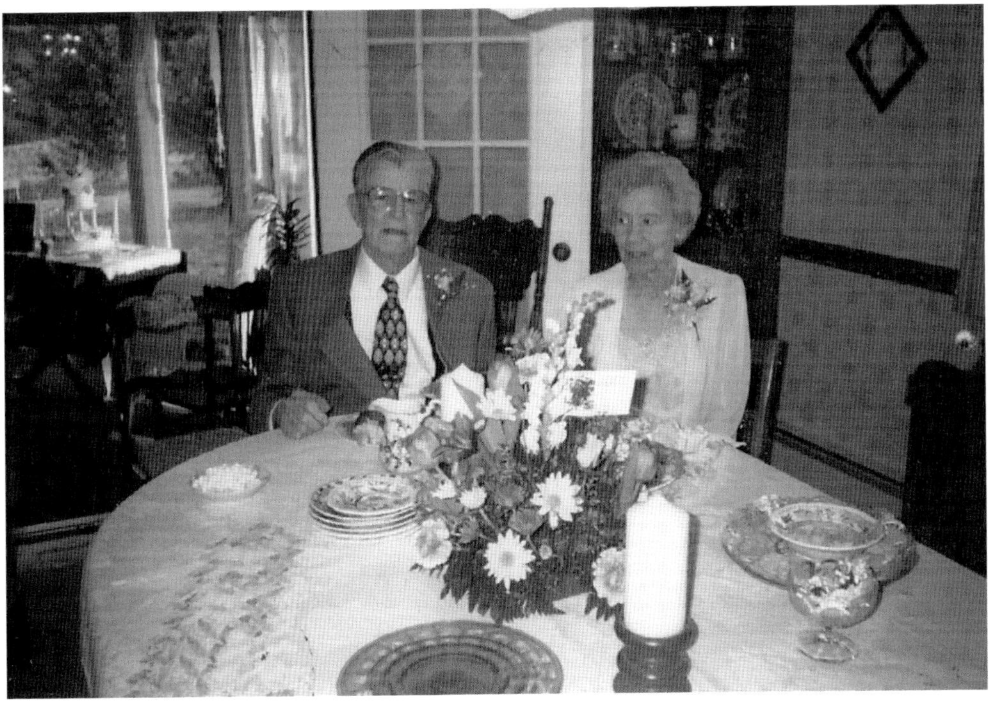

**H. Julian Hill**
A third-generation dairy farmer, Hill and his wife, Mary, owned and operated Rocky Mount Farm just outside of Kennedyville. The farm is designated a Maryland Century farm because of its continuous ownership and operation by a member of Hill family for 100 years. He was a founding member and first president of the Kennedyville Volunteer Fire Company and served on the Maryland Agricultural Commission. (Courtesy of the Hill family.)

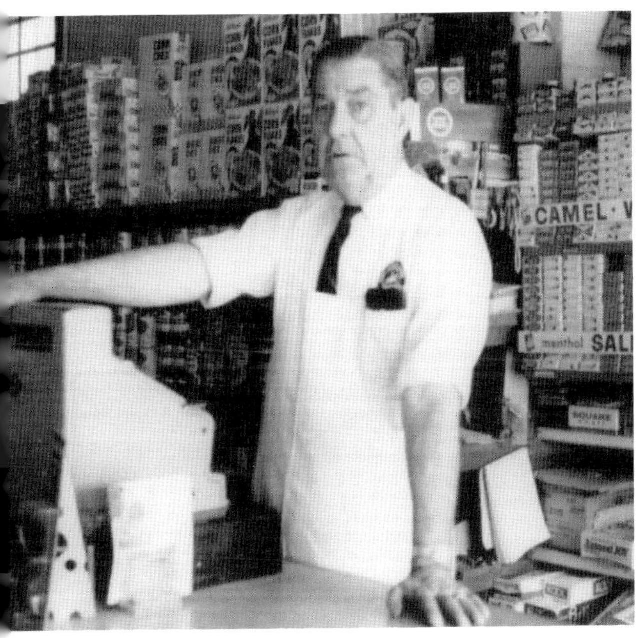


**Earl Kennard Jones**
Earl Kennard Jones was a lifetime resident and popular businessman in Still Pond for 40 years. He had been the Postmaster at Still Pond for 20 years at the time of his death in 1969. His grocery store was located in the center of Still Pond and housed the Still Pond Post Office. He was a director of Maryland National Bank and served as deputy sheriff of Kent County. (Courtesy of Willis K. Jones.)

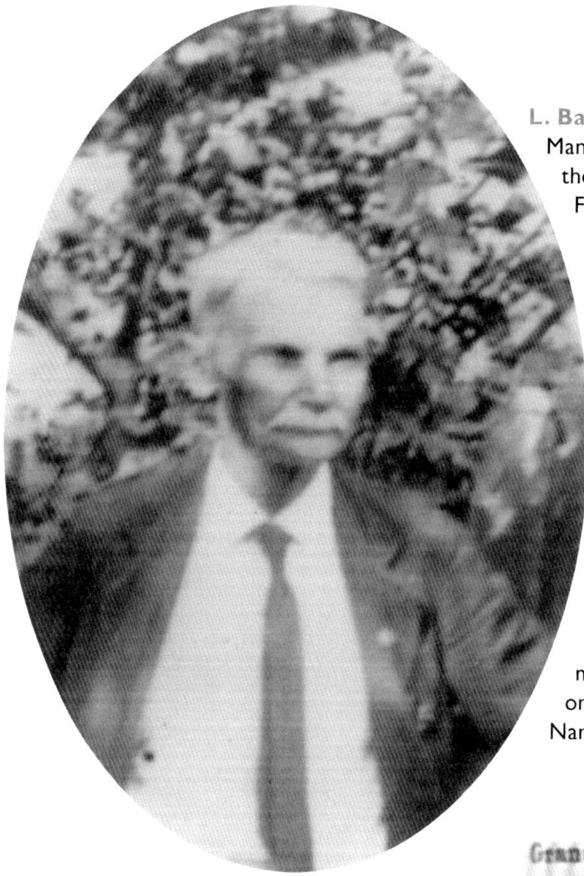

**L. Bates Russell**

Many Chestertown businesses closed during the hour of L. Bates Russell's funeral in February 1942 out of respect. He was a banker, automobile dealer, and newspaper publisher and brought the movies—the New Lyceum picture parlor—to Chestertown. He supported many business ventures, including the Pepsimint Chemical Company, a digestive aid that was produced and bottled on the second floor of the Enterprise building located in downtown Chestertown beginning about 1905. Russell also served 12 years on the Kent County Board of Education, six of them as president. He was a Mason for nearly 50 years and at one time or another was affiliated with most of the local fraternal orders. He died on his 76th birthday. (Both, courtesy of Nancy Russell Morris.)

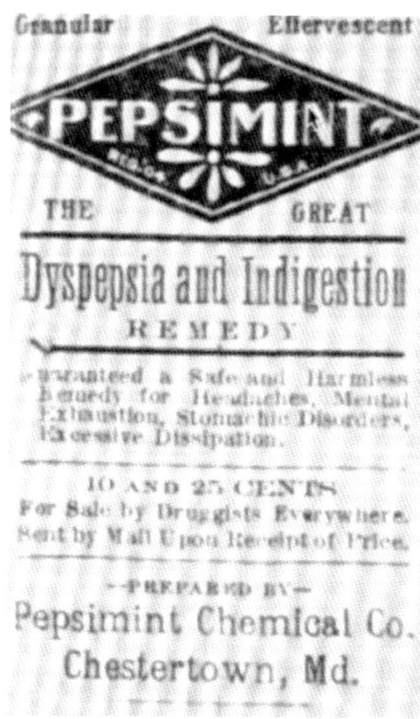

**John M. Luike Sr.**

"Jack" was born in Betterton. He started his career on the water when he was 13, quitting school to join his father as a commercial fisherman until he was drafted into the Army. He was sent to the South Pacific, where he was captain of a mechanized landing craft. After his service in World War II, he continued to be a commercial waterman. He started working at Aberdeen Proving Grounds in 1947 as a patrol-boat captain and also ferried other employees to Aberdeen on his boat, the *Clara Ann*. He retired after 42 years. He then began a job maintaining Betterton's beach. Luike also was a 64-year member of Betterton's volunteer fire department, which was next to his house. According to John M. Luike Jr., "He was always right there ready to roll when the whistle went off, he just had to hop the fence." (Courtesy of John M. Luike Jr.)

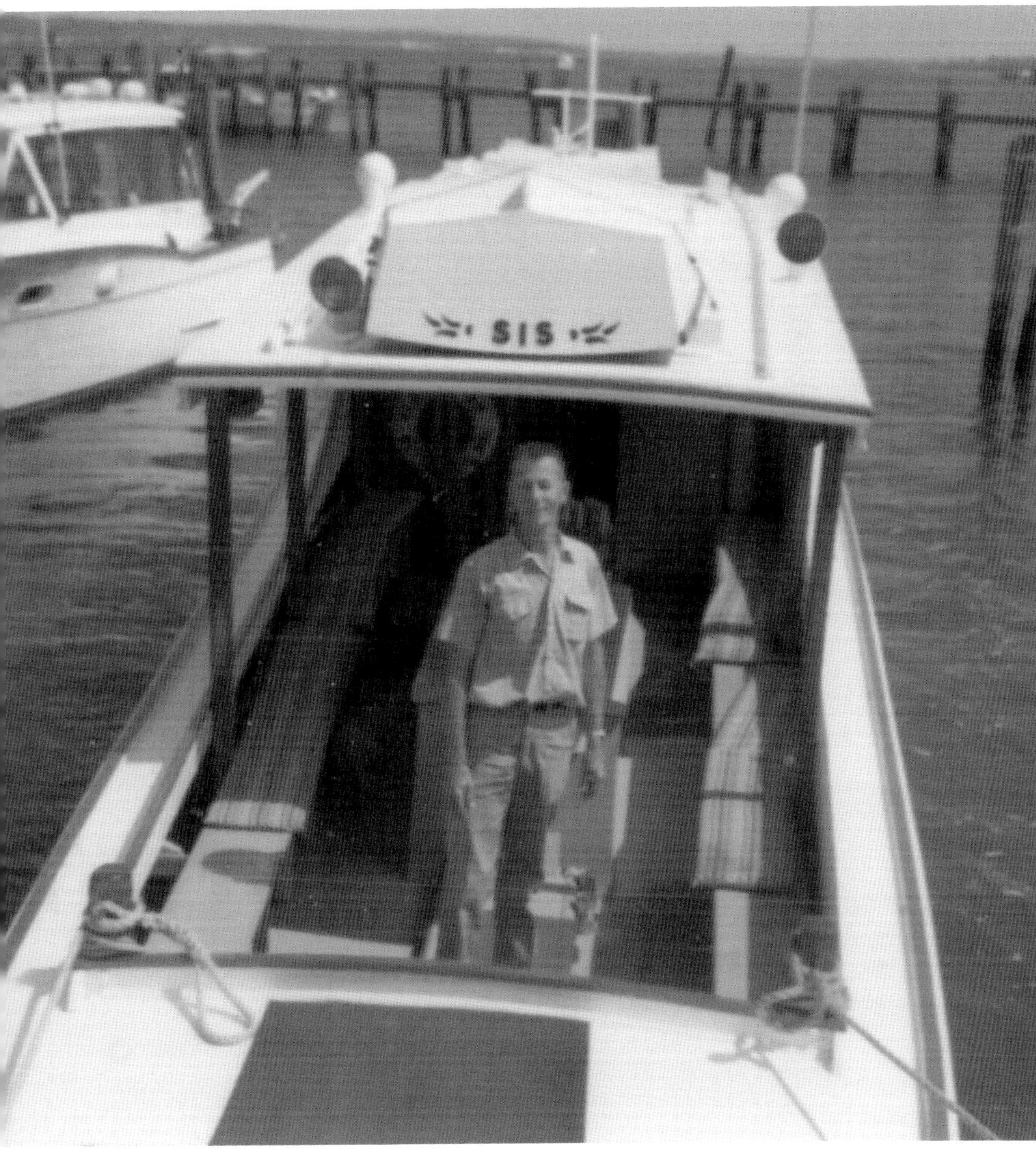

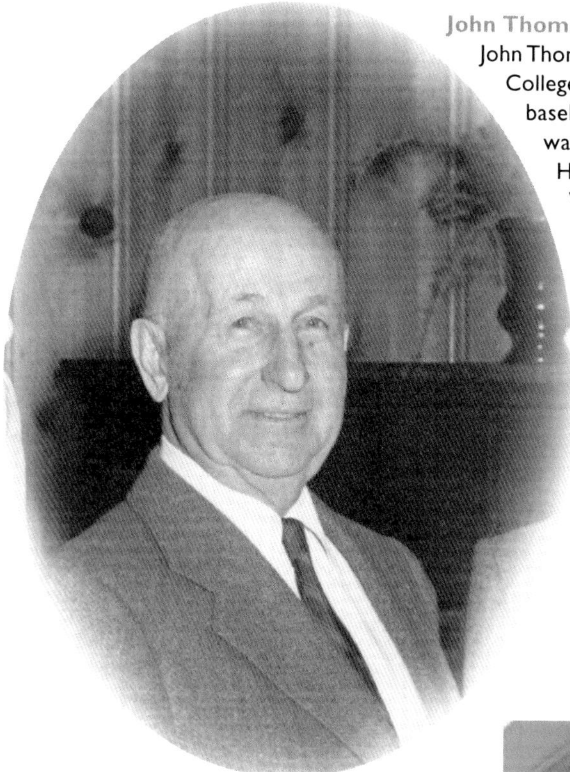

### John Thomas Kibler

John Thomas "Tom" Kibler was a coach at Washington College for over half a century. He coached the baseball, basketball, and football teams. Kibler was inducted into the Washington College Hall of Fame in 1981. He served in World War I, receiving many awards for his bravery, including the Silver Star, the Purple Heart, and the Distinguished Service Cross. (Courtesy of Jane K. Bristoll.)

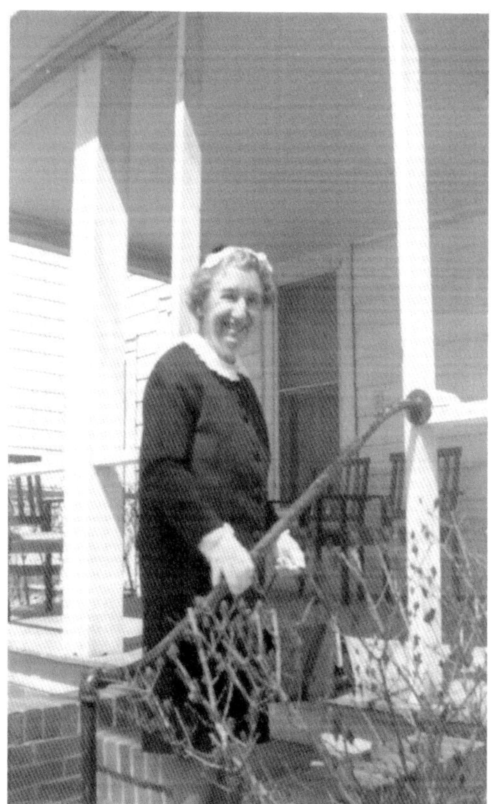

### Pollie Wickes Westcott Branham

Branham is remembered for Pollie's Column, published in the 1960s in the *Chester River Press* in which she shared her memories of Chestertown, where she grew up. She and her family lived in the Geddes-Piper House (formerly the home of the Historical Society of Kent County) for many years. (Courtesy of Robert Bryan.)

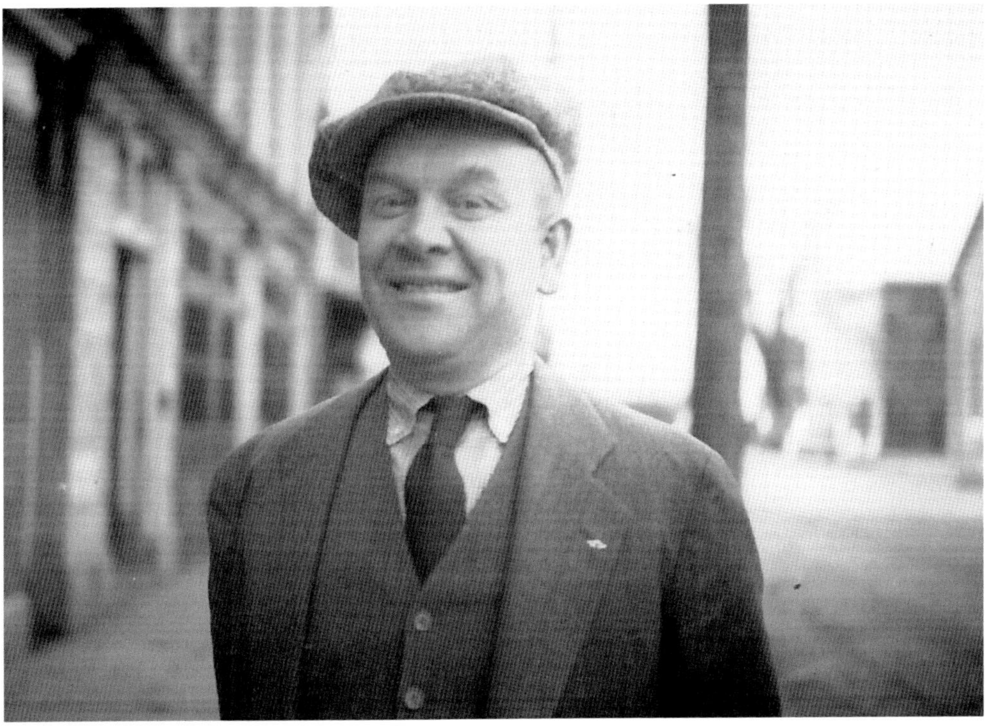

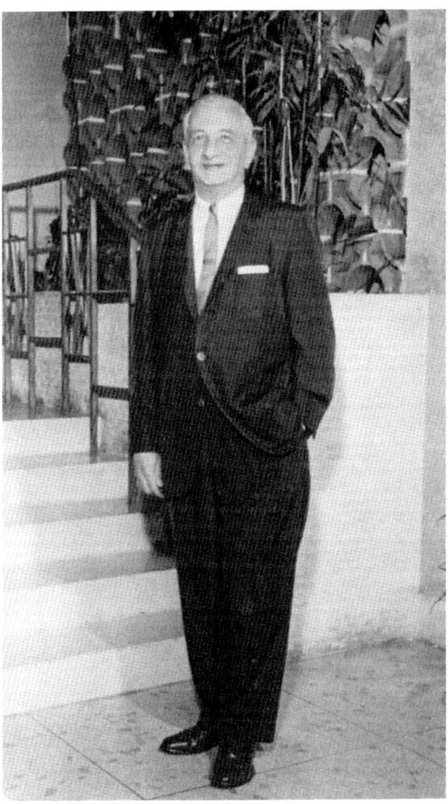

**Henry Gill**
Gill Bros. Ice Cream Factory and Dairy in Chestertown was owned by Henry Gill and his brother Charles Lee Gill. They made ice cream and operated a popular downtown restaurant called Gill Brothers with a marble-topped soda fountain and booths lining the walls. Downstairs was a small dance floor, more booths, and a nickelodeon that many remember. (Courtesy of the Historical Society of Kent County.)

**Henry Demain**
Vita Foods Corporation was in the pickle-manufacturing business when Henry Demain arrived in Chestertown in the late 1930s to open their canning and pickling plant on High Street (now the location of Dixon Valve and Coupling Company). He was their general manager until 1965. The Vita Food plant was a major employer in Kent County. Demain received the Outstanding Citizenship Award from the Chestertown Businessmen's Association. (Courtesy of the Historical Society of Kent County.)

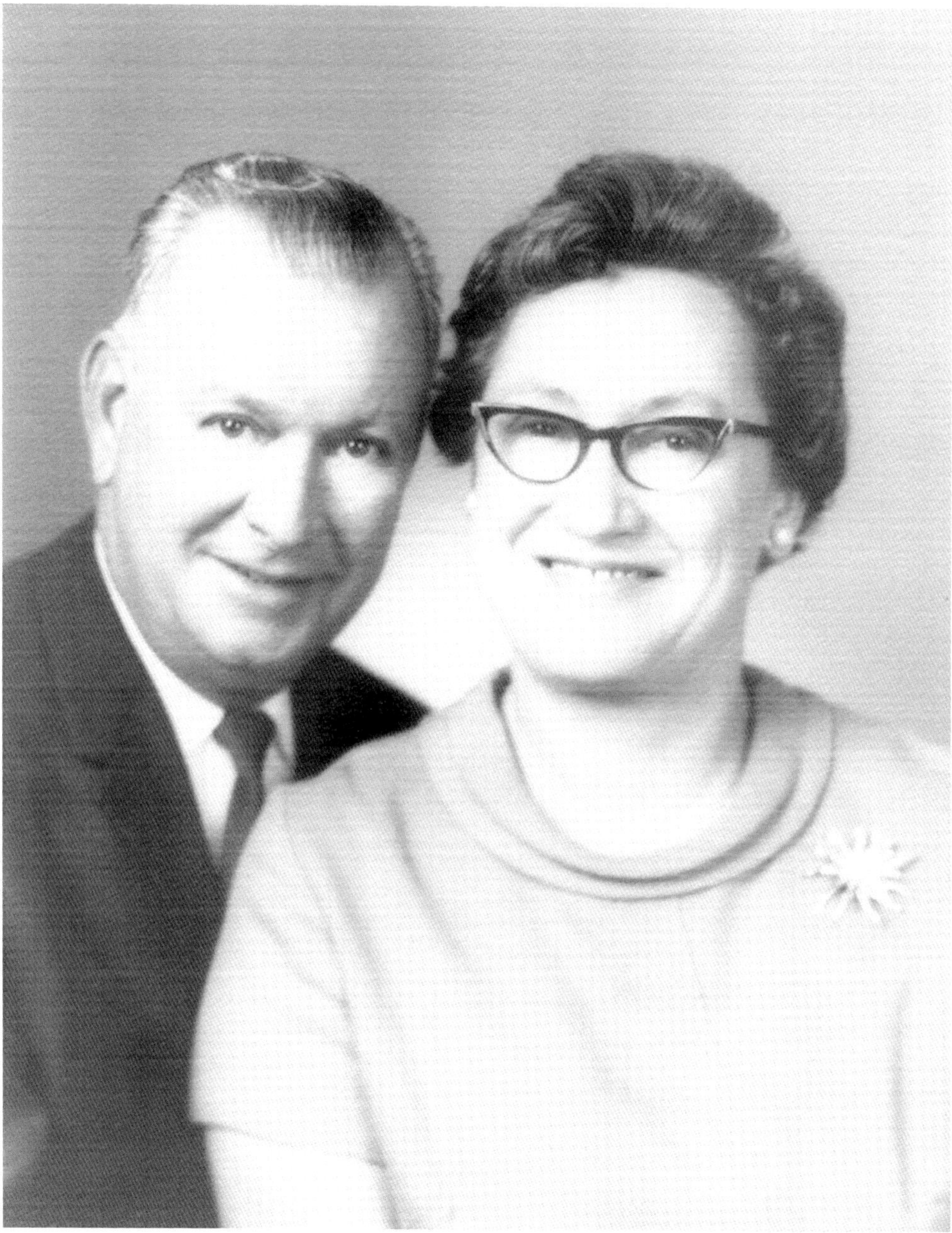

## Benjamin R. Fellows

Benjamin R. "B.R." Fellows opened a funeral home in Still Pond in 1916. B.R.'s son Edward "Eddie" Fellows and his wife, Mae Elizabeth "Betty" Shallcross Fellows, shown in the photograph, opened a Millington, Maryland, location in 1939. Eddie and Betty's oldest son, Howard, joined the business in 1962 until the early 1970s. Gary Fellows, Eddie and Betty's second son, and his wife, Gail, purchased the family business in 1979 and continued its operation until 1996, when the Fellows family, the Helfenbein family, and the Newnam family combined their funeral businesses to create Fellows, Helfenbein & Newnam Funeral Homes. Jason Fellows, Gary and Gail's oldest son, serves as the manager of the Millington location, which has been home to the Fellows family for four generations. (Courtesy of Gary Fellows.)

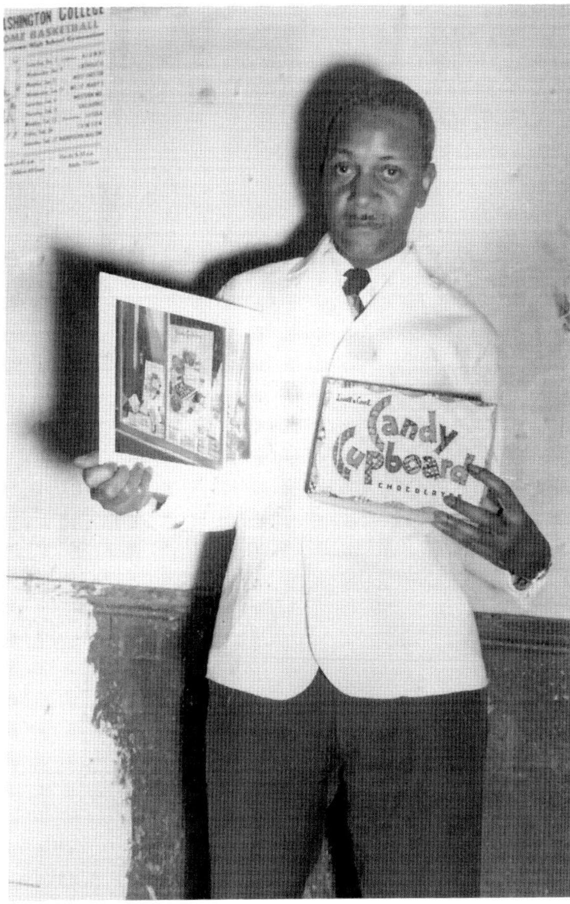


### James Chambers

Many remember James Chambers at Stam's Drug Store in downtown Chestertown, where he worked for many years. He was well versed in everything Stam's was selling, and delivered prescriptions around Chestertown on his bicycle. He was an expert in making the famous Stam's chocolate nut sundaes. Many local residents today still stop by Stam's for a treat from their soda fountain. (Courtesy of the Historical Society of Kent County.)

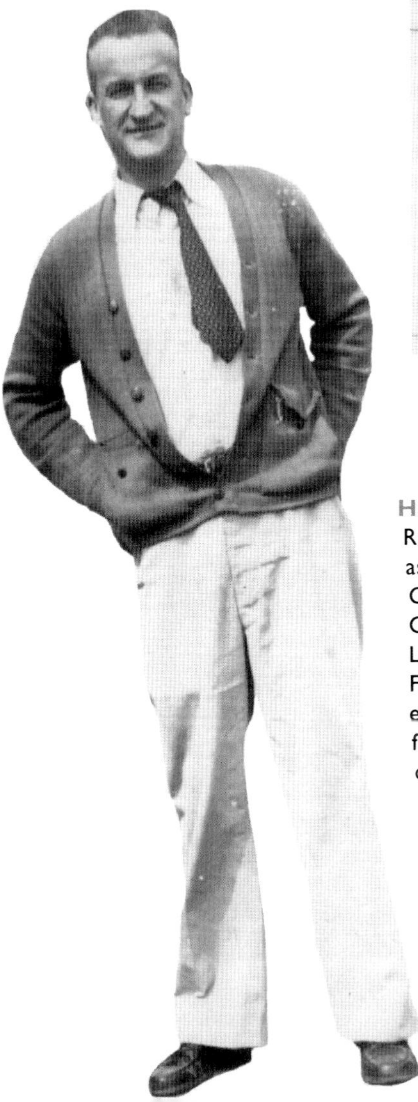

### Harry R. Rasin

Rasin was principal of Millington High School until it closed, assistant principal of Galena High School, judge of the Kent County Orphans Court, president of the Board of Millington Commissioners, president of the Millington Building and Loan Association, and member of the Millington Volunteer Fire Company. The Millington Lions Club recognized these efforts and still sponsors the Harry R. Rasin Scholarship Fund for motivated students from the Millington area. (Courtesy of G. Kevin Hemstock.)

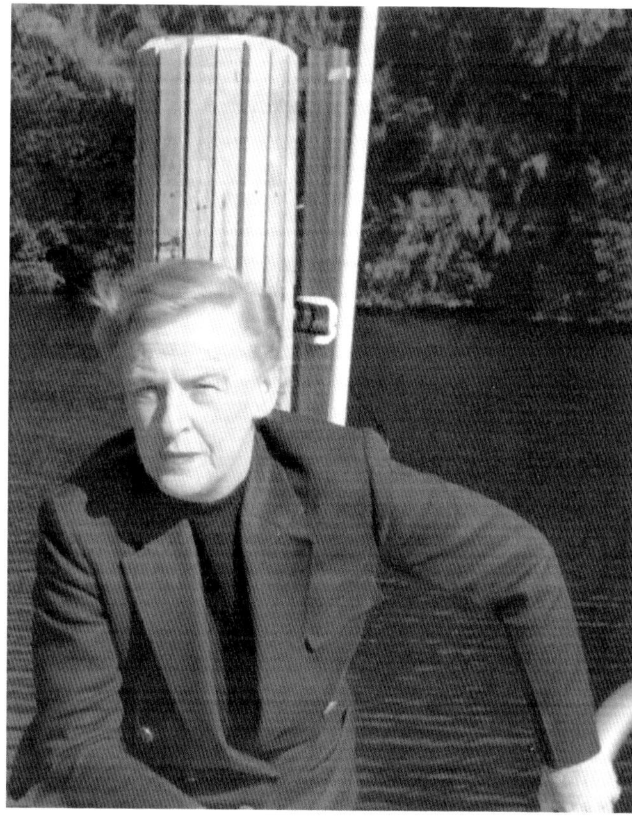

### Louisa d'Andelot Carpenter

DuPont heiress and philanthropist Louisa d'Andelot Carpenter, who owned Springfield Farm near Rock Hall, donated a farm near Chestertown for an Easter Seals Camp in 1953. Easter Seals Camp Fairlee is a camp that continues to offer children and adults with disabilities a camp experience today. She also donated 50 acres in Chestertown and arranged financing for a low-income housing project she named Washington Park. (Courtesy of Elmer E. Horsey.)

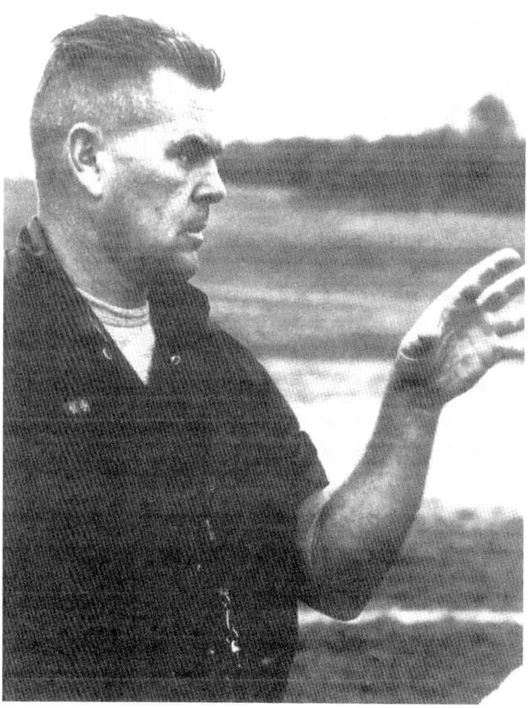

### Edward L. Athey

"Ed" was a professor and athletic director at Washington College for 38 years. He coached six varsity sports during his career. Washington College dedicated its new ballpark, Athey Park, in honor of his many years as baseball coach. Athey was inducted into the Athletic Halls of Fame of Washington College, Frostburg University, Allegany High School, the Maryland State Athletic Hall of Fame, and the Eastern Shore Slow Pitch Softball Hall of Fame. (Courtesy of Ron Athey.)

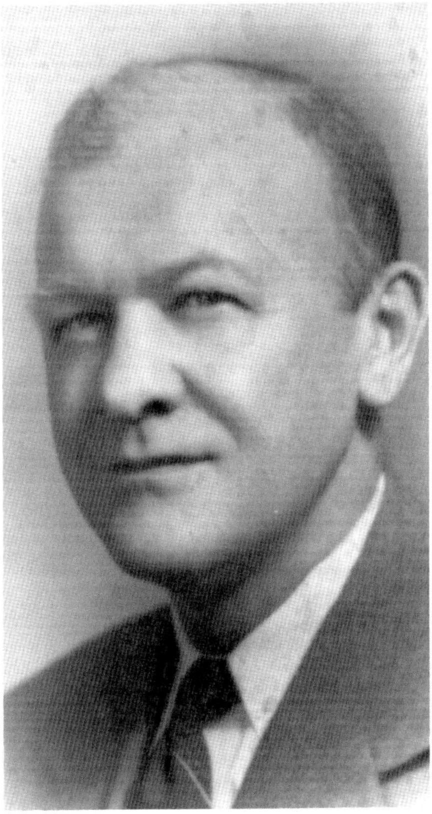

**Preston Patterson Heck**
Heck was an attorney for most of the governmental agencies in Kent County. "Pete" practiced law on Court Street in Chestertown (where his son Samuel L. Heck, Esq. practices today) for over 30 years. He was an instructor of law at Washington College, served as attorney and director for the Millington Bank, and was a longtime member of the vestry at Emmanuel Episcopal Church. (Courtesy of Samuel L. Heck, Esq.)

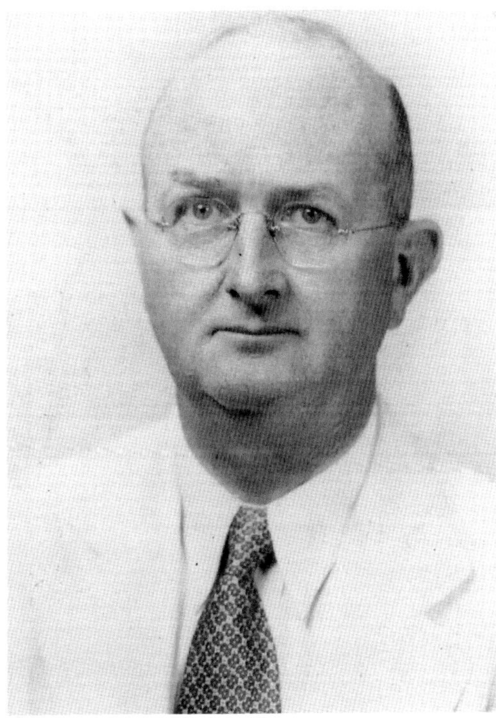

**The Honorable Stephen R. Collins**
Collins was often referred to as a lawyer's judge because he had a way of getting to the point. He did not use a lot of words when he wrote his court opinions. Judge Collins was born in Chestertown, and he retired after serving 17 years on the Maryland Court of Appeals. He was a World War I Army veteran and served on the vestry at Emmanuel Episcopal Church in Chestertown. (Courtesy of Richard LaMotte.)

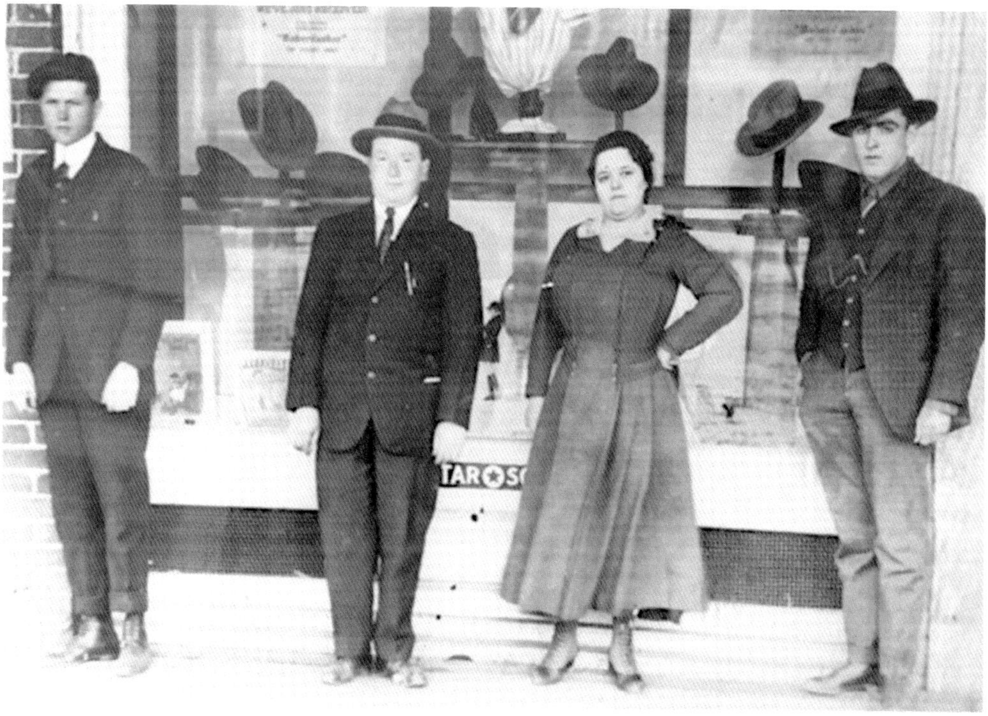

### The Bonnett Family

Ben L. and Yetta Dahne Bonnett arrived in Chestertown in 1922 and purchased a business owned by A. Sacks. Bonnett's Department Store stayed in business in downtown Chestertown for 58 years. Ben L. Bonnett retired in 1956 and his son Norton Bonnett and his wife, Edythe, continued the family business in downtown Chestertown until 1980. Norton Bonnett was also a popular podiatrist. Ben and Yetta are pictured here between two unidentified men. (Courtesy of Jan Bonnett Gavin.)

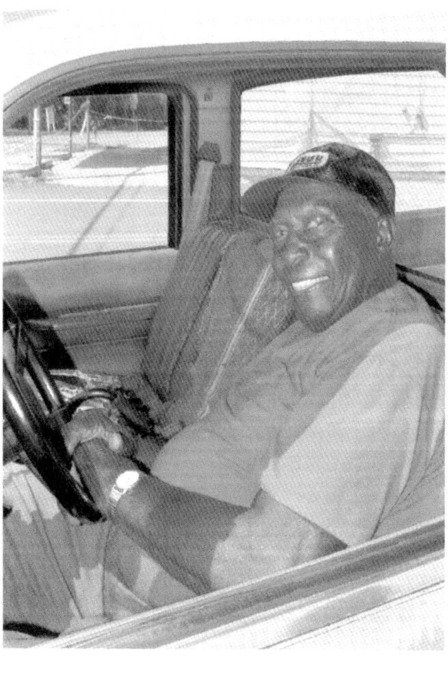

### Lewis Wilson

Many called him the mayor of Still Pond. "Mr. Perry" was a fixture at the Still Pond Store while it was open, and he had his own chair. He worked nearly his whole life, beginning at the age of 12, and earned the respect of everyone for his kindness, honesty, integrity, and hard work. (Courtesy of Walter Bowie, © 2011.)

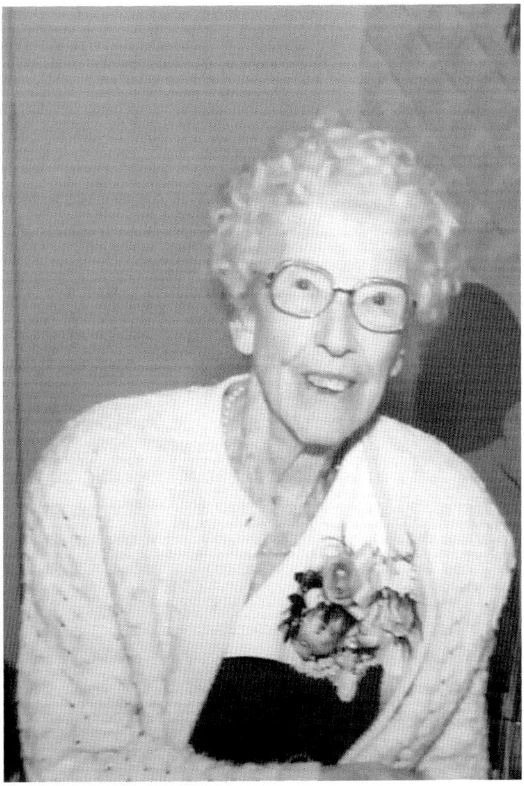

**Harriette Staples Welch**
The Jack and Jill Kindergarten was opened by "Miss Welch" in the Sophie Fisher Inn in Chestertown in 1943. Her grandmother had operated a kindergarten in the early 1900s, believing in the importance of an early education. She eventually moved the school to Emmanuel Episcopal Church until she retired in the late 1960s. The Jack and Jill Kindergarten was the first school for many Kent Countians. (Courtesy of Kathryn Cumiskey Schaefer.)

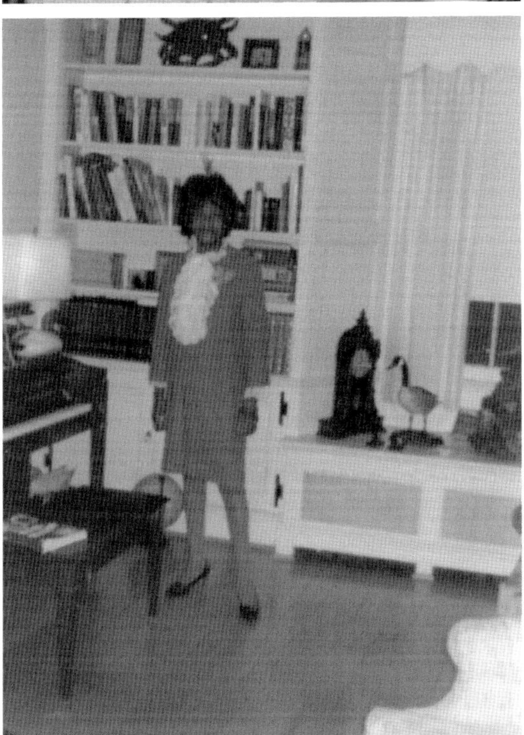

**Nellie D. Jackson**
Jackson was known for her outgoing personality. She began working for many Chestertown families in the 1930s and often entertained them with her piano skills. Nellie loved to stroll up and down High Street in downtown Chestertown in her high heels, greeting all of her friends. She died in 1994 at age 87. (Courtesy of the Horsey family.)

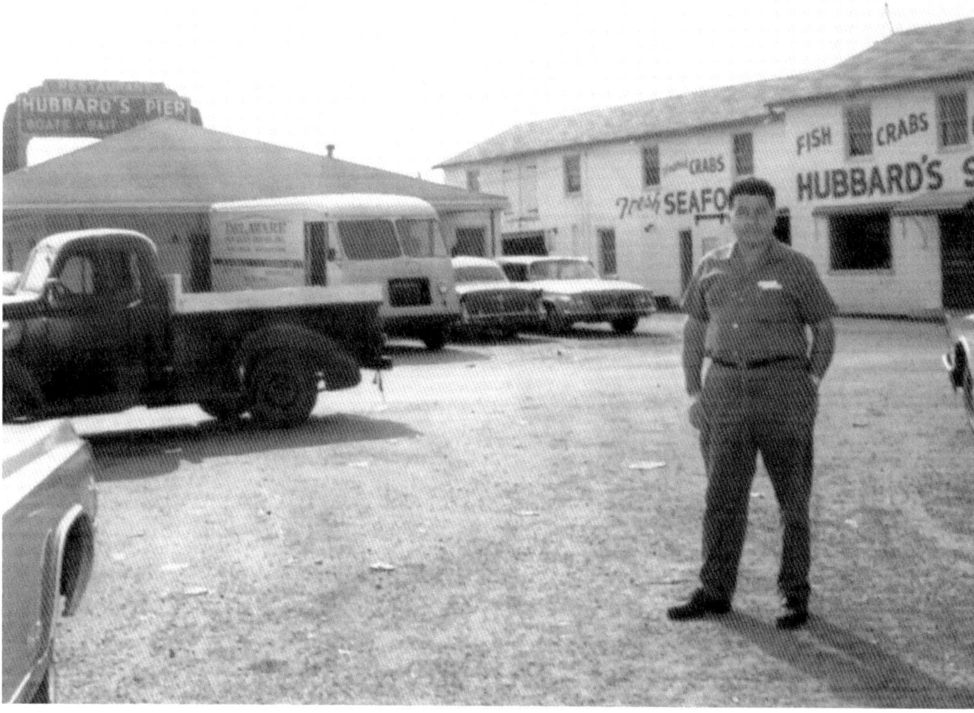


### George Wilkins Hubbard and Alonza C. Hubbard

Brothers Wilkins (above) and "Cope"(below), along with their father, Alonza, purchased a Rock Hall waterfront property in 1952, which later became Hubbard's Pier and Seafood Inc., a wholesale and retail seafood business. They also operated a restaurant on the property. Wilkins managed the company while Alonza and Cope were involved in the commercial fishing business. Wilkins passed away, but in 1962 Cope continued on his own as a waterman and farmer. He bought Bud Hubbard's Restaurant and Seafood in Chestertown in 1969 and continued to operate the business until 1977, continuing to work on the water until he retired in 2008. He was selected to be the grand marshal of Rock Hall's Fourth of July parade in 2007. (Above, courtesy of Edna Marie Dierker Hubbard Sutton; below, courtesy of Donna Hubbard Edwards.)

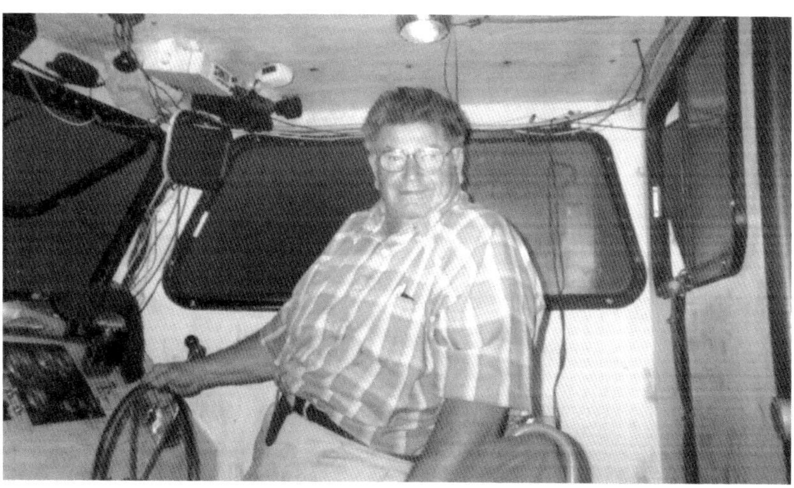

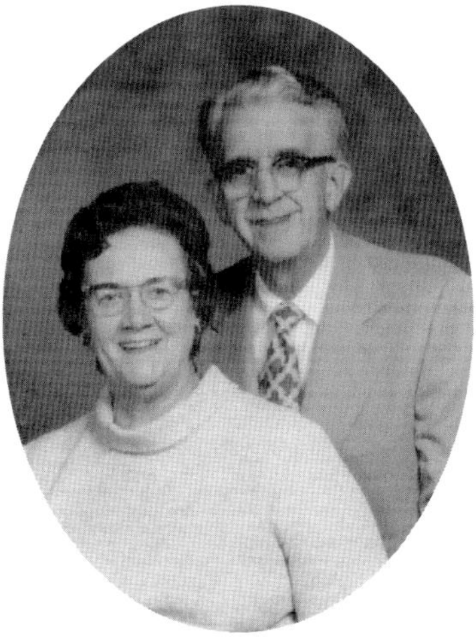

### Dr. Robert W. Farr

Farr was named *Good Housekeeping*'s Maryland Family Doctor of the Year in 1981. Farr, shown with his wife, Elsie, served as a captain in World War II. He began his medical practice in Chestertown in the late 1930s, retiring in 1991. He served as chief of staff at the Kent & Queen Anne's Hospital for several years and as Kent County medical examiner. (Courtesy of Joyce Farr.)

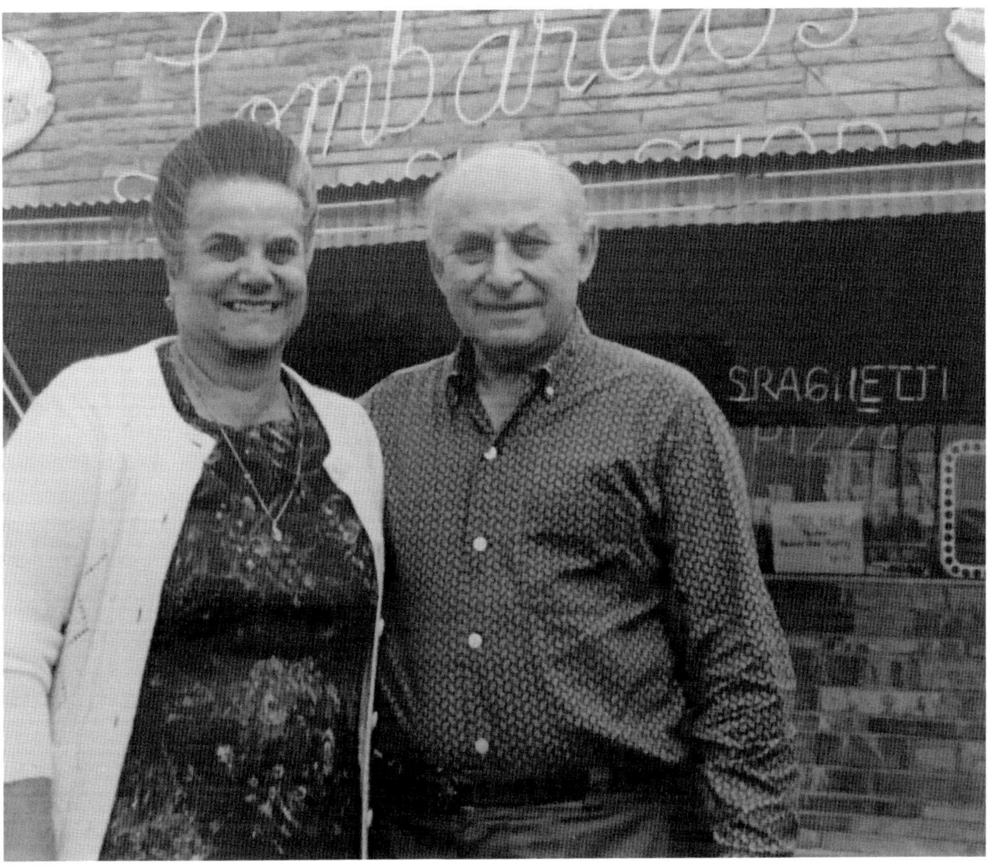


### John and Enza Lombardo

Lombardo's Sub Shop, a family restaurant in Chestertown, was owned and operated by John and Enza Lombardo for 32 years. Lombardo's had the best subs, steaks, and pizzas. John enjoyed writing, singing songs, and playing the guitar. He had a beautiful voice, as he sang songs in the crooner Bing Crosby's style. Enza was a natural born cook. Everyone enjoyed sampling her homemade Italian delights. (Courtesy of Tanina Lombardo Godar.)

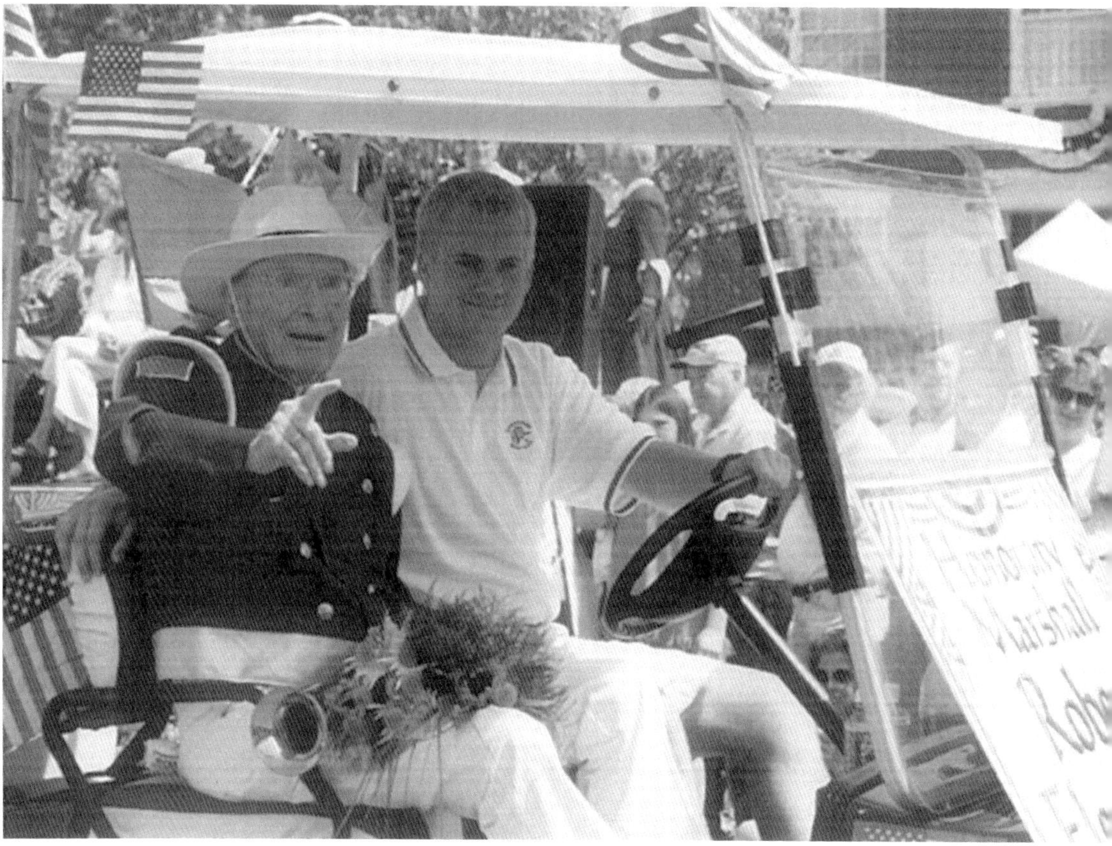

**Robert Townsend Fleetwood**

Fleetwood taught mathematics, chemistry, and many other subjects at Chestertown High School until 1945. In 1946, he opened the Kirby-Fleetwood Insurance Company with Jim Kirby. This company evolved into the current FAM&M Insurance Agency in Chestertown, where his grandson Creg is currently an agent. Fleetwood played the trumpet in the Chestertown Band and also served as their director. He was one of the original members of the award-winning Kent County Community Marching Band, playing the trumpet and marching well into his 80s. He also played "Taps" at many funerals. As a self-taught oil painter, Fleetwood painted local landscapes, portraits, and still-life paintings. He served as president of the Chestertown Chamber of Commerce and as a board member of Chestertown Volunteer Fire Company as well as the Chester River Yacht and Country Club. An avid golfer, "Bob" Fleetwood was club champion at the Chester River Yacht and Country Club five times and won numerous other trophies at tournaments throughout the Delmarva Peninsula. He served as the golf pro at Chester River Yacht and Country Club in 1949 and was a patron of the Masters Golf Tournament at the Augusta National Golf Club for over 40 years. Pictured here are Robert Townsend Fleetwood (left), honorary marshal of the Chestertown Tea Party parade, and his grandson Richard Cregar "Creg" Fleetwood Jr.. (Courtesy of Richard Fleetwood.)

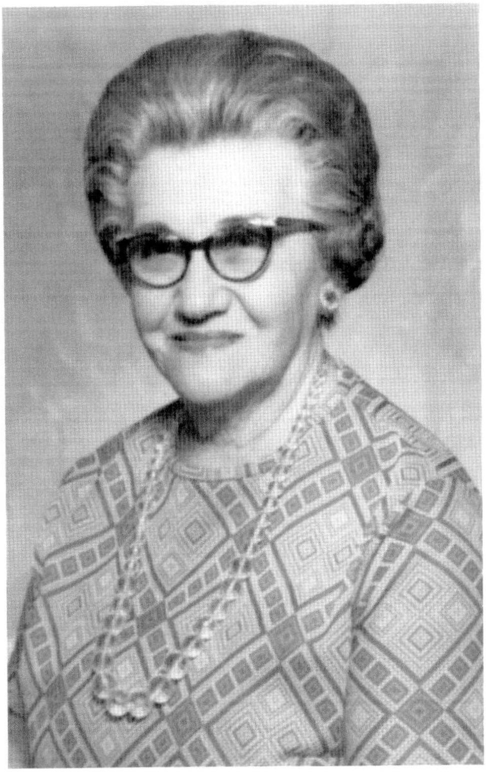

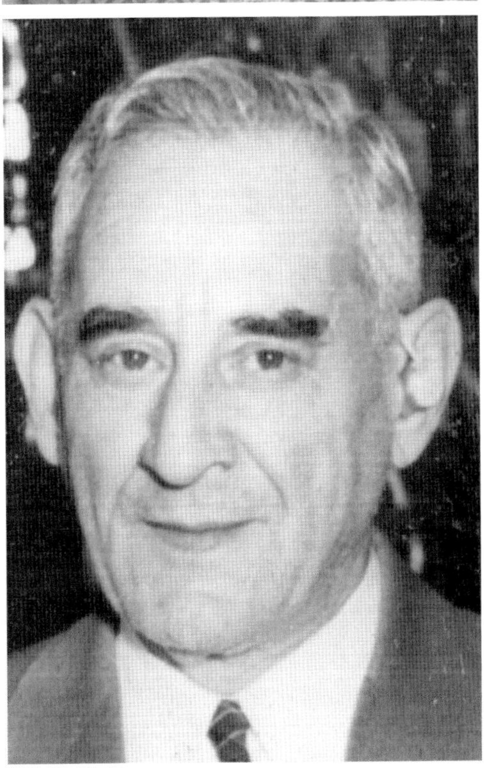

**Baurice and Jeanette Fox**
Fox's Five Cent to One Dollar variety store was opened on Cross Street in Chestertown by Baurice Fox and his wife, Jeanette, in 1923. They later moved the store to a High Street location where it remained until they retired after 40 years in business. They also opened Fox's Furniture Store, the Yardstick, and the Family Shoe Store, all on High Street in downtown Chestertown. (Both, courtesy of Frances Goldstein Sindler.)

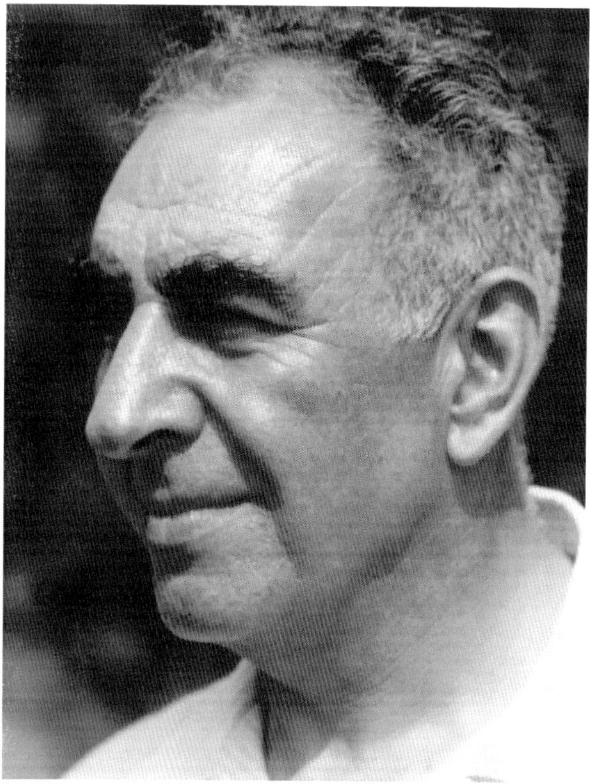

**Joseph P. Linduska**

An internationally respected conservationist, Linduska of Chestertown was known for his humorous writing in the *Kent County News*, which won him awards and a devoted following on the Eastern Shore. He was a research scientist and pioneered federal studies that exposed the fatal link between pesticides and wildlife reproduction. He worked for the Department of Agriculture, the US Fish and Wildlife Service, the National Audubon Society as vice president for science, and as the director of public relations and wildlife management for Remington Arms Company in Chestertown. Linduska was the author of two books, including his collected work, *A Writer's Voice*, edited by Louise E. Dove, which pulls together many of the articles he wrote for the *Kent County News*, over 50 technical papers, and over 300 popular articles about the outdoors. He was also a columnist for *Sports Afield* magazine. (Courtesy of Kent Price III.)

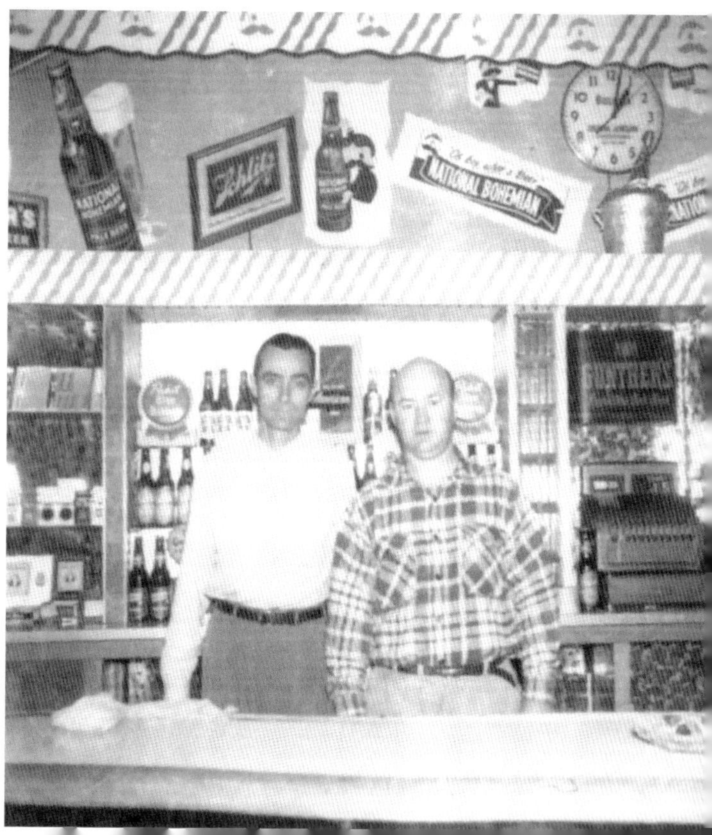


**Francis Gibson**

The Blue Bird, Chestertown's landmark tavern and restaurant, was built by "Gibby" in 1937. He owned and operated it until it was sold in the early 1980s and also worked for the *Kent County News* as their courier for 17 years. Gibby (right) and Milford Dukes (left) were well known to generations of Kent Countians as well as Washington College students and visitors. (Courtesy of Beverly and Francis Gibson.)

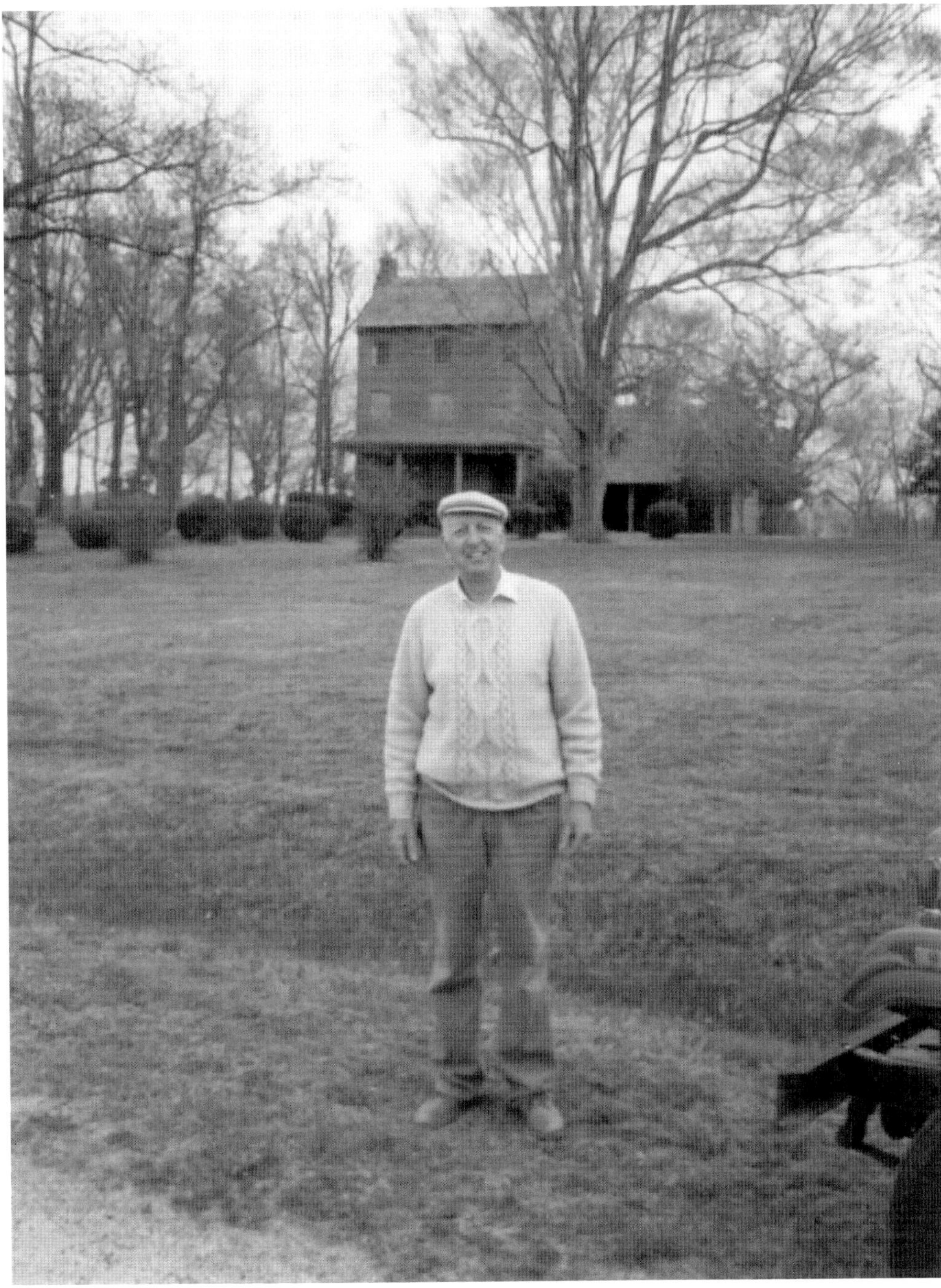

Walter Barrett Harris Jr.
Harris promoted and pioneered no-till farming and was instrumental in developing Camp Howell, a Boy Scout retreat. Harris devoted his life to Blooming Neck Farm and the Chesapeake Bay in Kent County. He was a founder and past president of the Kent County Heritage Trust and founder of Kent County Museum Inc. He was awarded the title Admiral of the Chesapeake Bay in 2000 by the State of Maryland. (Courtesy of Dolly Harris.)

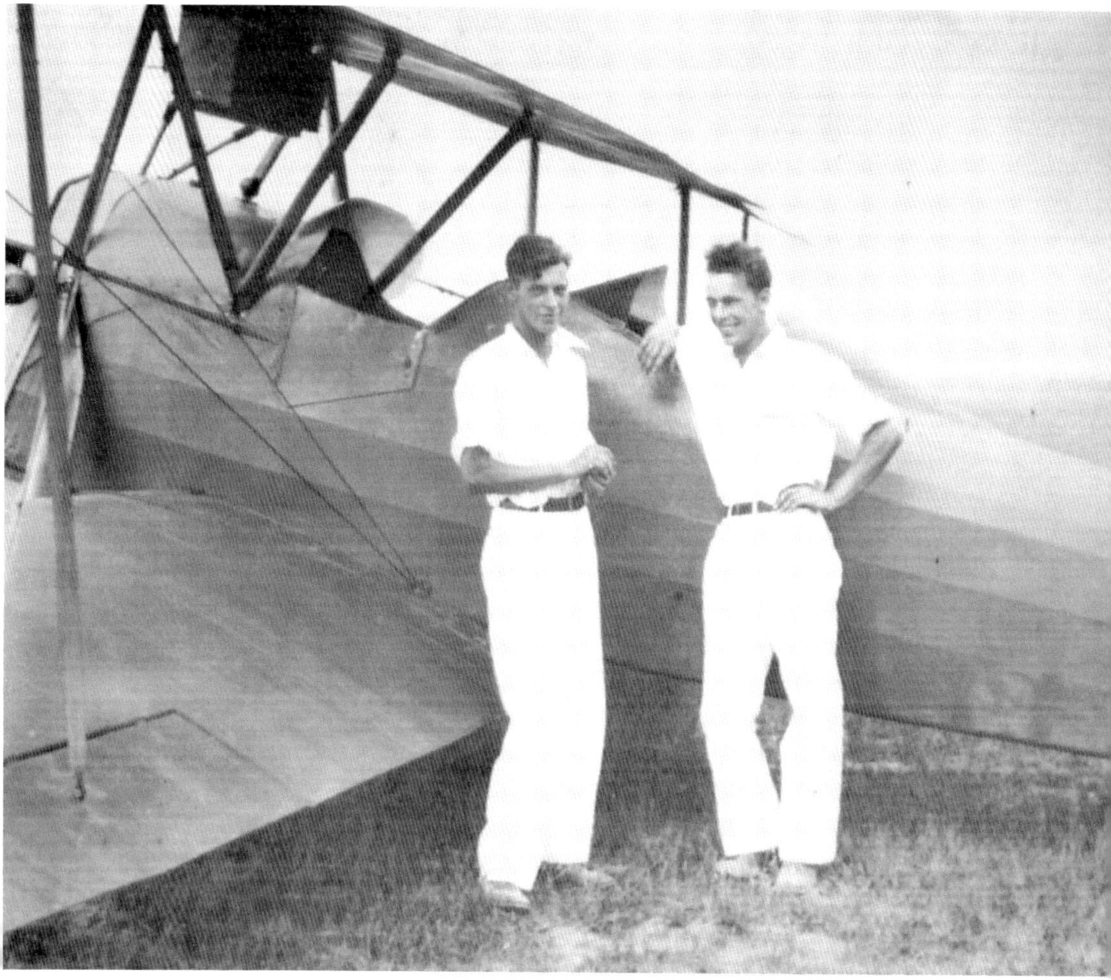

**Arthur Livingston "Mike" Harris and John Baynard "Blackie" Harris**
Brothers Mike (right) and Blackie (left) introduced many Kent Countians to the age of flight. They grew up on the family farm near Betterton on the Chesapeake Bay. Mike purchased a bi-wing Waco plane, hopped passengers sometimes at a penny a pound for a ride, and attracted a crowd when he and Blackie performed aerial acrobatics and wing walking. There were few airports around so Mike would land on almost any flat field long enough to accommodate takeoffs. If it got too dark, lanterns were placed on each end of the runway to help with the landing. The Waco met its end in a dispute with a thunderstorm in 1936. Blackie's red parachute was cut into pieces and made into dresses for the girls in his family. Mike and Blackie later visited many states in a 1947 Bellanca airplane. (Courtesy of Anne Livingston Harris.)

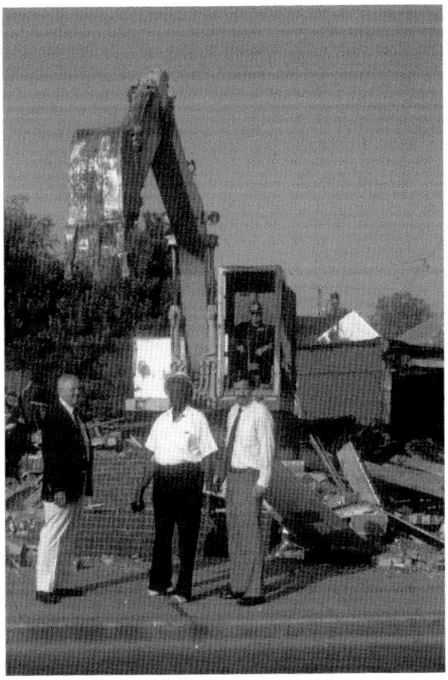

**Charles Graves**
"Charlie" owned and operated the Uptown Club in Chestertown and hosted many up-and-coming entertainers, including Ray Charles, B.B. King, Fats Domino, Little Richard, and Otis Redding as well as many local acts such as Chestertown's own Jazz Johnson. The property was purchased by the Town of Chestertown for housing in 1988. Pictured here are, from left to right, Mayor Elmer Horsey, Graves, town manager Bill Ingersoll, and 'Tuck' Davidson in the cab. (Courtesy of Heather R. Davidson.)

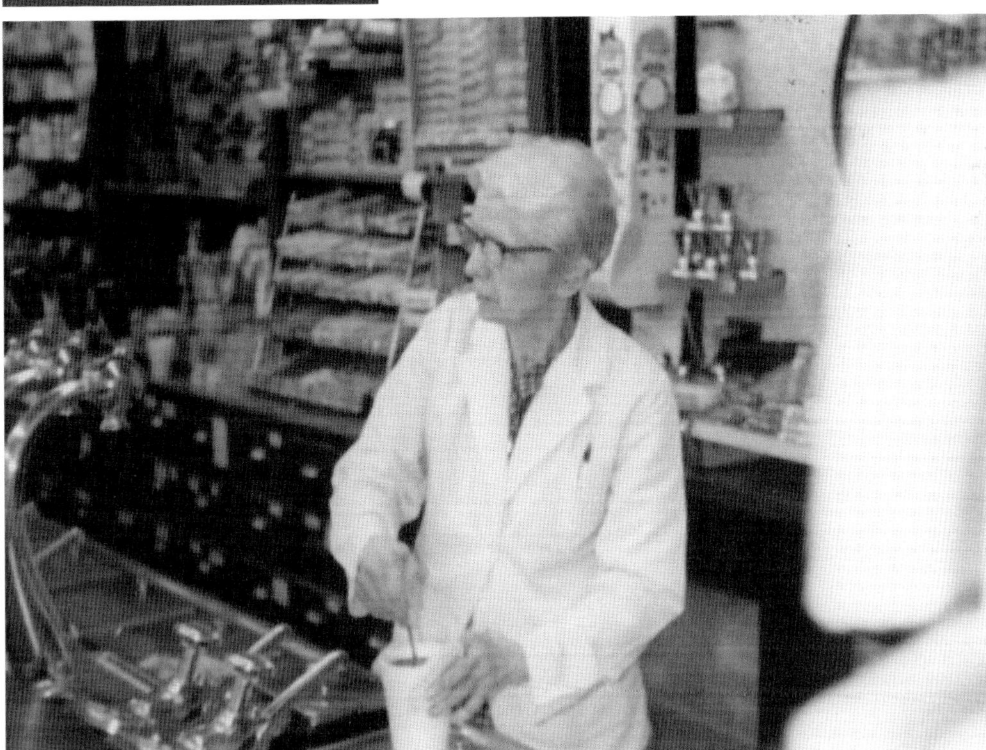

**Harriet Frances Skirven**
She was called an institution, fixture, and legend. A faithful employee of Stam's Drug Store in downtown Chestertown for 57 years, "Miss Harriet" was also known as "Doc" Skirven to many. She joined Stam's in 1924 right out of high school and lived in an apartment over the store. She received the Outstanding Community Service Award from the Kent County Chamber of Commerce for her hundreds of simple acts of kindness. (Courtesy of Buster Pitts.)

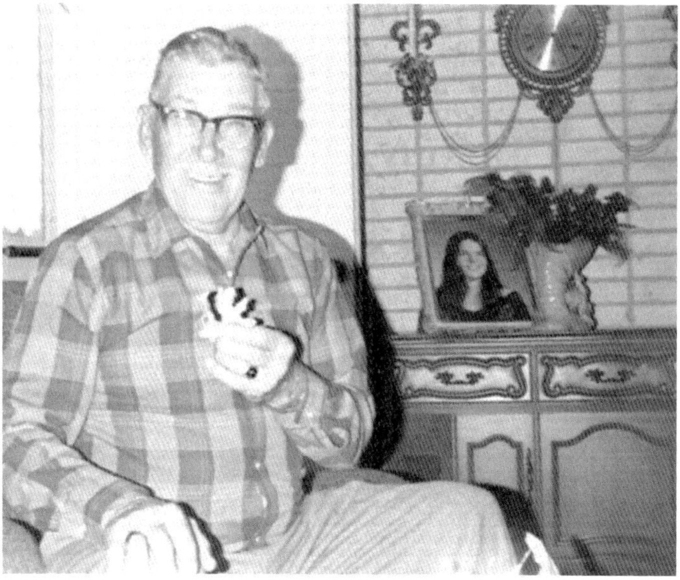

### George Wallace

Wallace umpired baseball and softball games in various leagues from Wilmington, Delaware, to Cambridge, Maryland, for 50 years. A lifetime resident of Millington, he played semipro baseball for two years and received honors from the Kent Independent League, the Kent County Women's League, and the Independent League of Queen Anne's County. In 1997, he was inducted as an umpire into Maryland's American Softball Association Hall of Fame. (Courtesy of Bonnie Wallace Massey.)

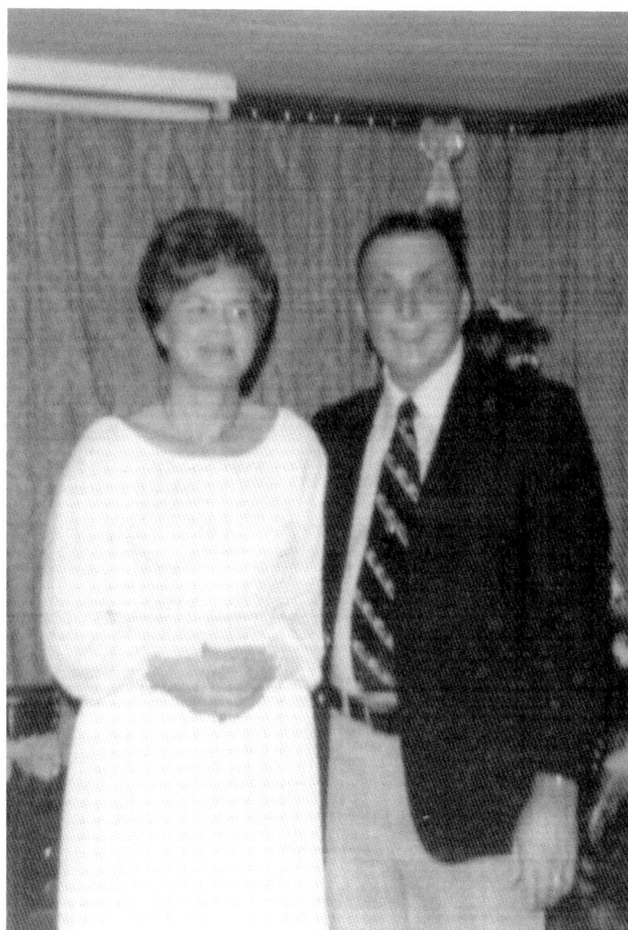

### Herman W. Voshell Jr.

Voshell's Luncheonette in Millington, owned and operated by Barbara and Herman W. Voshell Jr., was a gathering place for the local people for 27 years until 1990, when the business closed. Voshell also drove a Kent County public school bus for over 35 years. He was a life member of the Millington Volunteer Fire Department. At the age of 20, in 1956, he was severely burned while fighting a fire at the Kent Oil Company in Galena. (Courtesy of Barbara Voshell.)

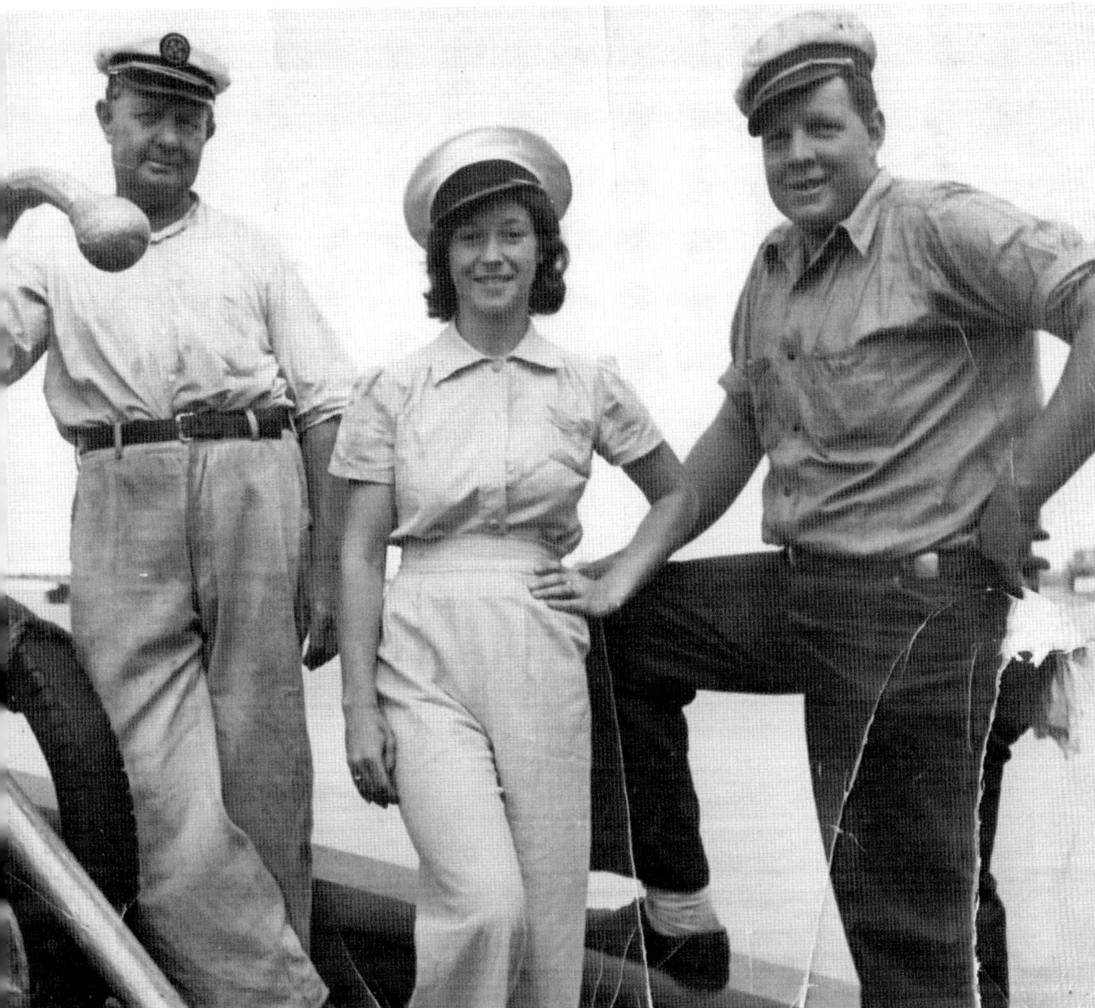

**Lillie Mae Capel Flowers Meredith**

At 22, Meredith was the youngest female sea captain to navigate in rivers, bays, and oceanic waters. Meredith, who was born at Buckingham Farm near Chestertown, received her captain's license in 1939 after five years of apprenticeship with her father-in-law Captain Flowers. A pioneer in her profession, the US Department of Commerce's Bureau of Marine Inspection and Navigation issued her license No. 1 on June 30, 1939, "to operate or navigate vessels not more than 65 feet in length propelled by machinery and carrying passengers for hire and vessels of 15 gross tons or less, propelled in whole or in part by gas, gasoline, petroleum, naphtha, fluid, or electricity and carrying passengers for hire". Meredith is flanked by the skipper of the *Chester* on the left and her husband and engineer, Otis Flowers, on the right. (Courtesy of Betty Hardman.)

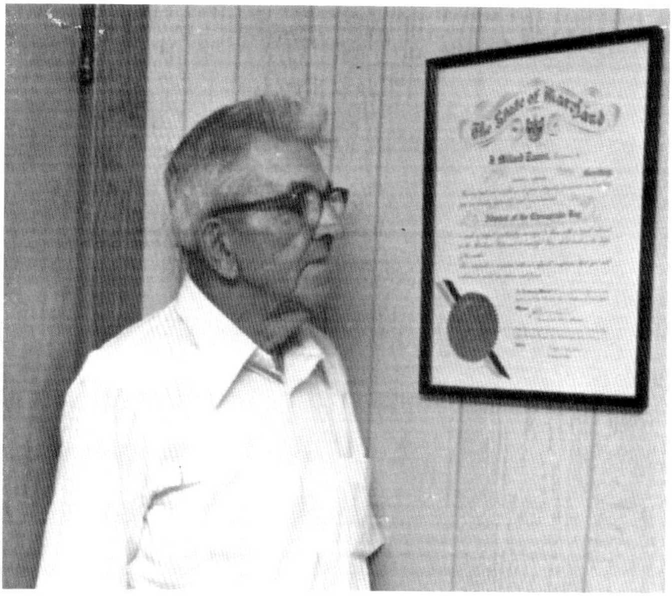

**Irving Crouch**
A lifetime waterman and commercial fisherman, "Captain" Crouch of Rock Hall was a former president of the Maryland Waterman's Association and named Admiral of the Chesapeake Bay by Maryland governor Millard Tawes in 1968. He named his fishing boat after his daughter Joyce. (Courtesy of the Historical Society of Kent County.)

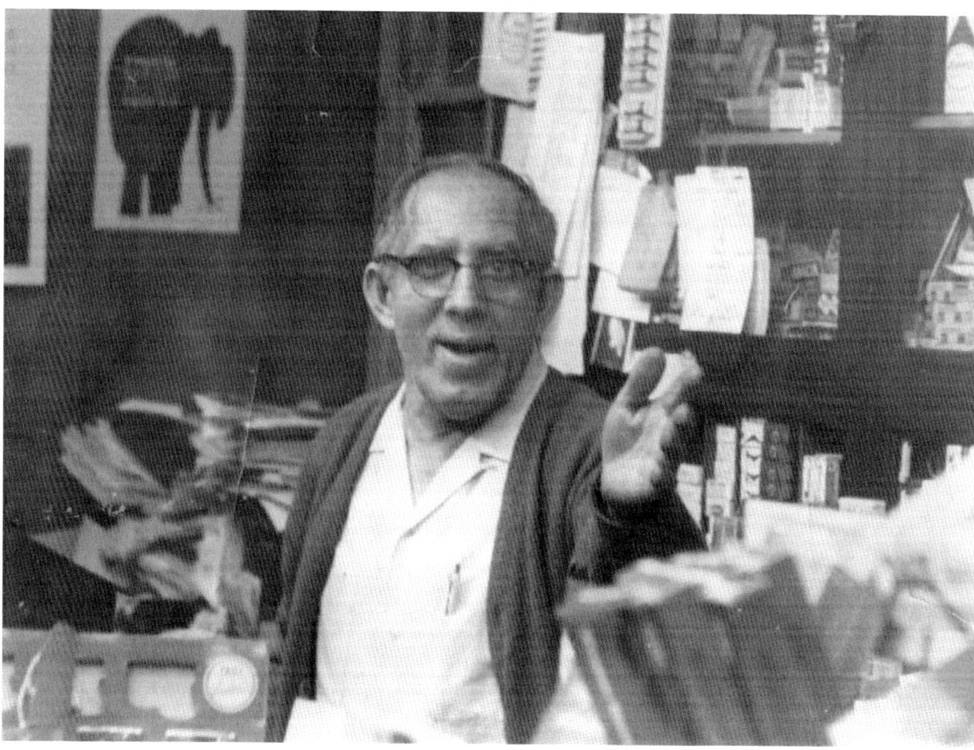

**Paul Sipala**
Paul's Shoe Store had its beginnings as a shoe-repair shop in Chestertown in 1927. Sipala retired in 1974 when his son Michele took over the business, closing it in 2014 after 40 more years. He was elected Second Ward Chestertown Councilman and played in the Chestertown Volunteer Fire Company Band before three presidents visiting Washington College. He and his wife, Edith, founded the P&E News Agency in the 1960s, closing it in the early 1980s. (Courtesy of Michele Sipala.)

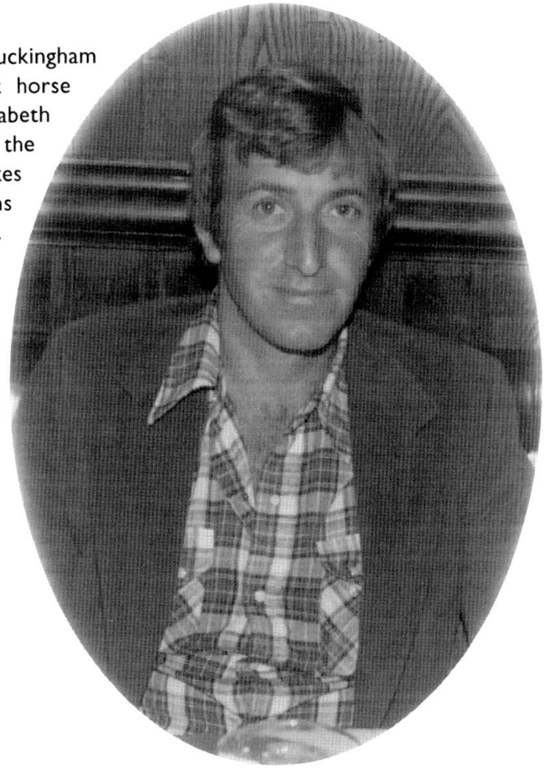

**E. Edward Houghton**

Longtime resident E. Edward Houghton of Buckingham Farm near Chestertown was a prominent horse breeder and fox hunter. He and his wife, Elizabeth "Binnie," bred, raised, and raced some of the nation's finest horses, including over 40 stakes winners. Five of their Maryland-bred champions were winners of the Maryland Million Classic. The Houghtons were named Maryland Outstanding Owners in 1997. Houghton was an animal lover, outdoorsman, and environmentalist. (Courtesy of Elizabeth F. Houghton.)

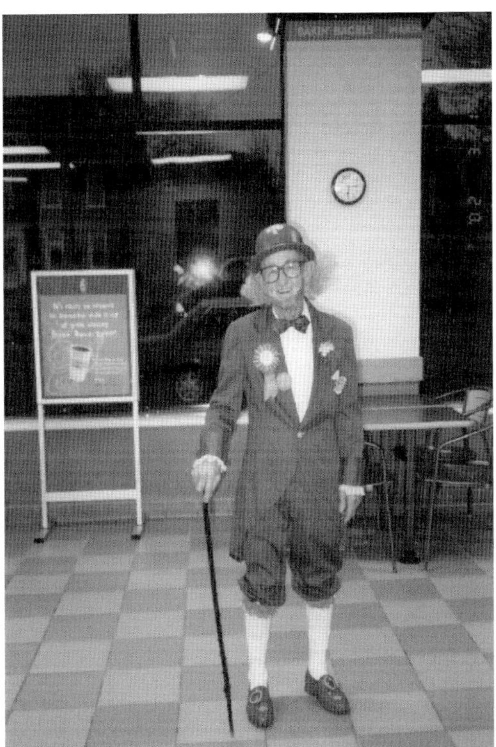

**Charles Henry Moloney**

During his career, "Charlie" was a jockey and Diamond Belt champion boxer. He was known to townspeople as Chestertown's leprechaun and could be seen out and about every St. Patrick's Day. He enjoyed fox hunting and woodworking and was an avid horseman and great supporter of the Washington College lacrosse program. (Courtesy of Doris Moloney.)

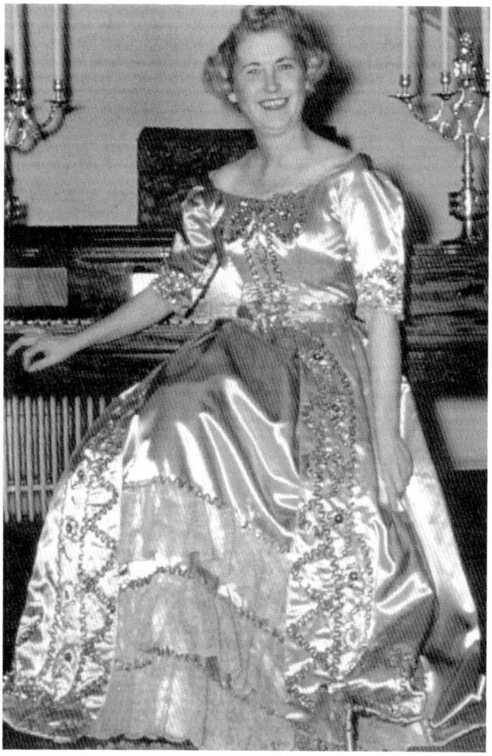

**Mabel Hawkins Deringer**
Known to her students as "Miss Mabel," Deringer lived in Chestertown and was well known for the dancing and etiquette classes she taught to young people in the 1950s into the 1970s. She also made smocked doll dresses for Hutzlers Department Store in Baltimore. (Courtesy of Mary Deringer Phelps.)

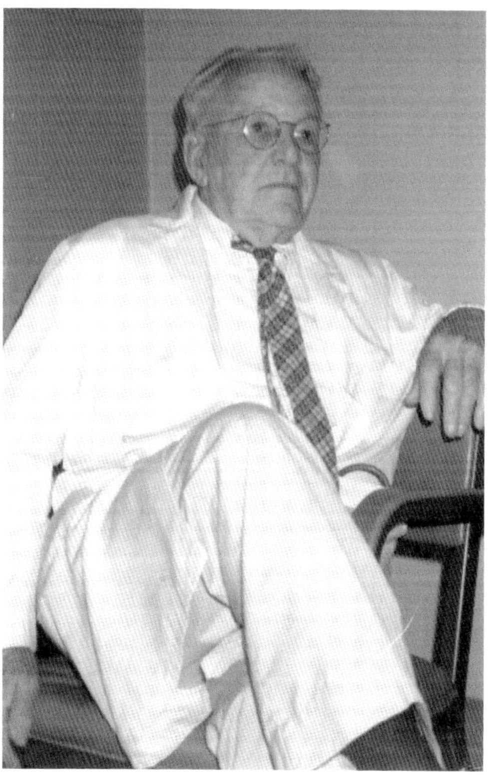

**Dr. Alexander Colclough Dick**
The first surgeon at the new Kent and Queen Anne's Hospital in Chestertown in 1935 was Dr. Dick. He made Kent County his home for over 50 years. Dr. Dick won the respect of all who knew him and was honored by his many friends in Chestertown, Kent County, and at Washington College, where he was inducted into the Washington College Athletic Hall of Fame. (Courtesy of Nancy M. Dick.)

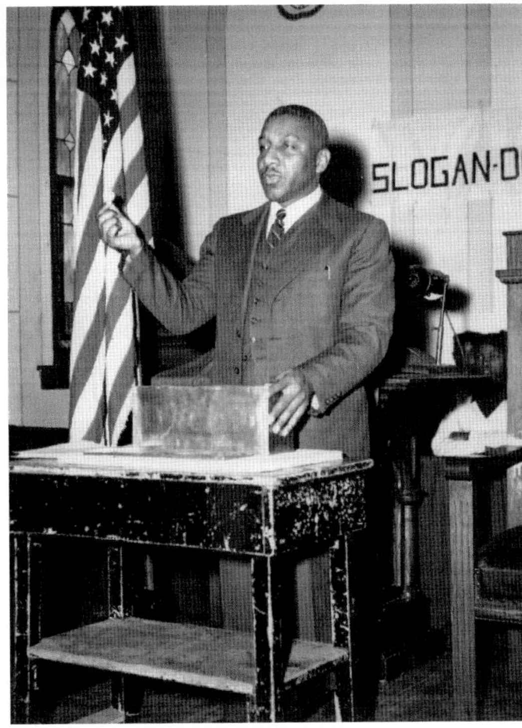

**Elmer Theodore Hawkins**
Arriving in Chestertown in 1926, Hawkins began his career as a teacher, and his wife, Marjorie Hawkins, who arrived in 1927, began her career as a nurse. Later that same year, Hawkins was hired as principal of Henry Highland Garnett Elementary and High School, then a school for Chestertown's African American children. He remained principal of Garnett until June 1967, when the school became part of an integrated Kent County school system. Garnett became the first Chestertown Middle School, and Hawkins was appointed principal. He retired in 1972 just six months before his death in 1973. The school is known today as the H.H. Garnett Elementary School. The Kent County community honored him in ceremonies commemorating a street in his name. Elmer T. Hawkins Drive is located in the Calvert Heights development in Chestertown. (Courtesy of the Henry Highland Garnett Alumni Association, Peggy Brown.)

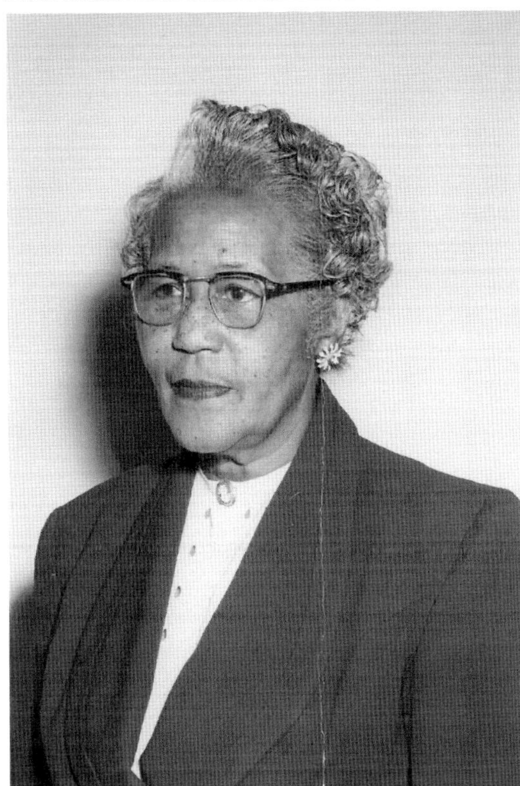

**Marjorie Hawkins**
Hawkins delivered hundreds of babies in Kent County and worked to promote the wellbeing of children and infants. She also worked to advance the values of scientific nursing and sanitary practices. Among her other duties, she gave children vaccinations for smallpox and shots to protect them from tetanus, typhoid, measles, and polio. Hawkins came to Kent County in 1927 as a public-health nurse and worked for 38 years among the County's residents. (Courtesy of the Historical Society of Kent County.)

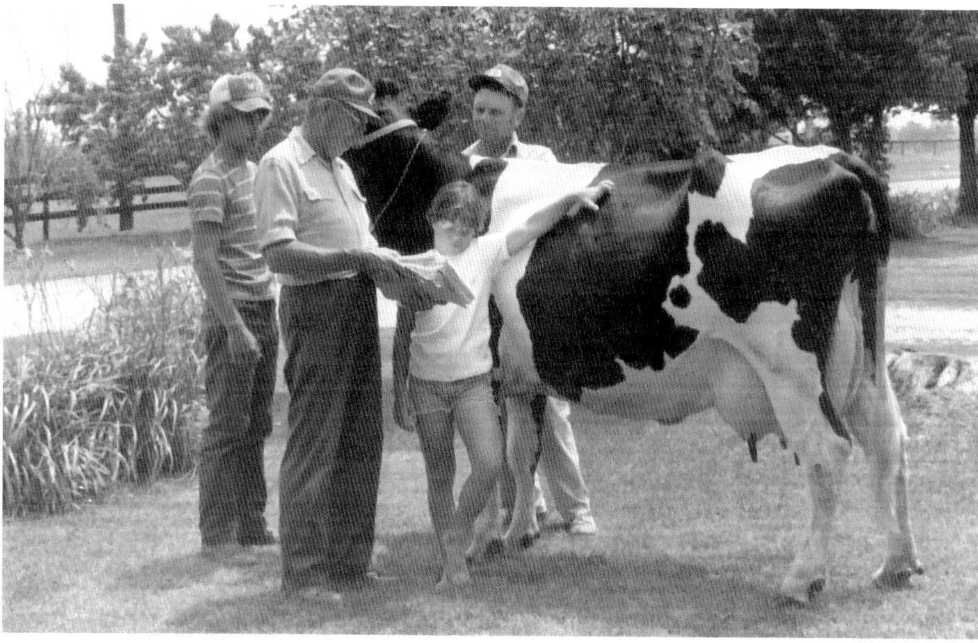

**Stanley B. Sutton**
Sutton's Bittersweet Farm near Chestertown is now operated by third-generation family members. The Suttons have been designated master farmers by *Pennsylvania Farm* magazine and were named Maryland Farm Family of the Year in 1996. Sutton served as Kent County's assistant cooperative extension agent for 40 years and was a local leader in the 4-H movement. Pictured here from left to right are William S. Sutton III, Stanley B. Sutton, Susan Sutton Nickerson, and William S. Sutton Jr. (Courtesy of William S. Sutton.)

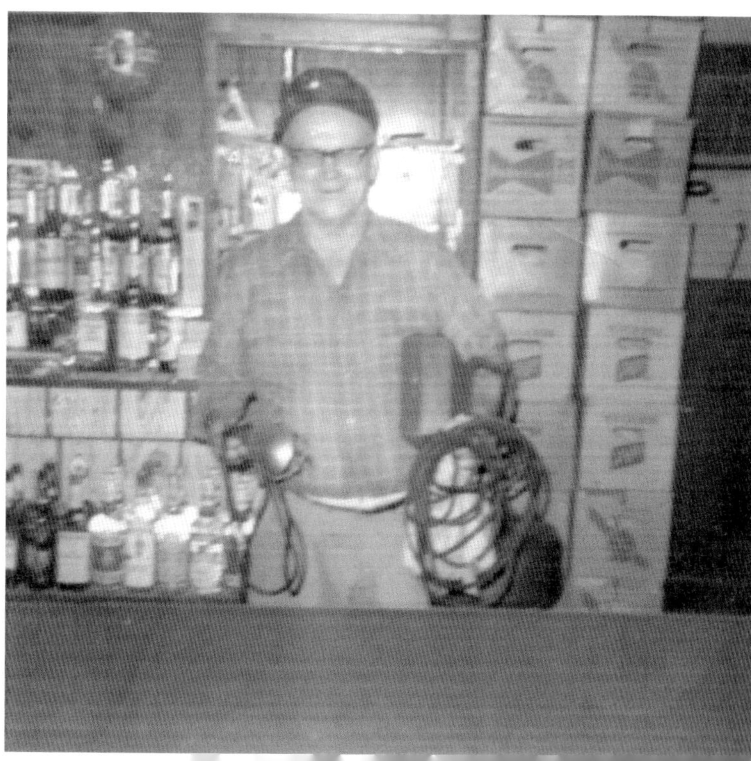

**Edgar A. Harris**
The Village Tavern in Chestertown was operated by "Eddie" Harris for over 30 years. He opened the tavern as a bar and restaurant in 1947. It became just a bar in the 1950s and was one of the most popular gathering places for many local patrons as well as Washington College students. (Courtesy of Charles Price.)

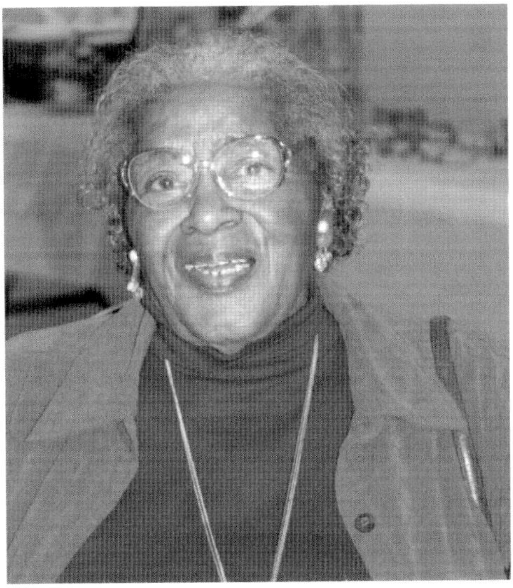

**Ruth Briscoe**
A lifelong resident of Kent County, Ruth Briscoe received the Washington College President's Distinguished Service Award for her many contributions to various organizations in Kent County. She was involved in the Kent County Chapter of the American Red Cross, the Kent and Queen Anne's Hospital/Chester River Hospital Auxiliary, and American Cancer Society Relay for Life. (Courtesy of Glenda Dierker.)

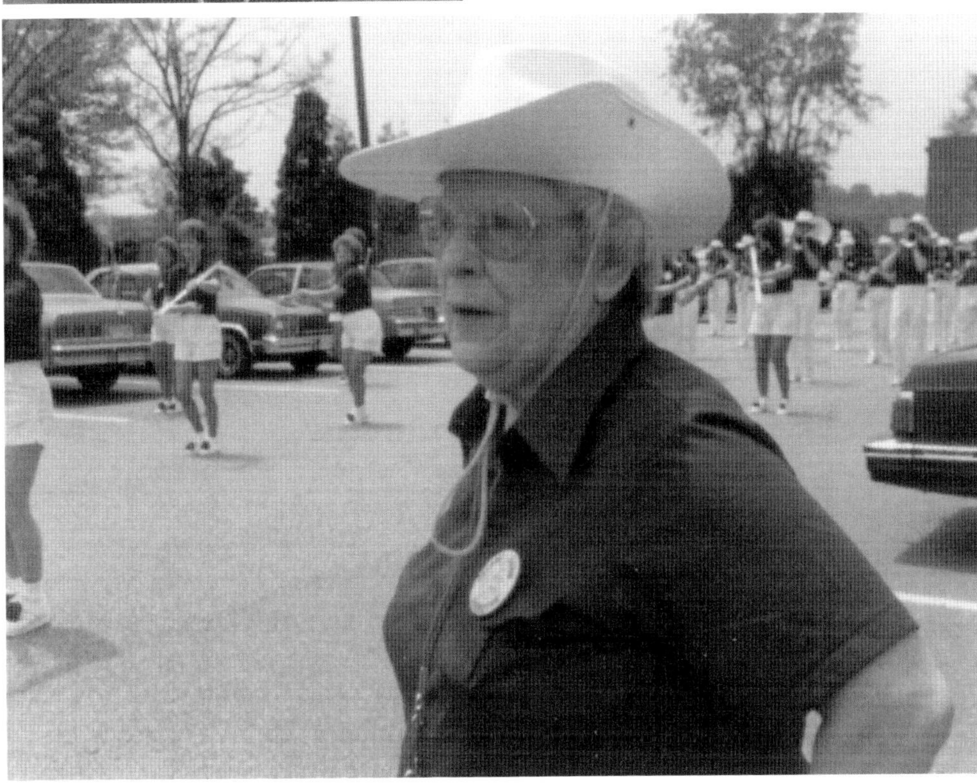

**Leone Yohe Woodall**
A longtime local teacher, Leone Yohe Woodall, of Chestertown, was the chorus and band director at Galena High School for many years. She was a gifted teacher who loved music. She organized and directed, with the help of her former students, a Galena High School Alumni Band that eventually became the Kent County Community Marching Band. A monument next to the Galena Town Hall honors Woodall. She was also named to the Maryland Music Educators Association Hall of Fame. (Courtesy of Dorothy Schauber Mench.)

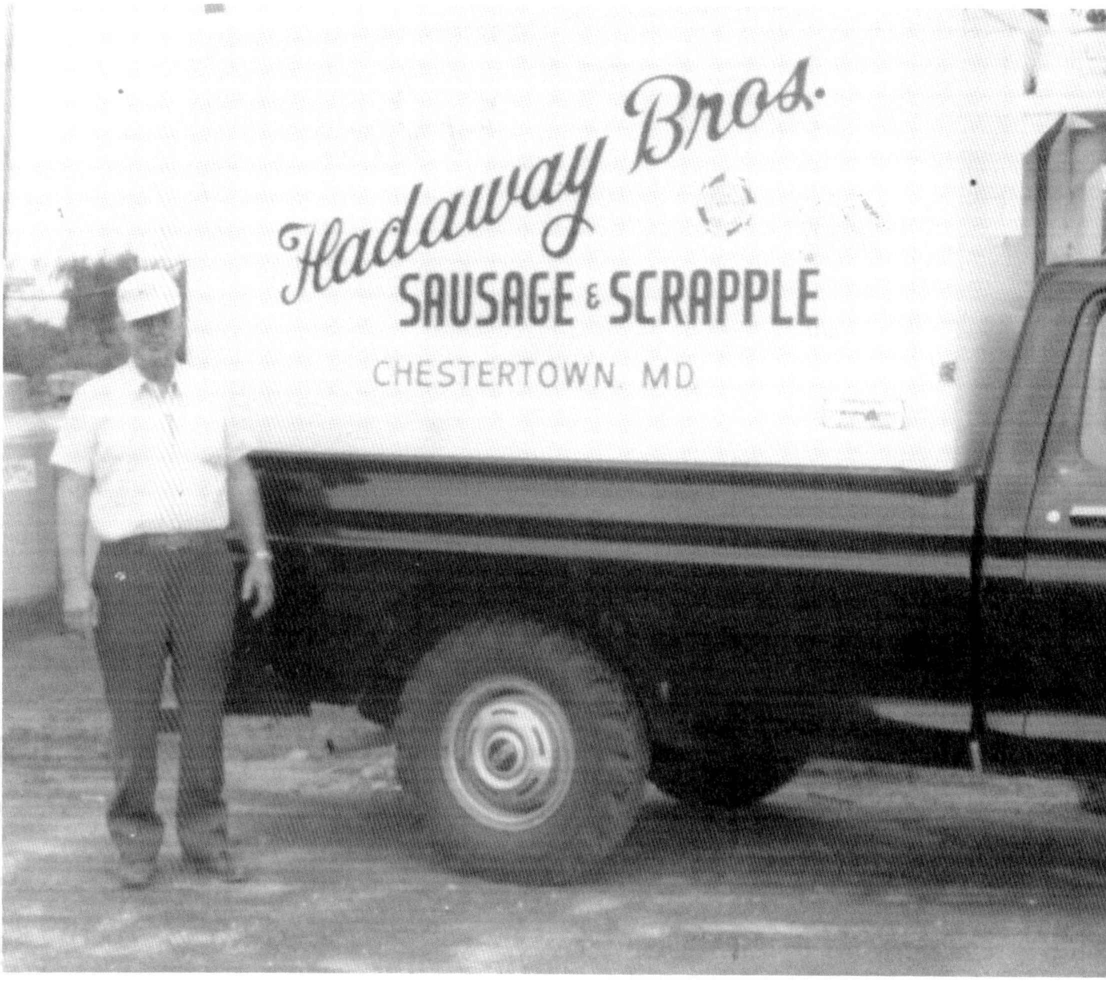


**Jesse G. Hadaway Sr.**
Hadaway Bros. sausage and scrapple were two popular breakfast items in Kent County and surrounding areas for many years. Jesse G. Hadaway Sr., shown standing next to his delivery truck, operated Hadaway Bros. Sausage and Scrapple in Chestertown until he retired in 1976. He bought the business from his brothers Gilbert and William Hadaway. The first scrapple was made from a family recipe in the kitchen of his sister Suzy Hadaway Robinson and delivered locally by Hadaway. The cooking and packing plant was built behind Hadaway's home on Cannon Street in Chestertown. Hadaway Bros. raised their own hogs. For over 50 years, deliveries were made all over the Upper Shore area. Hadaway was involved in the operation of Radcliffe Park, where harness-racing meets were held. He hosted many recreational ventures at the park, including a greased-pig contest for local children. In 1946, he created a second softball diamond across from the Chestertown Armory at Radcliffe Park and hosted day and night games. (Courtesy of Judy Hadaway Thompson.)

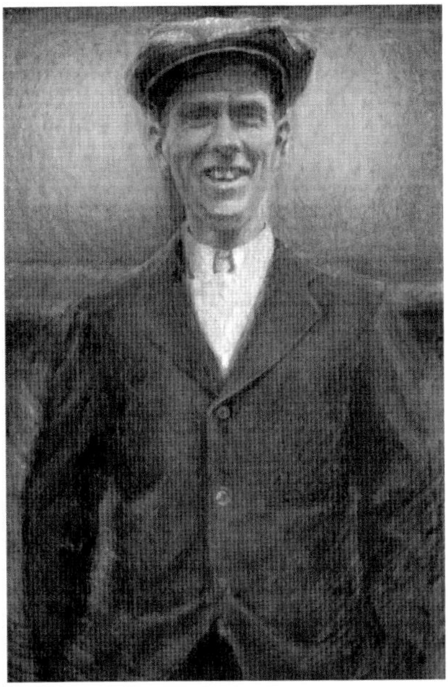

**Carl Leonard Brown**

Brown is remembered by many families as their local handyman, always ready to help those in need. "Mike," a carpenter, lived in the Quaker Neck area of Kent County his entire life. He was an entertaining storyteller, and his recollections of family and neighbors were often enriched by impersonating their voices. (Painting by Daniel Brown, courtesy of Carl G. Brown.)

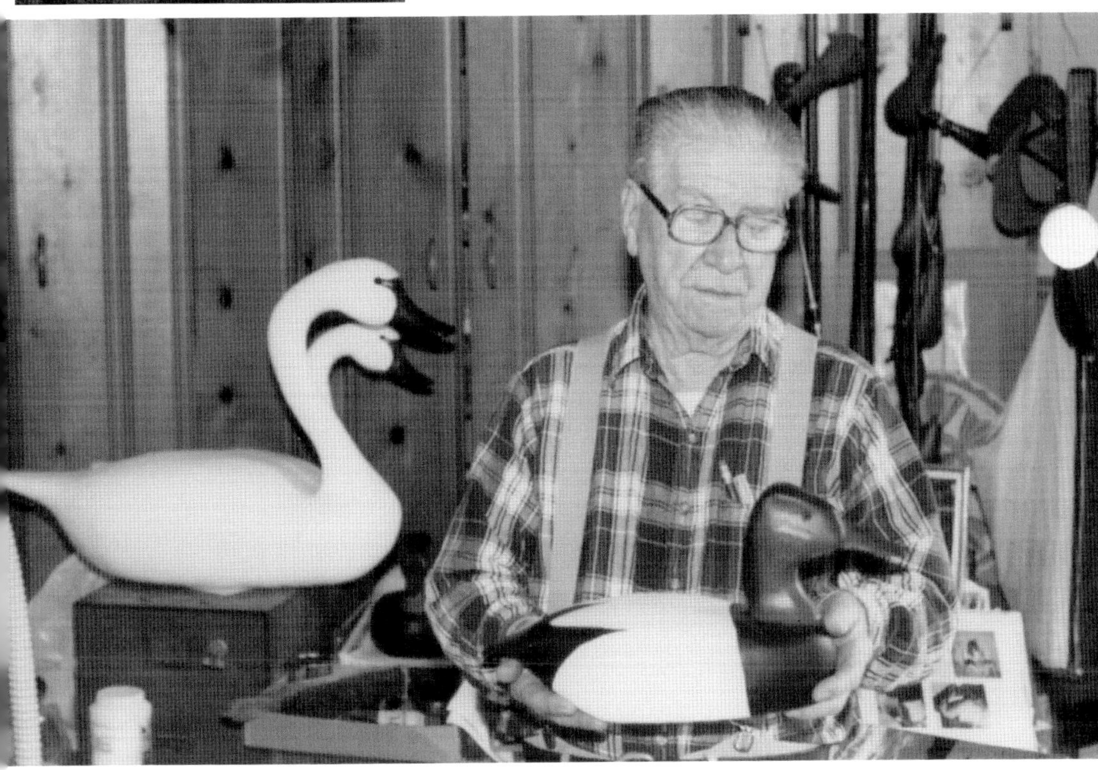

**George "Clifton" Simns**

Simns was a self-employed barber in Rock Hall, where he lived for 69 years. He loved to hunt, boat, and fish and took out fishing parties when he was not in his barber shop. Simns was an accomplished photographer and worked for the *Kent County News*, taking photographs of community events. He was also a skilled decoy carver. (Courtesy of William F. Schauber.)

### Harry S. Russell

A newspaperman for 47 years, Russell was the editor of the *Kent County News* when he died in 1972. He grew up in Chestertown, where his father founded the *Enterprise* in 1893. Russell was the editor of the *Enterprise* until it stopped publication in 1955. He then became editor of the *Kent County News*. Russell operated the New Lyceum Theater Corporation, a business founded by his father. The building, which is located in downtown Chestertown, is now the Garfield Center for the Arts at the Prince Theater. Russell was a graduate of Washington College, where he served as a coach, chair of their athletic council, and member of their Board of Visitors and Governors. He was a founder of the Chester River Yacht and Country Club and served as the club's manager and secretary for a number of years. (Courtesy of the Historical Society of Kent County.)

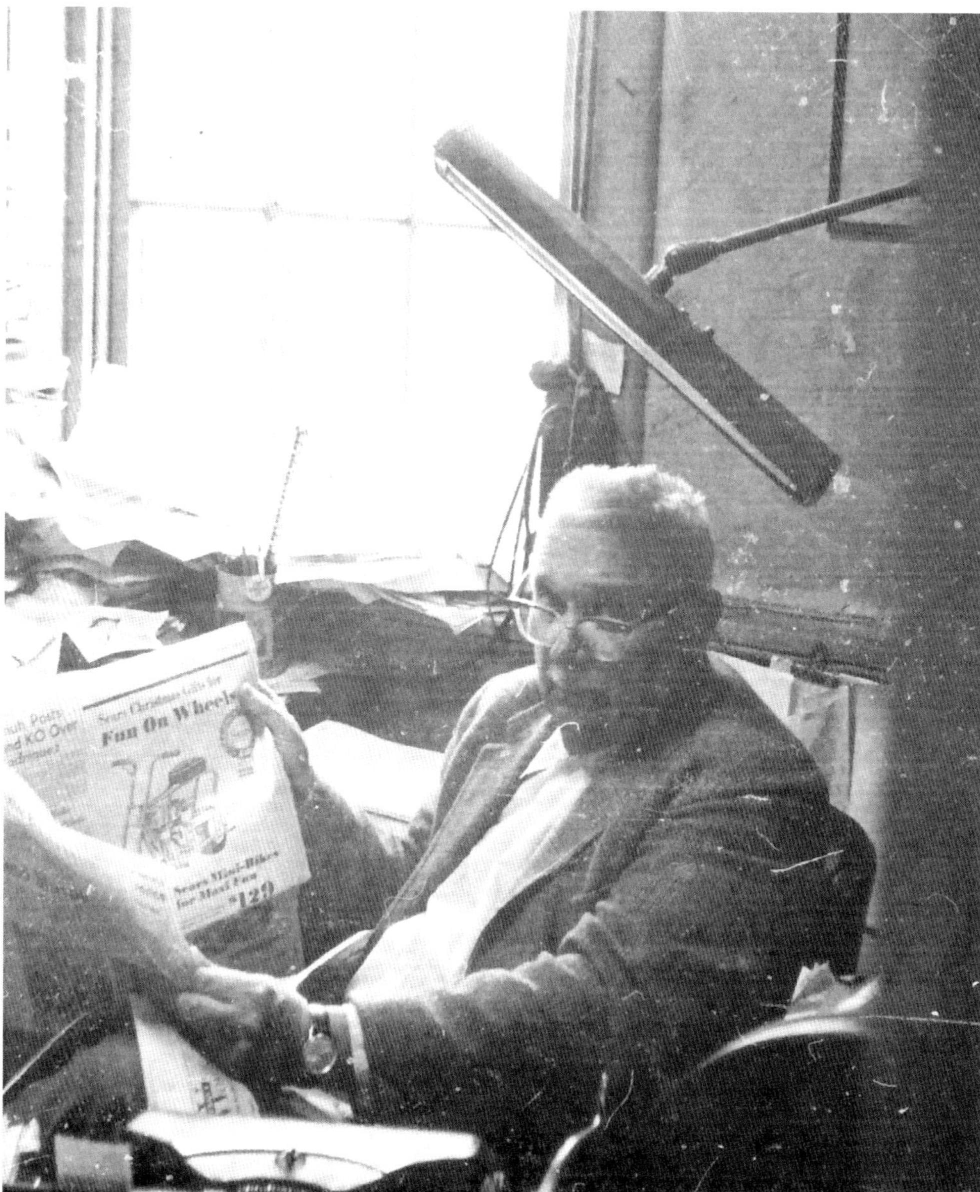

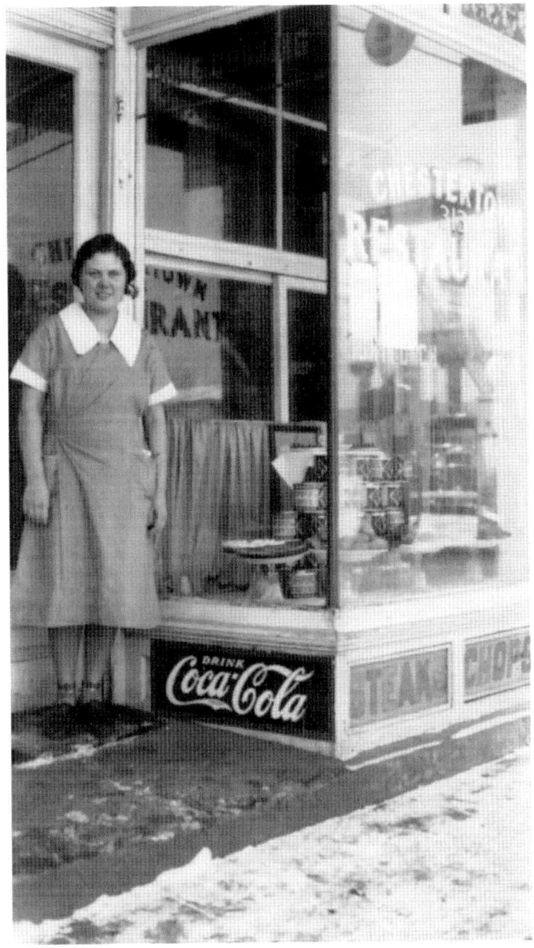


**George Evangelos Kellas**
Born in Greece, Kellas arrived in America in 1909 and opened the Chestertown Restaurant on High Street in downtown Chestertown in 1930. Kellas moved the restaurant from Chestertown to Kings Town in a building on the Chester River in 1957 and called it Riverview Restaurant. He closed the restaurant and opened Riverview Liquors, retiring at age 89. His wife, Katherine Batchelor Kellas, is shown in front of the downtown restaurant. (Courtesy of Angela K. Councell.)

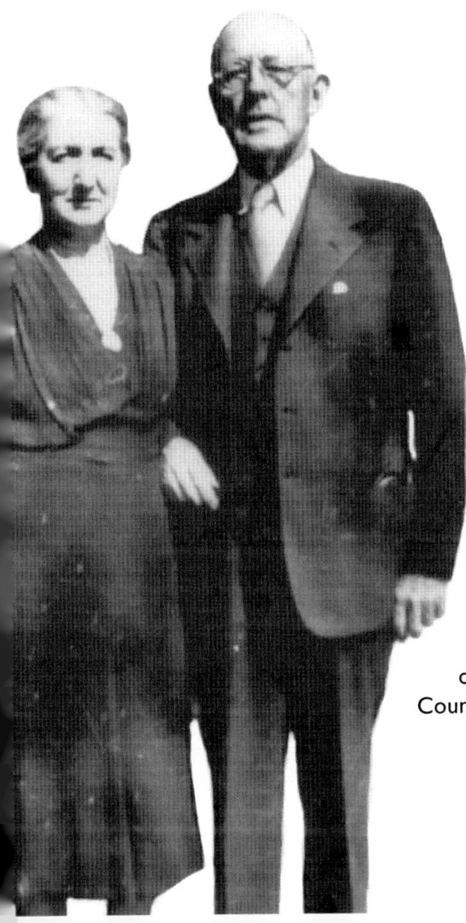

**Dr. Frank W. Smith**
Born in Chestertown, Dr. Smith practiced medicine in Kent County for 49 years. Shown with his wife, Eva, he served as chief of staff of the Kent and Queen Anne's Hospital, medical examiner for Kent County, president of the Kent County Medical Society, register of wills for Kent County, and vice president of the Kent County Savings Bank. (Courtesy of Louan Smith Waddell.)

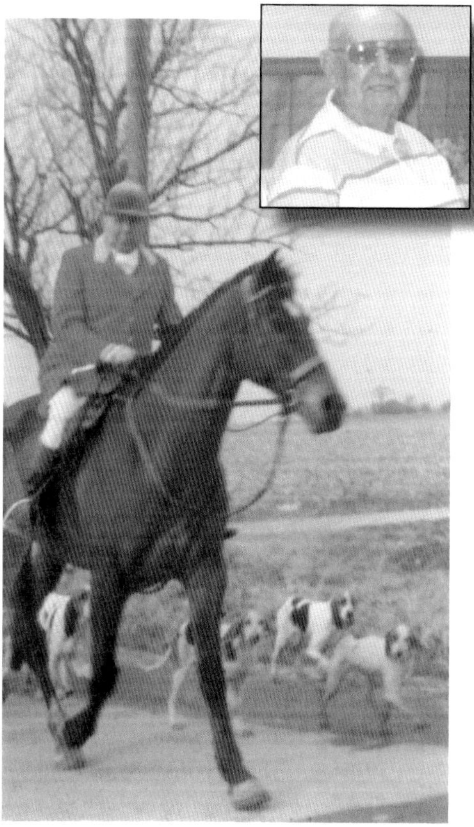

**Howard A. Brown**

"Hound Dog" enjoyed foxhounds, the horses, and the hunts. He hunted fox in the traditional English manner up and down the East Coast. He bred foxhounds, raised and cared for the horses, and orchestrated fox hunts. Hound Dog was a member of several fox-hunting organizations and worked as a huntsman. He was also known for his homemade scrapple feasts. (Courtesy of Dickie Brown.)

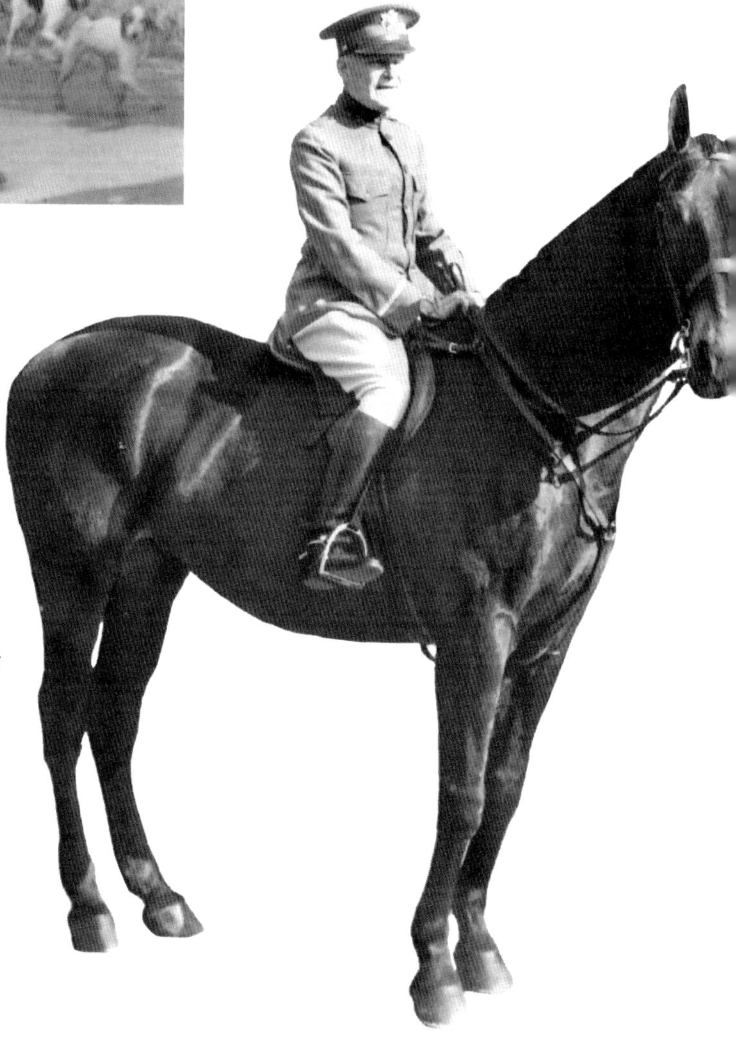

**Wilbur Ross Hubbard**

Hubbard was believed to have been the oldest master of foxhounds in the world at age 97. He was widely known for his historical preservation efforts in Kent County and dancing expertise. He lived at Widehall, one of Chestertown's premier historic homes. (Courtesy of the Historical Society of Kent County.)

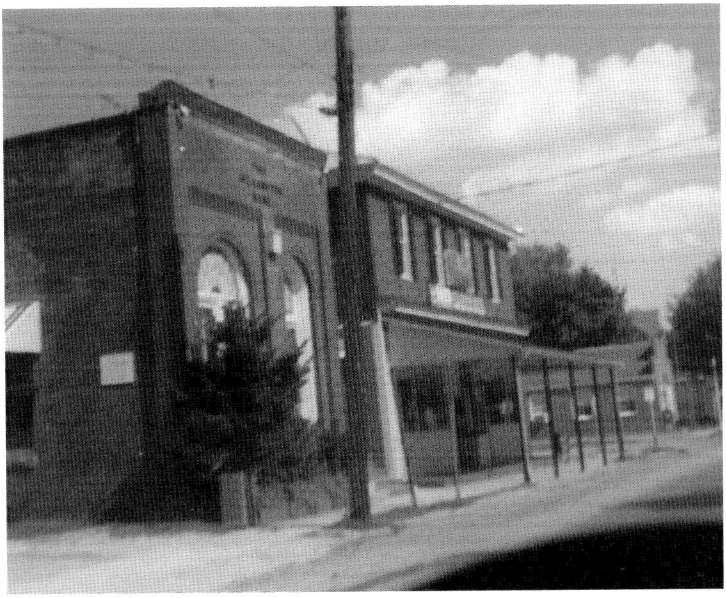

**Morton I. and Flora Hollins**
For approximately 100 years, the Hollins family had a country department store in Millington. Started by a young Baltimorian, Isaac Hollins, at the turn of the 20th century, the I. Hollins Department Store (above) provided everything anyone needed, except groceries: rugs, furniture, shoes, clothing, jewelry, dry goods, toys, school supplies, and more. This small country department store eventually was run by Isaac's son Morton Hollins with his wife, Flora, and daughters Paula and Susan. The store closed a few years after the death of Hollins in 1970, was bought by the bank next door, and demolished to create parking. In the early years, Isaac and his wife had a house next to the store. Two of his six children were born in Millington, Shirley Hollins (Freedman) of Baltimore, now 96, and Morton. Pictured here are, from left to right, Susan Hollins, Paula Hollins, Flora Hollins, and Morton Hollins. (Both, courtesy of Susan Hollins.)

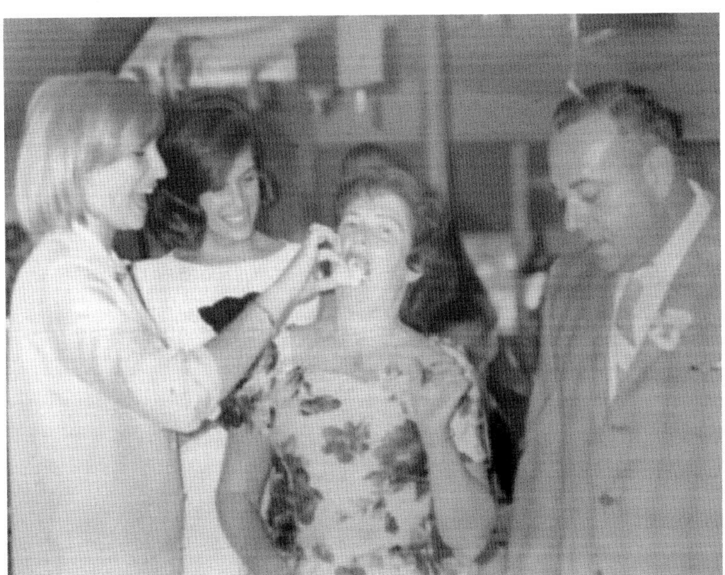

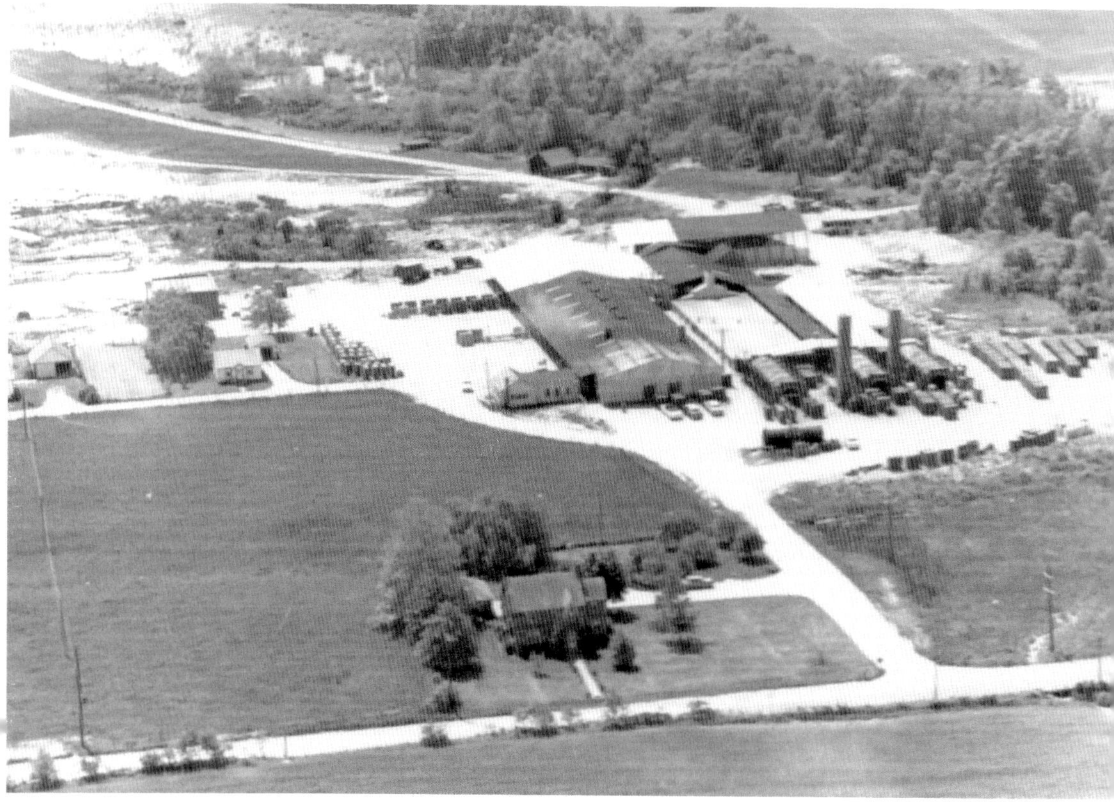

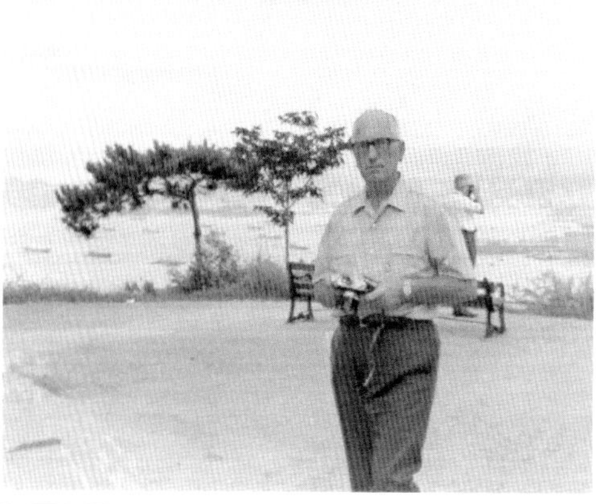

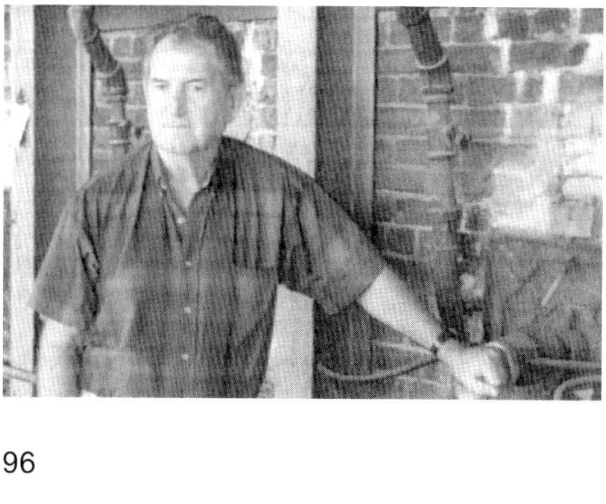

## Richard F. Schauber

"Dick" took over the operation and management of the Chestertown Brick Company in 1933. Dick's father, John, and his uncle George started the company in 1924. The first kiln was built from brick from an old paper mill. A tunnel kiln was built in 1958. Bricks from the company were used to build the Chestertown Post Office in 1935. Dick remained active in the business until he retired in 1980 when his son Richard E. Schauber became president. He and his brother James upgraded the plant with a cleaner-burning kiln, producing products to serve residential and architectural markets. One of the last architectural jobs was the oncology building on the Johns Hopkins campus. They operated the company until it was sold to Delaware Brick Co. Dick Schauber was also the owner, developer, and engineer for the College Heights area of Chestertown. Above is an aerial view of the Chestertown Brick Company; on the left are Richard F. Schauber (left, above) and Richard E. Schauber. (Both, courtesy of Dorothy Schauber Mench and Richard E. Schauber.)

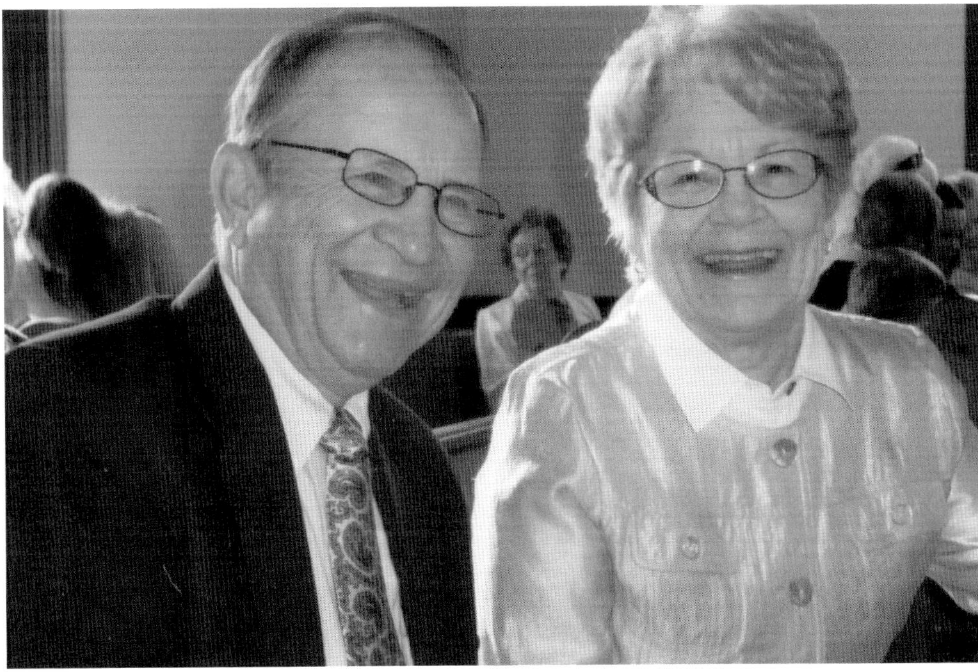

**Harry Thomas Williams II**

"Harry T" of Worton was a fourth-generation Kent County farmer of Red Acres Farm, designated a Maryland Century farm. His son Bryan Williams operates the farm today, still producing crops as the farm did in the 1850s. Williams served as a Kent County judge of the orphans court for 28 years. He received the Martin Luther King Jr. Humanitarian Award in 2012. Harry T. Williams is pictured here with his wife, Elizabeth "Sis." (Courtesy of Elizabeth "Sis" Williams.)

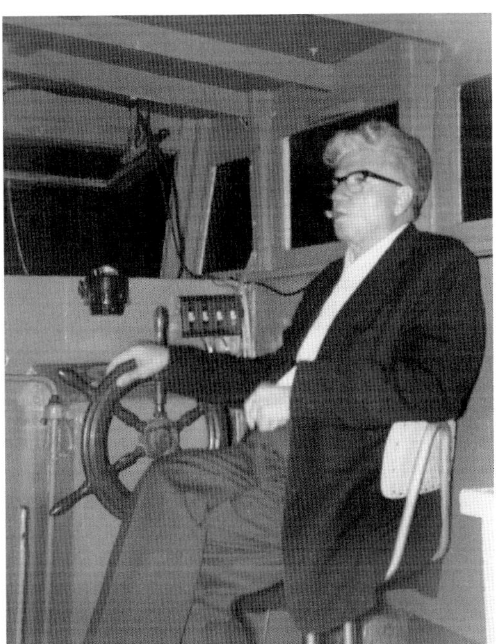

**Grover C. Hubbard**

Known among sportsmen and watermen, "Bud" was the founder and proprietor of Bud's Restaurant in Chestertown, one of the Eastern Shore's most notable eating places. He originally opened a filling station on the site of the restaurant in Chestertown in the early 1930s. He began selling hot dogs and hamburgers along with gas, and soon the business grew into the popular restaurant. (Courtesy of Donna Hubbard Edwards.)

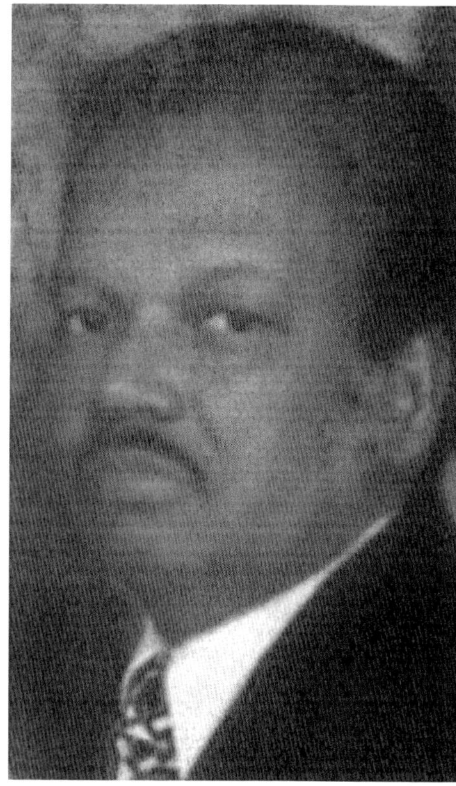

### Kenneth Walley Sr.

A lifelong resident of Kent County, Walley was a funeral director and embalmer in Chestertown for over 40 years. He served his apprenticeship under the Willis Wells Funeral Home. He served in the US Army and was past commander of the Parker White American Legion Post 143, Chestertown. Walley was a member of Bay City Lodge No. 1490 and the Thomas H. Kiah Lodge No. 181. (Courtesy of Joyce Walley.)

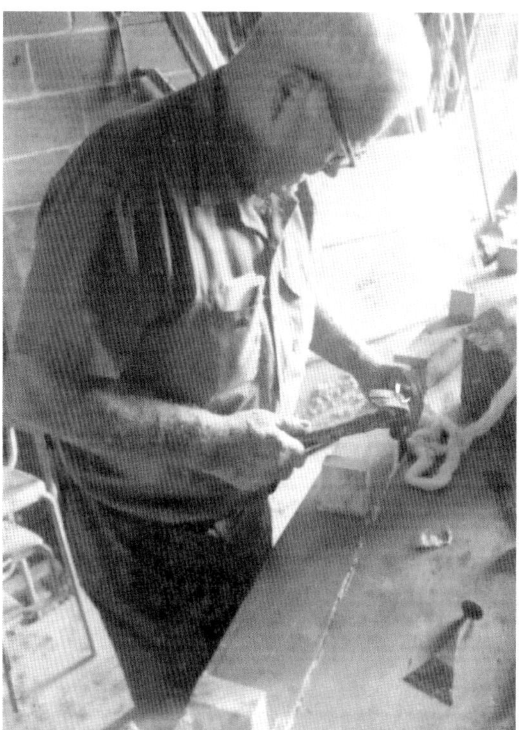

### Stanley Francis Vansant

Hundreds of the 3,000 work and head boats "Captain" Vansant built still work the Chesapeake Bay, its coves, and harbors. Vansant spent most of his 81 years as a waterman and master boat builder in Piney Neck, Rock Hall. He owned the Stanley Vansant Boatyard. A statue named *Oysterman* was modeled after him and dedicated to the watermen and other working people of the Chesapeake Bay area. (Courtesy of Ron Fithian.)

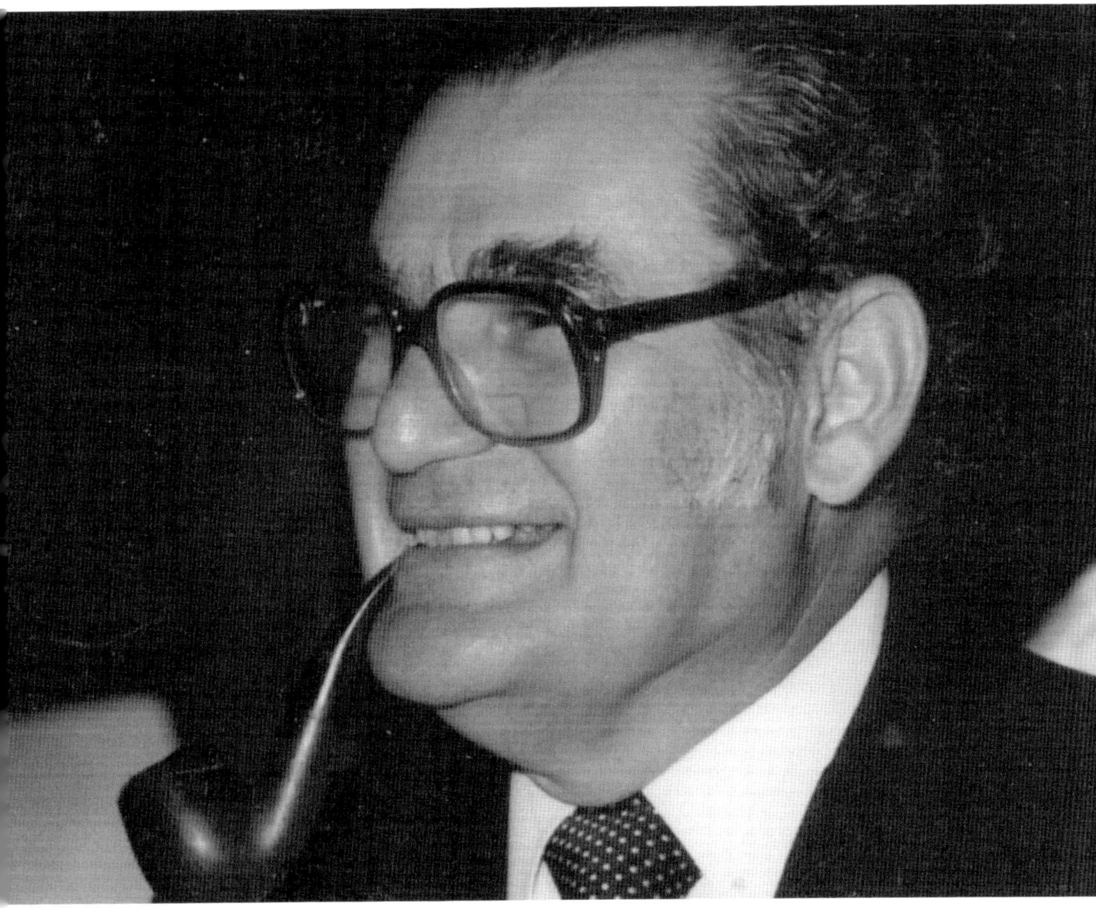

**Frank Rudnick**

After his discharge from the US Army Air Corps in 1946, where he served during World War II, Rudnick began working with his brother Joe at their father's auction house in Galena, Harry Rudnick & Sons. They ran a livestock auction and sold farm equipment and real estate, eventually adding furniture and antique auctions. He and his brother Joe sold the business in 1994. Rudnick served on the board of directors of Magnolia Hall (now University of Maryland Shore Nursing and Rehabilitation Center), Kent & Queen Anne's Hospital (now University of Maryland Shore Medical Center at Chestertown), and the Millington Bank branch of Farmer's National Bank. Family and friends remember Frank for his pipe and the ever-present smell of Half & Half tobacco, his evening cocktail of a gin martini on the rocks with an olive, his love of the "sale place," and his constant presence at the lunch counter at Twinny's in Galena. (Courtesy of Anita Rudnick.)

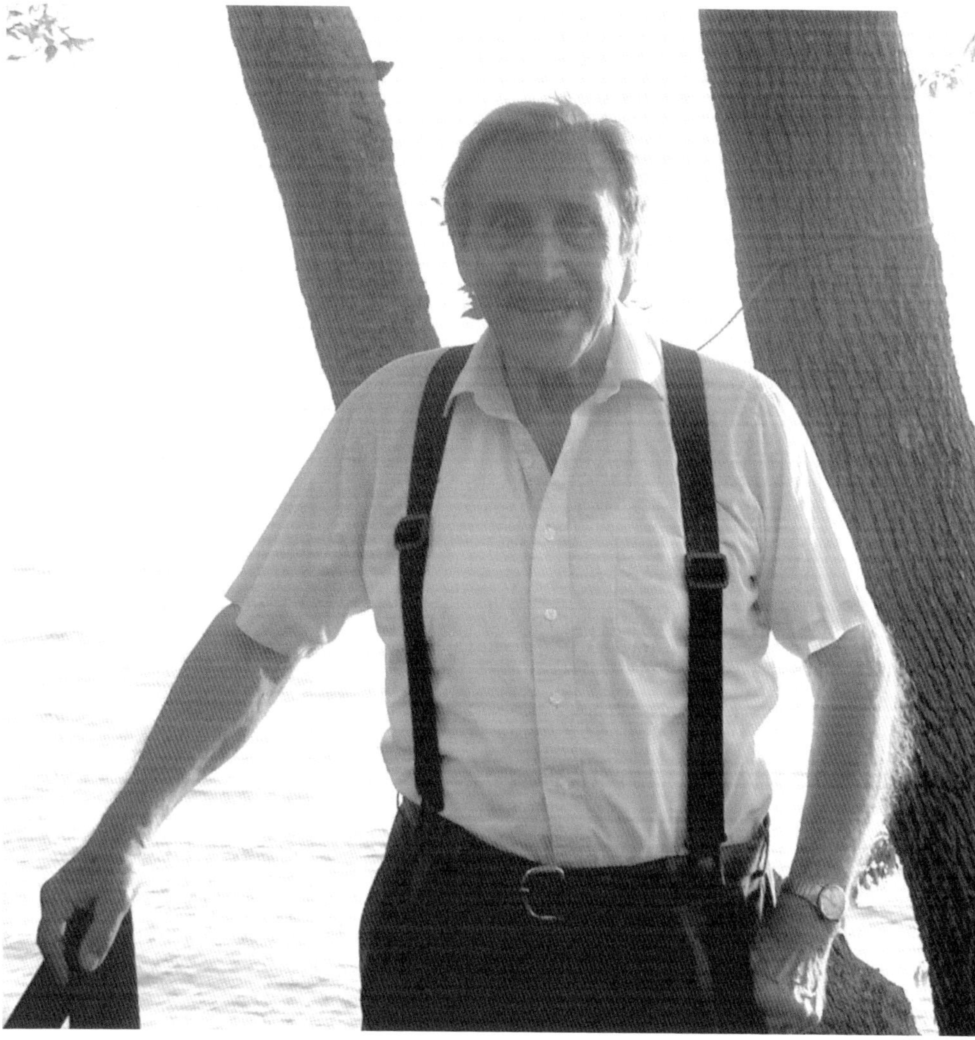

**Vincent Martin Raimond**

Arriving in Kent County in the early 1950s after serving in World War II and graduating from the University of Alaska with a civil-engineering degree, "Vince" was a partner in Wilson, Nuttall, Raimond Engineering Inc. (WNRE), a research and development company that specialized in designing off-road vehicles. In 1958, Raimond established Ambulitter Corporation to manufacture the off-road vehicles whose designs they held. These vehicles were built for Aberdeen Proving Ground, Imperial Oil of Canada, Gulf Oil, and the US Army Transportation Corps, among others. Raimond also held a long love and appreciation for the arts and founded and became the executive director of the Kent County Arts Council. In addition to encouraging individuals and groups to participate in the arts, he founded Actors Community Theater, a long-lived and successful community theatre organization. His interest in historical preservation led him to rescue over 20 structures destined for the bulldozer that were examples of 18th-century Vernacular architecture throughout Kent County. From these materials, he built Toad Hall, his home at the head of Still Pond Creek. (Courtesy of Leslie Prince Raimond.)

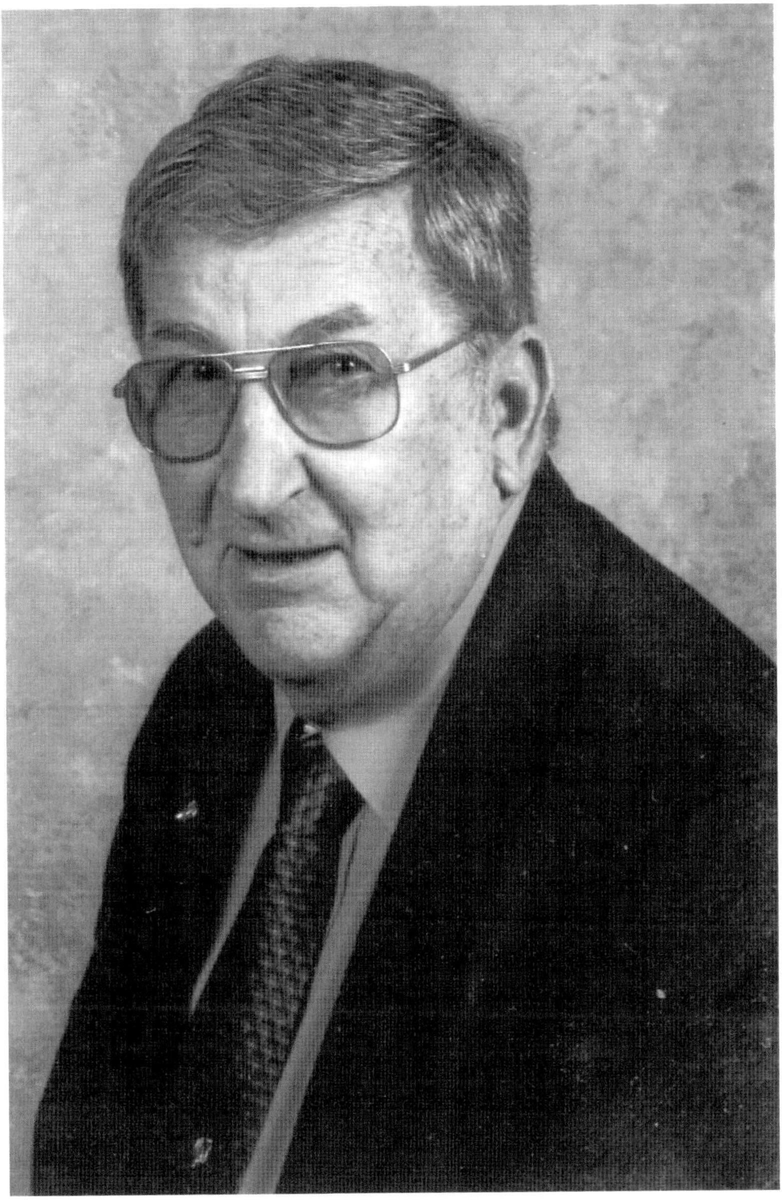

**Larry William Simns**

Simns was initiated into the life, work, soul, and spirit of a waterman by his great-grandfather Capt. Willie Stevens. He developed a keen sense of how and where to fish and learned to consider the elements, methods, and regulations that would forever change and sometimes damage the Chesapeake Bay and watermen's communities. Simns established and became president of the Maryland Watermen's Association in 1973 and served until his death in 2013. He was often recognized as the most important advocate for watermen and the Chesapeake Bay and worked tirelessly with people and organizations on controversial issues such as the rockfish moratorium, oyster and bed management, and regulations on harvesting female blue crabs with resolution, consensus, equity, preservation, and conservation in the forefront. He received the prestigious Admiral of the Chesapeake Bay award in 2012 from Maryland's governor Martin O'Malley. (Courtesy of Susan Barnhardt.)

### William Barger Usilton III

"Billy" and his wife, Perry, were a significant presence in the newspaper history of Kent County for half a century. He was the last in a newspaper dynasty commencing before the Civil War, when the first William Barger Usilton became copublisher of the *Kent News*. W.B. Usilton and his sons (Fred Usilton and William Barger Usilton Jr.) published its paper well into the 20th century. Billy graduated from Chestertown High School and Washington College where he was editor in chief of the college newspaper. He was inducted into Washington College's Hall of Fame in 1986. He moved to New York City in 1929 to work in the publicity department for the entertainment corporate giant RKO (Radio-Keith-Orpheum). Billy and his glamorous bride, Evelyn Perry, a star performer in a nationally renowned touring dance troupe, returned to Chestertown and the *Kent News* in 1932. He replaced her first name with her maiden surname "Perry" and sometimes affectionately called her Miss P.U. Soon, Billy took over management of the *Kent News* with Perry working by his side in charge of circulation. When Usilton returned from war service in 1945, little Chestertown supported three weekly newspapers: the *Kent News*, the *Transcript*, owned by brothers Rich and Will Collins, and the *Enterprise*, owned by Harry Russell. He was a prime mover in the merger of the newspapers with the formation of the Kent Publishing Company that included himself and Rich and Will Collins. Kent Publishing bought out Harry Russell of the *Enterprise*. The *Kent County News* supplanted the *Kent News* and the *Transcript*. The *Enterprise* remained in publication until 1955. The weekly *Kent County News* is still published today. Billy was general editor, and Harry Russell was news editor. The paper was blessed with two popular entertaining newsworthy columns: Billy's Looking' Em Over and Harry's the Lancer. Billy passed on to the "Great Newsroom in the Sky" in 1982. Miss P.U. died in 2013 at the age of 101. (Courtesy of W. Porter Ellington.)

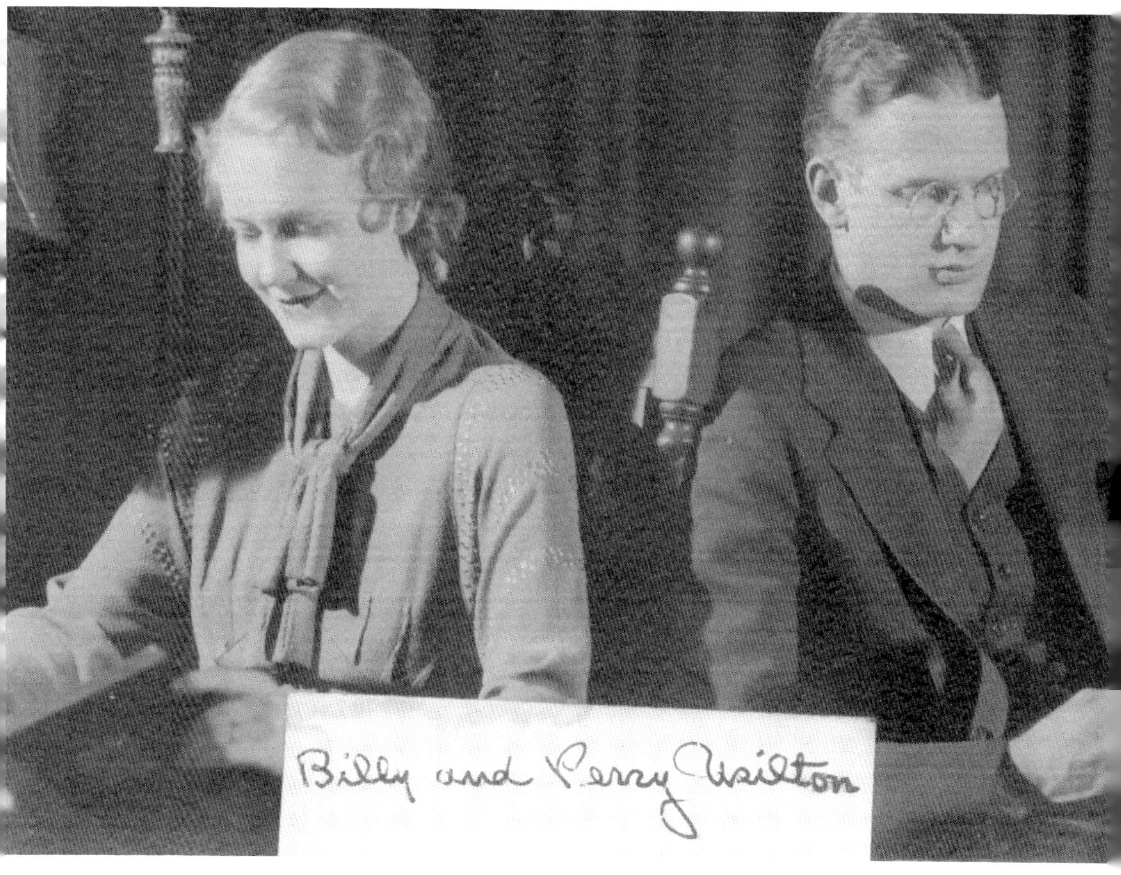

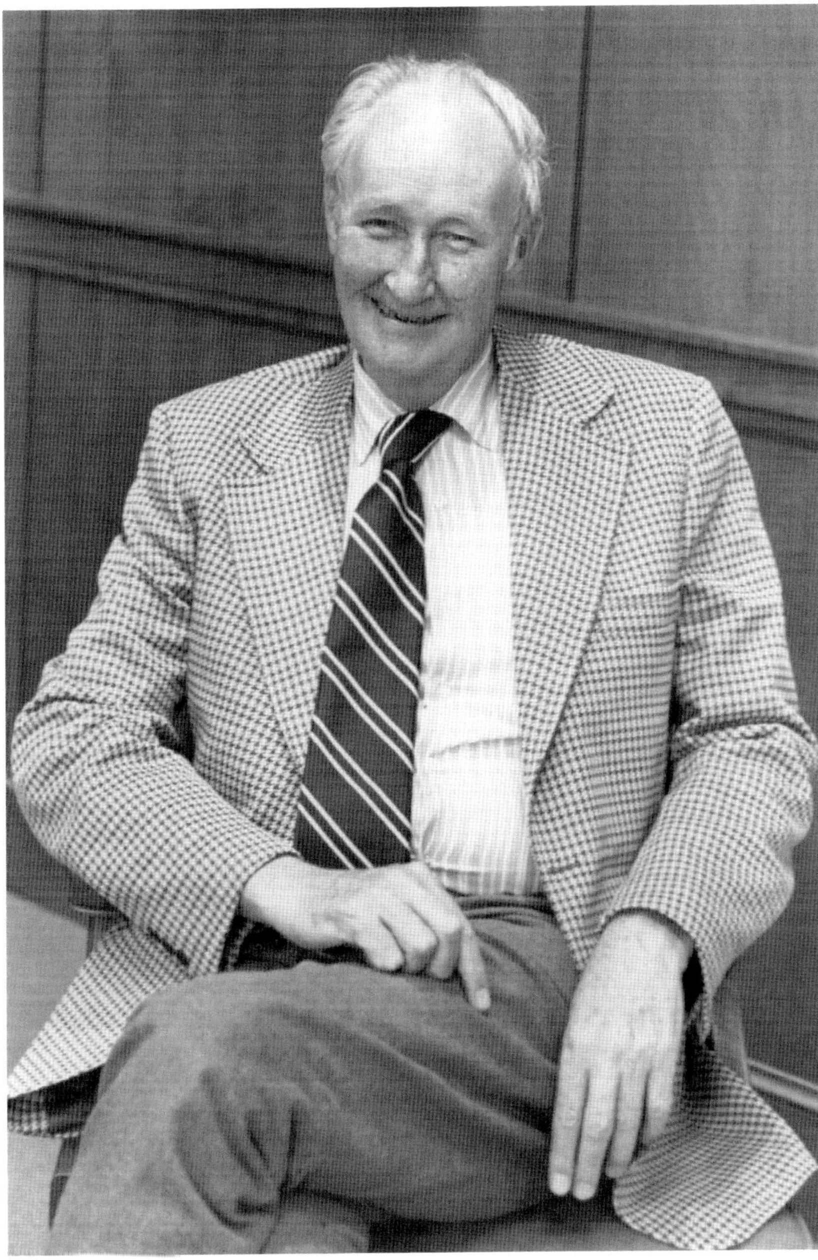

**Dr. Joseph H. McLain**
"Joe" joined the faculty at Washington College in Chestertown in 1946 as a chemistry professor and became head of the department in 1955. Dr. McLain served as the acting dean at the college for a time, and in 1973 he became the 22nd president of Washington College and the first alumnus to hold that position. He was inducted into Washington College's Athletic Hall of Fame in 2004. He was widely known for his expertise in solid-state chemistry and pyrotechnics and patented more than 30 inventions, including smoke grenades used by the Army to camouflage advancing troops. He wrote three textbooks on pyrotechnics and helped develop rocket-propellant formulas and devices used for stage separations in space flights. (Courtesy of Lynn McLain.)

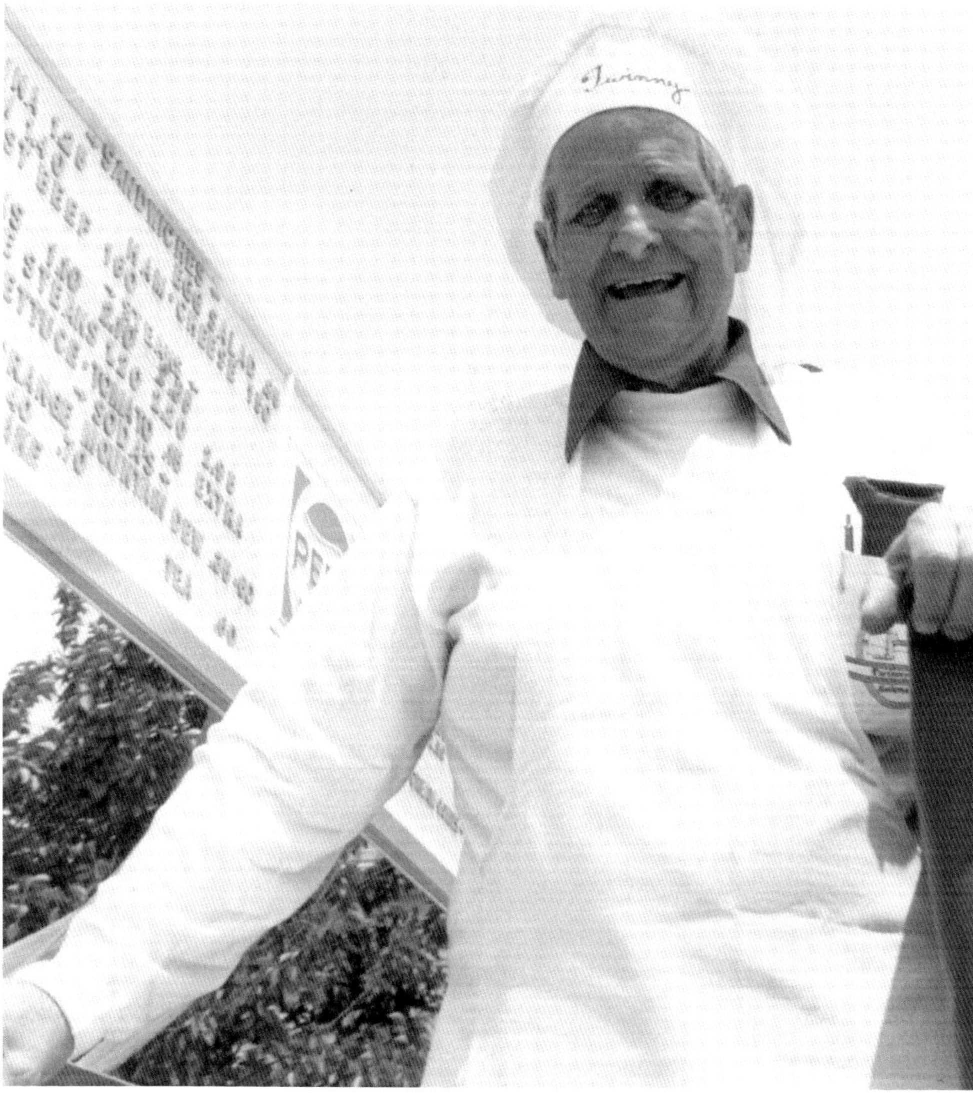

**Alan Price**

The operation of Twinny's Restaurant in Galena is a family affair. Alan Price, whose identical twin brother was named Alvah, opened his first restaurant in Galena in 1950 and called it Price's Place. He operated Price's Place until 1966, when he began working for Alvah as a salesman for Cecil Auto Sales. He returned to the restaurant business in 1980 at the current Galena location and called the restaurant Twinny's. His daughter Alice Newnam kept the books, waitressed, and later managed the business for her father and mother. She bought Twinny's in 2005 after they had both passed away. It is still a family business with Alice's sister Joanne Price, her daughter Jennifer Willey, and several cousins all working there. (Courtesy of Alice Newnam.)

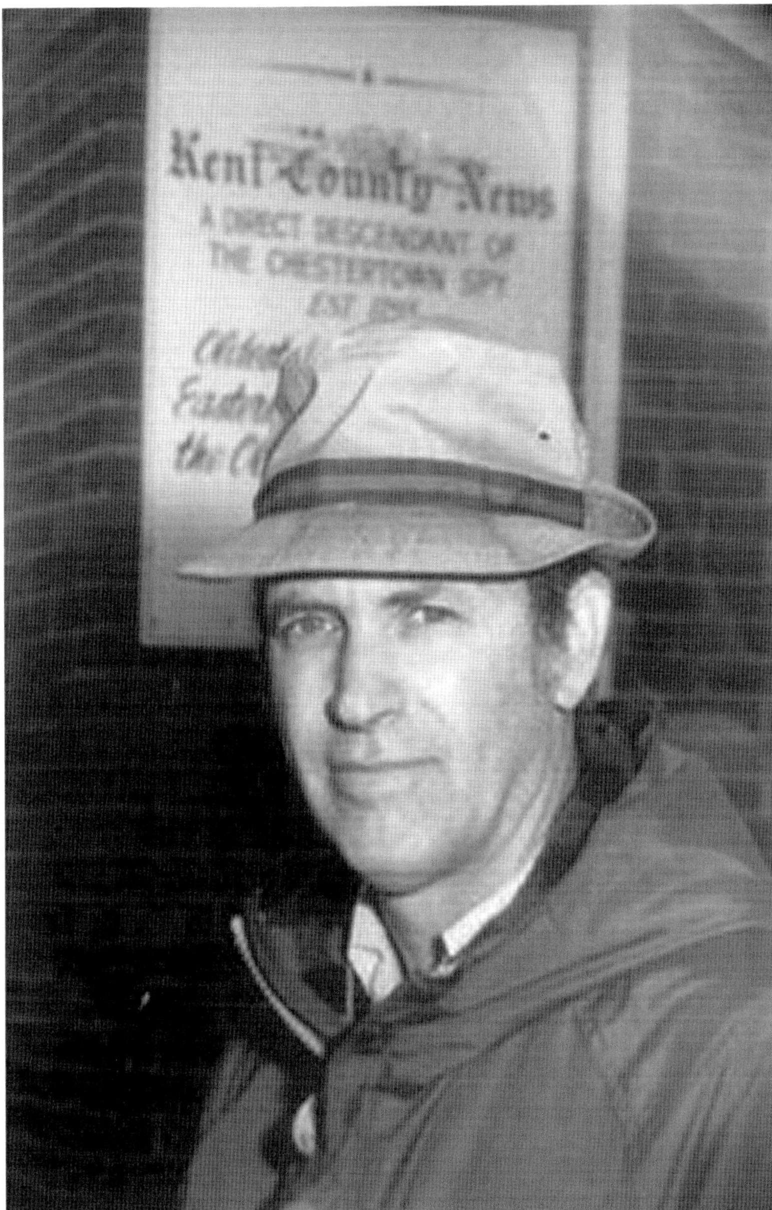


**Harry Hurtt Deringer**
He called himself "the old curmudgeon" and brought his passion for Kent County and sports history to his news jobs. Deringer was editor of the *Chester River Press* before becoming director of the news bureau and sports information at Washington College, later serving as assistant to the vice president for development and public relations and director of public relations at Washington College. He left Washington College to work as editor of the *Kent County News* and was named publisher of that newspaper in 1976, a position he held until retiring in 1994. Deringer was inducted into the Washington College Athletic Hall of Fame. He served as councilman for the town of Chestertown, was a board member of Kent Savings and Loan, coached Little League baseball, and served as master of ceremonies for many civic events. (Courtesy of Judy Ashworth.)

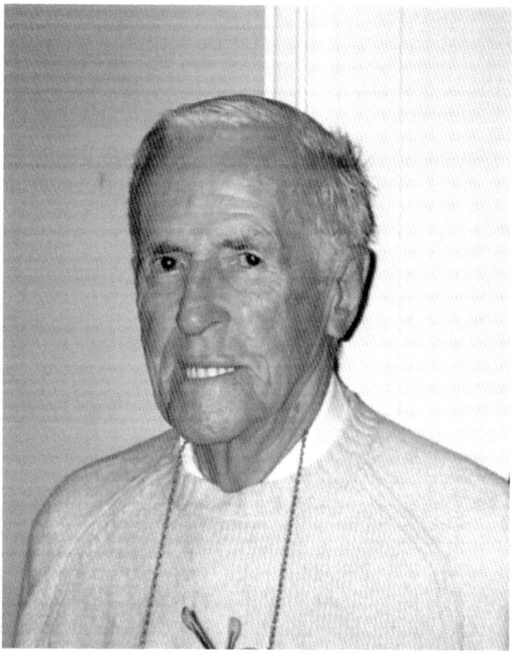

### Thomas Walker Eliason

For 75 years, Thomas Walker Eliason was the weather observer for the National Weather Service and published his recordings weekly in the *Kent County News*. He was a lifetime resident of Chestertown and a 1942 graduate of Washington College, whose tennis team he coached through the 1960s. Eliason served with the US Army Air Corps during World War II and afterwards worked as an accountant. (Courtesy of Nancy E. Drazga.)

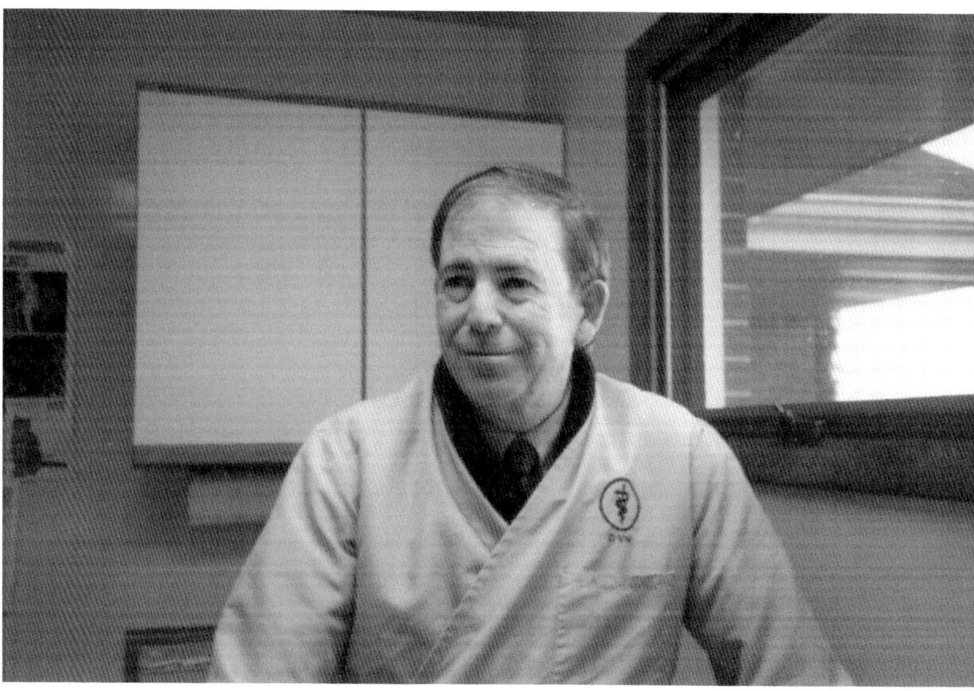

### Dr. Michael Forney

"Mike" was a veterinarian for 45 years, serving the upper Eastern Shore. He had served in the US Air Force as a weather specialist in South Korea before he and Dr. Ralph Buckel founded the Chestertown Animal Hospital in 1969. Dr. Forney was a consulting veterinarian in Ecuador in South America for 10 years. His interest in travel took him to more than 60 countries. (Courtesy of the Chestertown Animal Hospital.)

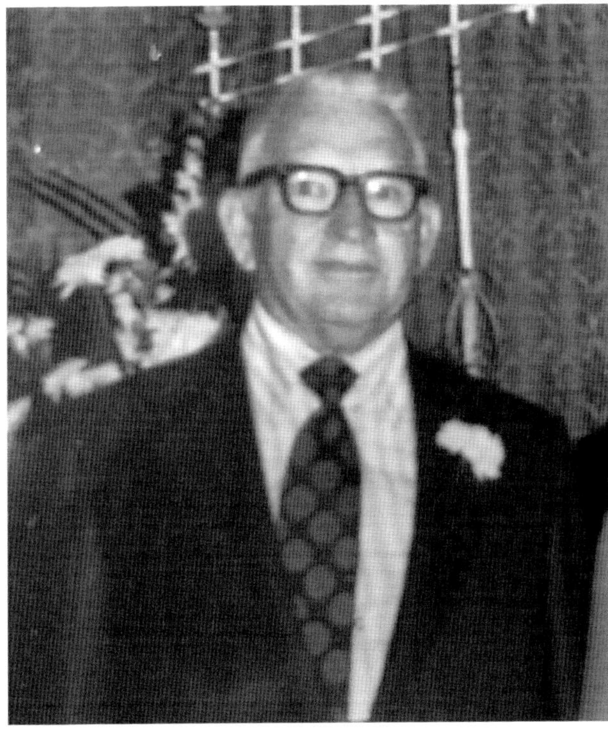

**Edward Walters Vansant**
A contractor and builder for over 30 years, "Pappy" said what he built had to be bulldozed down because he used so many nails. He served as chief and president of the Millington Fire Company, was a charter member of the Millington Lions Club, and served as worshipful master and lecturer of Chester Lodge No. 115 in Chestertown. He built the ammunition buildings in Chestertown during World War II. (Courtesy of Betty and Ken Vansant.)

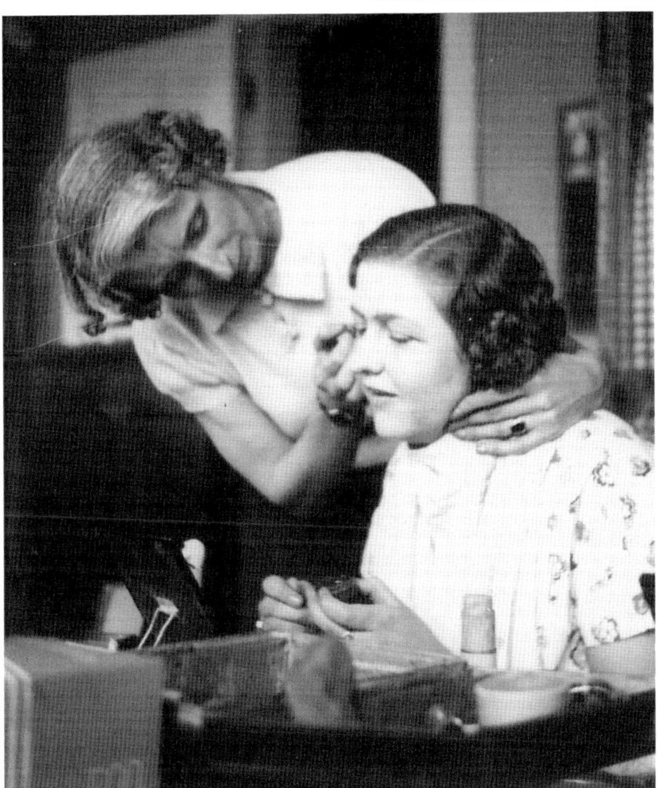

**Doris Thistle Bell**
"Miss Doris" of Chestertown was the first instructor of women's physical training at Washington College. She was awarded the college's Gold Pentagon in 1958 and inducted into the Washington College Athletic Hall of Fame in 1981. She remained at Washington College for 44 years. Bell is pictured on the left with Washington College student Carrie E. Schreiber. (Courtesy of the Historical Society of Kent County.)

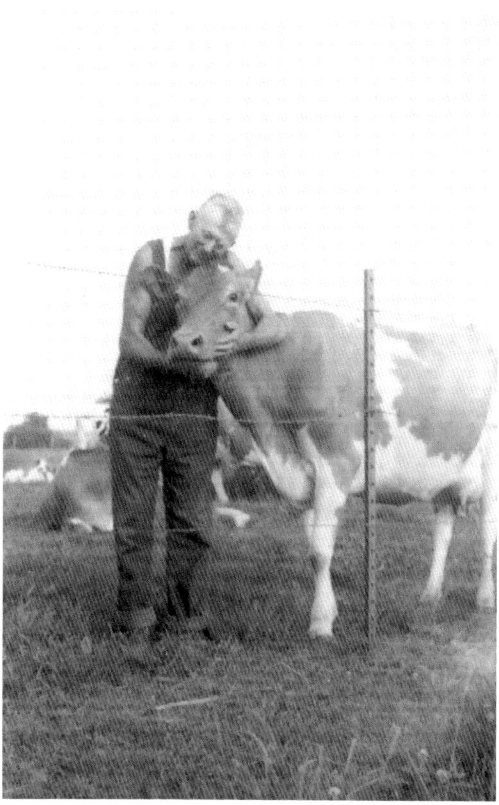

**Adam Schauber and Schauber Milk**
Milk bottles from all of the Kent County Schauber dairies are sought after by bottle collectors today. George Schauber began the Imperial Dairy about 1907. Adam Schauber (pictured) started the Fairy Meadow Dairy about 1915. John Schauber opened Hopewell Dairy in 1931, followed by Frank Schauber's Worrell Dairy in 1935. Brad Schauber started the Schauber Dairy about 1940. (Courtesy of William A. Schauber.)

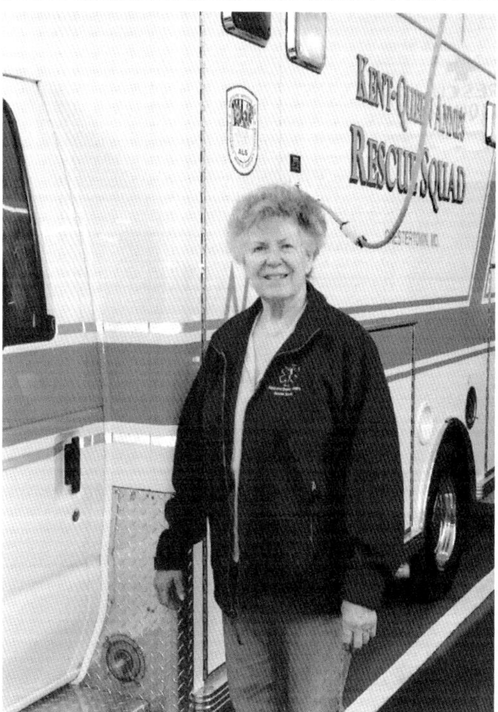


**Mary Hurd Grussing**
Since 1982, Grussing has been a volunteer with the Kent and Queen Anne's Rescue Squad delivering emergency care to Kent and Queen Anne's County residents. Her tremendous commitment was evident in 1999 when she answered 794 calls and in 2004 when she answered 1,143 calls and was top responder. She was honored as Kent County's Maryland, You Are Beautiful volunteer in 2005. (Author's collection.)

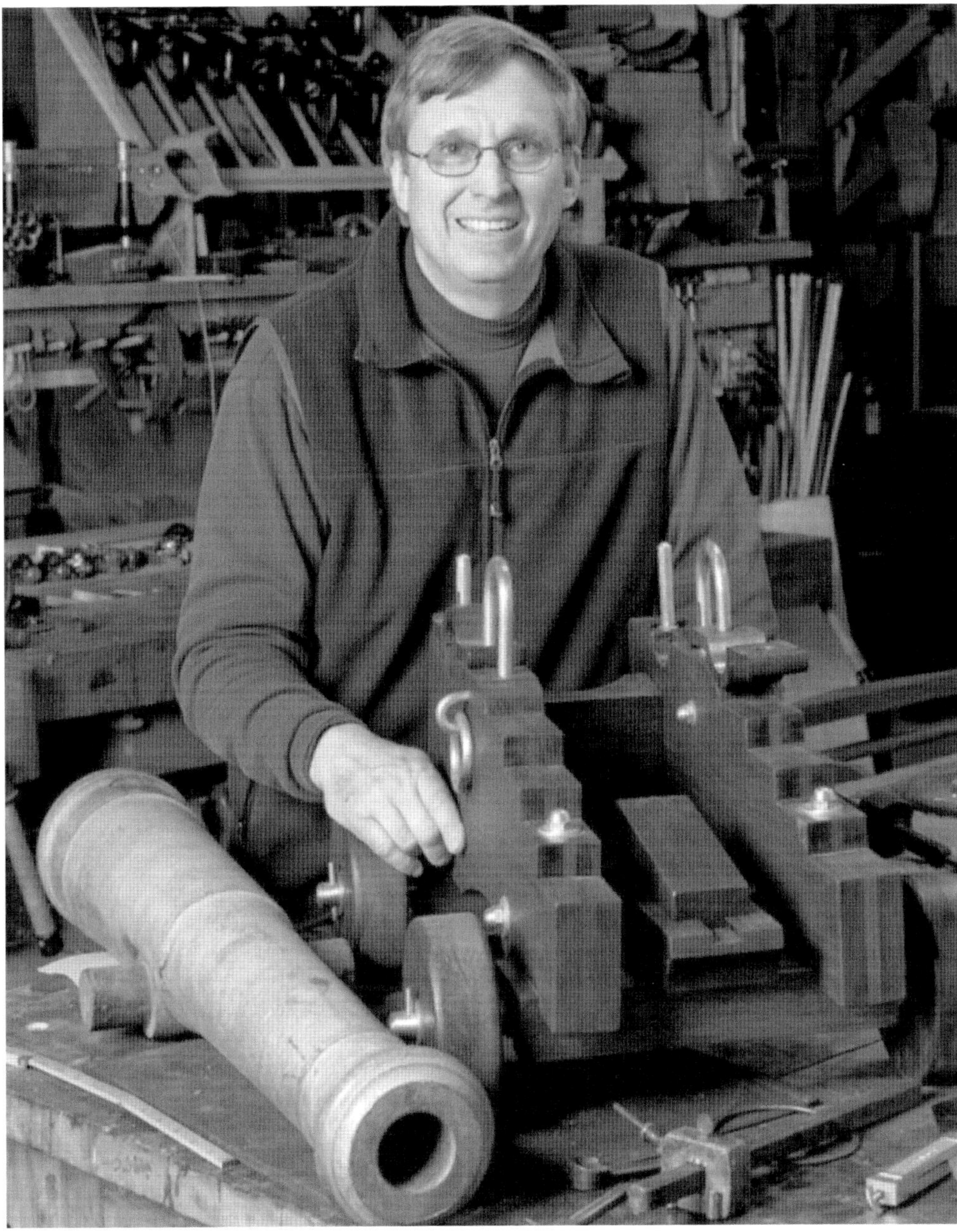

**Frank B. Rhodes Jr.**

Rhodes is the grandson of Col. Edgar William and Bernice Chrysler Garbisch, who assembled one of the truly great collections of American nave (primitive) paintings and furniture, and he has been building notable American furniture in Chestertown since 1983. Many of the pieces Rhodes, one of the few remaining heirs of Walter P. Chrysler, the founder of the Chrysler automobile company, builds are from the Garbisch family and other private collections. His shop is home to a miniature museum that includes the Chrysler family archives. He also produces fine furniture of his own design and specializes in repair, restoration, refinishing, and upholstery of antique as well as more contemporary furniture and marine interiors. Rhodes is also an avid train collector. (Courtesy of Frank B. Rhodes Jr.)

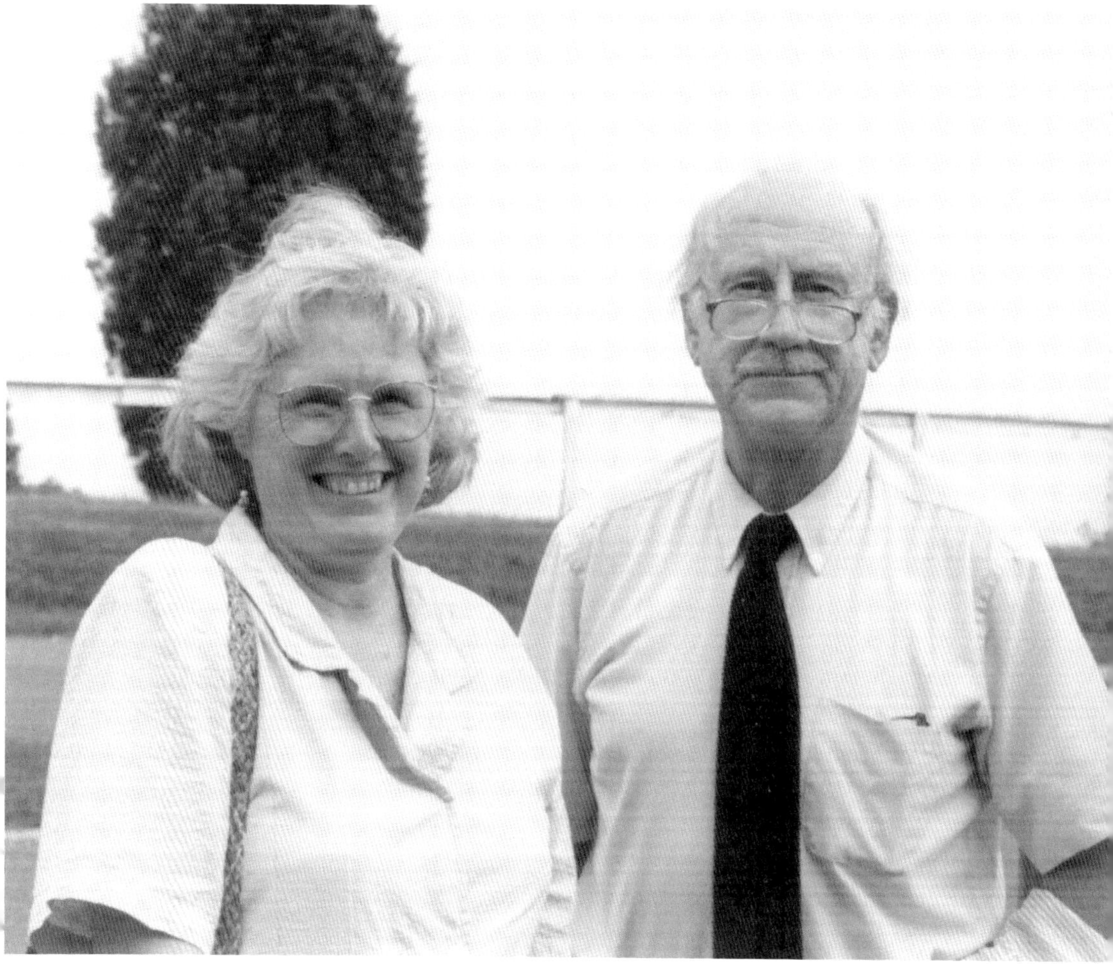

**Kathleen Brackett and Maynard Pressley White Jr.**
Maynard Pressley "Press" White Jr. was a history professor at the University of Delaware and very active in historical endeavors in Kent County. He proposed and organized Chestertown's Historic District and its zoning and was one of the first Chestertown Historic District members. Press was also one of the organizers of Preservation Inc., an advisory group interested in preservation and restoration in Kent County. His wife, Kathleen, "Kakie," researched properties for the Chestertown Historic Survey. In addition, she also researched and nominated properties outside town limits for historic recognition. She taught with the Kent Learning Center in Chestertown and worked with international students at the Gunston School and later with students with learning differences at Wye River Upper School, both in Centreville. (Courtesy of Kathleen B. White.)

**Peter Rice Jr.**

In 1956, Peter Rice's parents sent him and his brother to Echo Hill Camp on Bloomingneck Farm in Kent County, overlooking the Chesapeake Bay. The camp experience was a turning point in his life. The Rices bought the camp business in 1966, and Peter went to work there full-time and became the camp director in 1970. In 1972, he founded Echo Hill Outdoor School to teach children an awareness and appreciation of the environment and the Chesapeake Bay. Over the past decades, his Quaker calm and love of kids has helped build one of the best camp and environmental-education programs in the country. Today, the camp hosts over 180 school and youth groups, bringing over 7,000 students and campers to the campus each year. Since 1984, nearly every student from the Kent County Public Schools system has taken classes and spent nights at Echo Hill. Radcliffe Creek School, Gunston, Kent School, and the Chestertown Christian Academy also participate in Echo Hill programs. (Courtesy of Peter Rice Jr.)

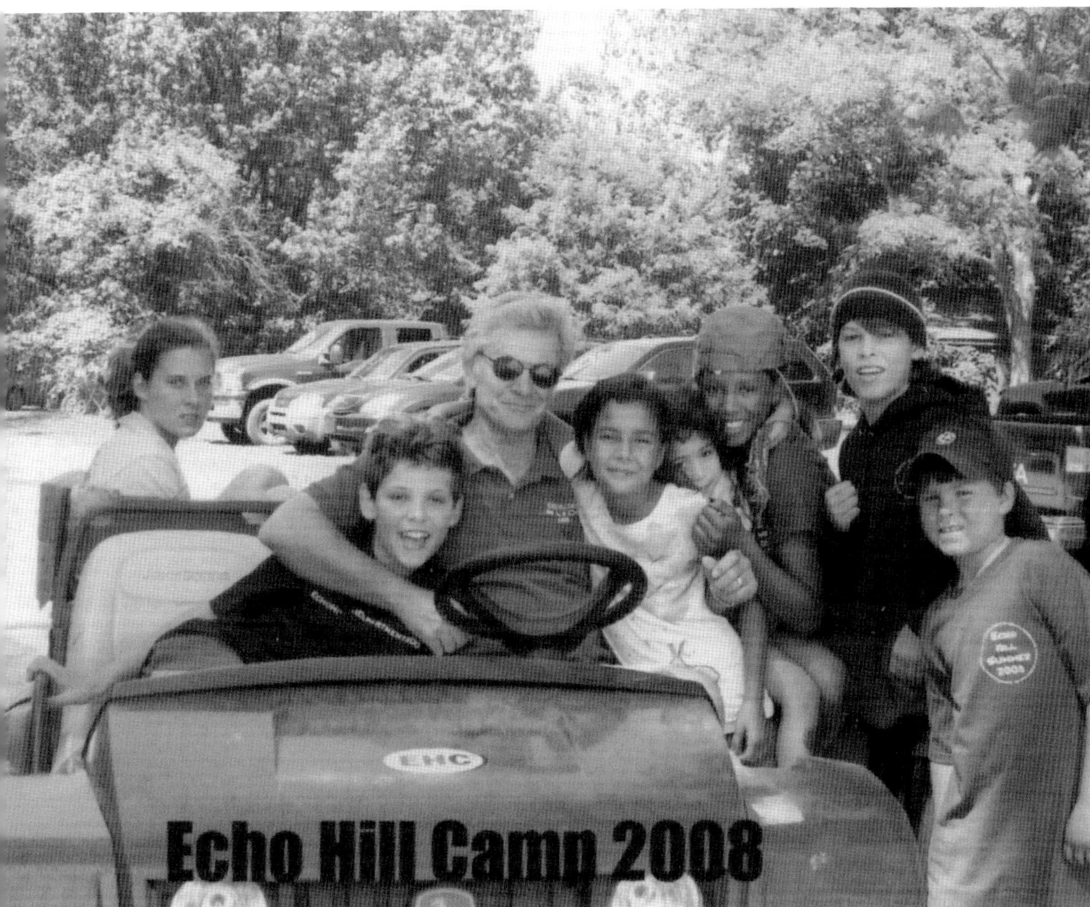

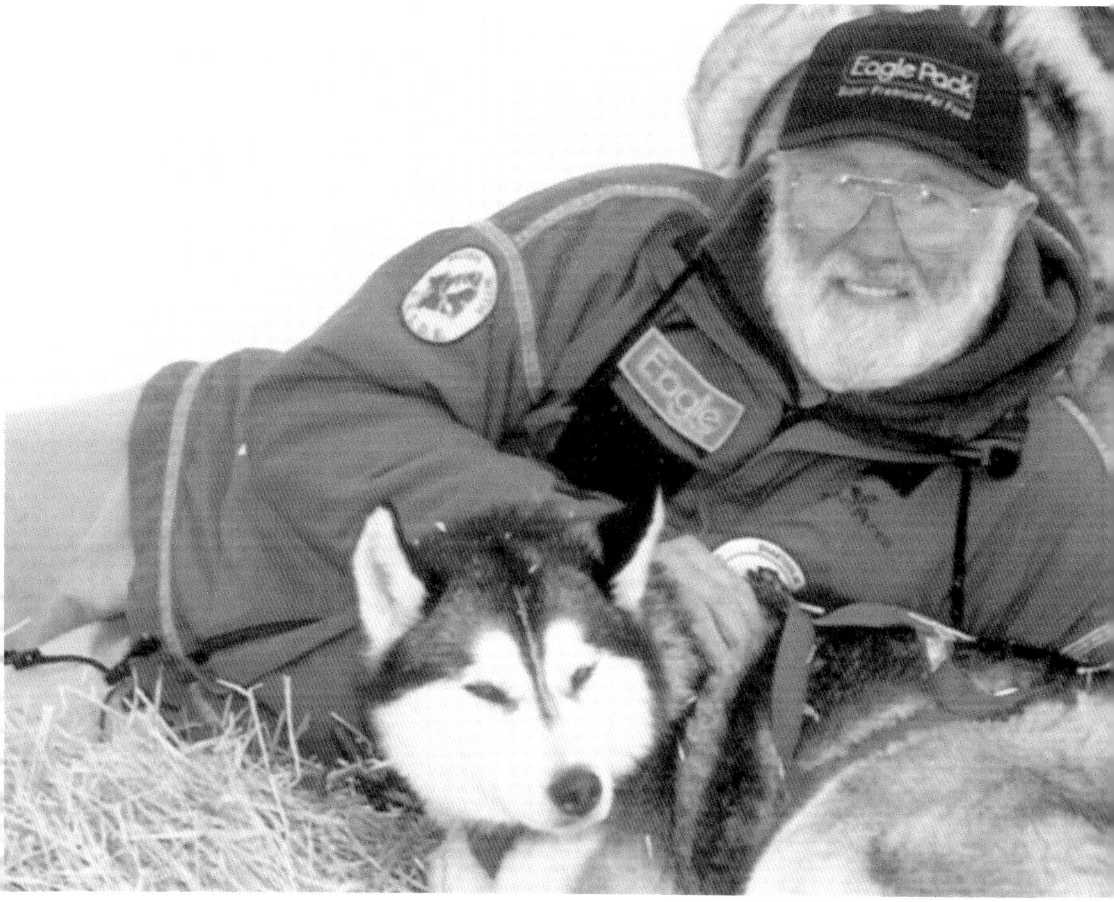


**Dr. Albert S. Townshend**

Born and raised in Chestertown, "Dr. Al" established the Eastern Shore Animal Hospital near Chestertown in 1972. He retired from active practice in 2006 when he became staff veterinarian for WellPet, a major pet-food manufacturer. He now travels the world promoting the value of good nutrition for pets. Dr. Al, shown above with his sled dog, has spent every winter in Alaska for the past 24 years where he volunteers as a trail veterinarian on the 1,000-mile Iditarod sled-dog race. He has received the coveted Golden Stethoscope Award from the Iditarod for contributions above and beyond the call of duty in bringing veterinary care to the dogs of the Iditarod. Dr. Townshend is also a contributing author to the text *Canine Sports Medicine*. (Courtesy of Dr. Al Townshend.)

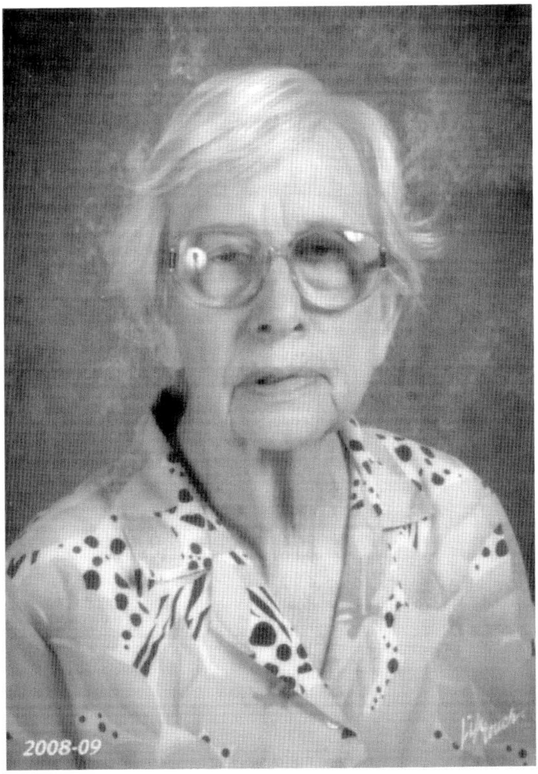


**Thelma O'Grady**
"Miss Nick" of Galena was chosen as Kent County's Most Outstanding Volunteer for 2003 as part of the Maryland You Are Beautiful Program. The award was given in recognition of her years of volunteer service and dedication to helping others in many activities, including volunteering at the Galena Middle School after retiring as a teacher for 43 years, her tutoring efforts, and her 64 years as a Girl Scout leader. (Courtesy of Thelma O'Grady.)

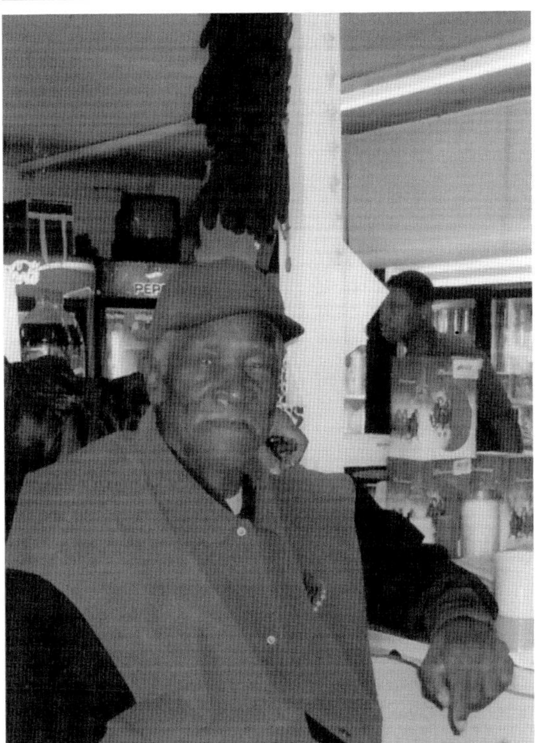

**Walter Samuel Murray Jr.**
In the 1940s, "Jonas" played catcher for a semiprofessional team called the Rock Hall Tigers. The Reverend Clarence Hawkins, a former Kent County Commissioner, commented, "Jonas and other members of the team were good enough to play professional ball and probably would have if the opportunity had been there." Jonas was a waterman and worked on the dock of Hubbard's Pier and Seafood in Rock Hall where he bought crabs, rockfish, and turtles from local watermen. (Courtesy of Peter Rice.)

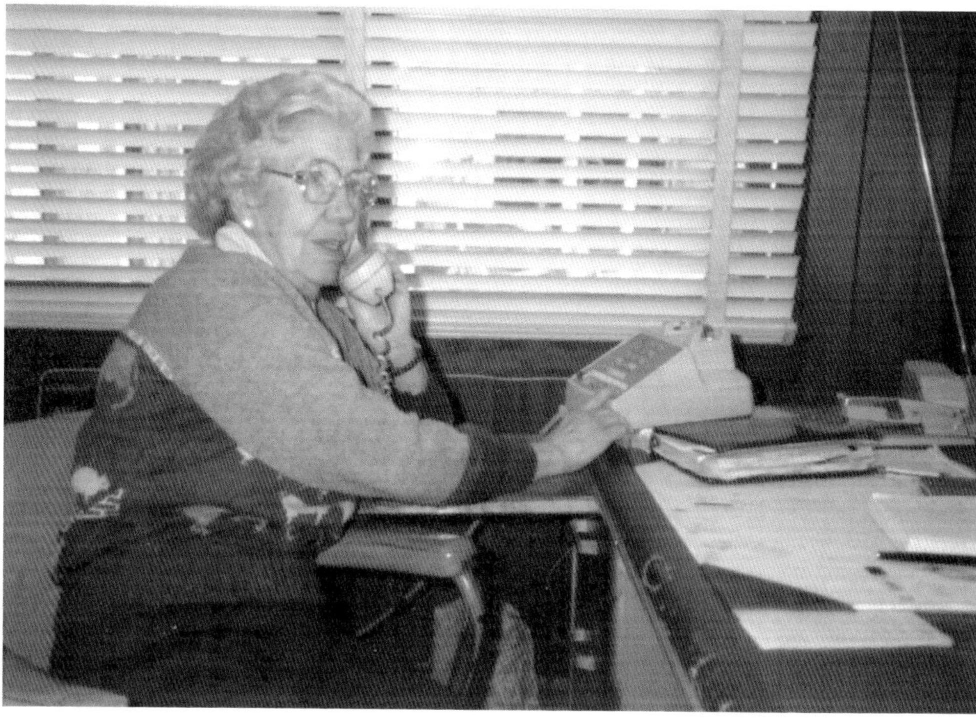

### Edna Marie Dierker Hubbard Sutton

Sutton worked with her husband, Wilkins, (see page 74) and his family at Hubbard's Pier and Seafood Inc. in Rock Hall, operating the restaurant and assuming bookkeeping duties for the restaurant and seafood business. Sutton served on the Rock Hall Board of Zoning Appeals and the Rock Hall Museum Board. She was honored in 2004 as the grand marshal of Rock Hall's Fourth of July parade. (Courtesy of Edna Marie Dierker Hubbard Sutton.)

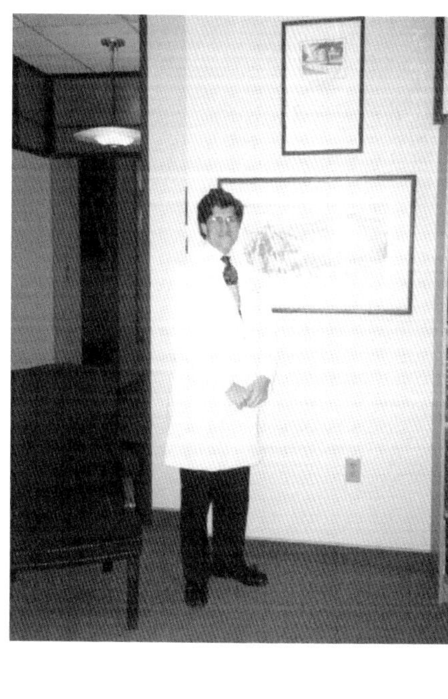

### Dr. George Wilkins Hubbard Jr.

The son of Edna Marie Dierker and the late George Wilkins Hubbard Sr. (see page 74), Dr. Hubbard grew up in Rock Hall, graduated from Rock Hall High School, and earned his medical degree from the University of Virginia. He holds many academic and professional positions within the medical field. He is a general and thoracic surgeon in Norfolk, Virginia. (Courtesy of Edna Marie Hubbard Sutton.)

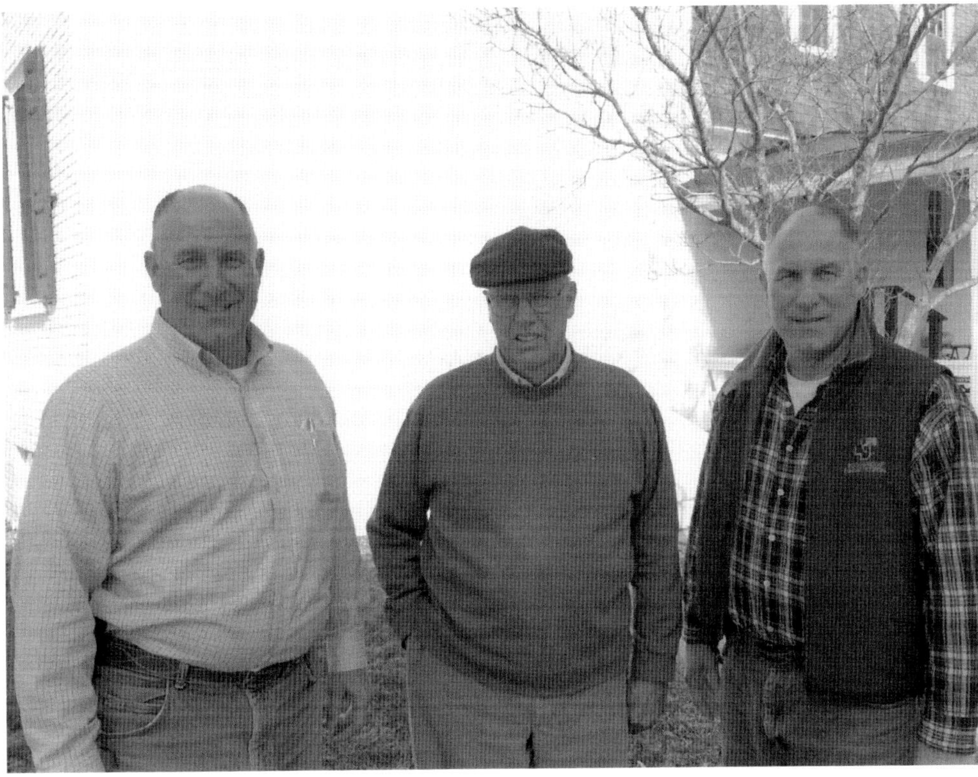

**The Olin Davis Family**

Rich Levels Farm just outside of Sassafras, Maryland, has been in the Davis family since Olin Davis Jr.'s grandfather purchased it about 1850. The rich land for which the house is named continues to be farmed by Davis, his identical twin sons Allen and Olin, and his grandchildren. The grain and poultry farm operates under the name of Rich Levels Grain Inc. Olin Davis Jr. is pictured standing between his twin sons, Allen on the left and Olin III on the right. (Courtesy of the Olin Davis family.)

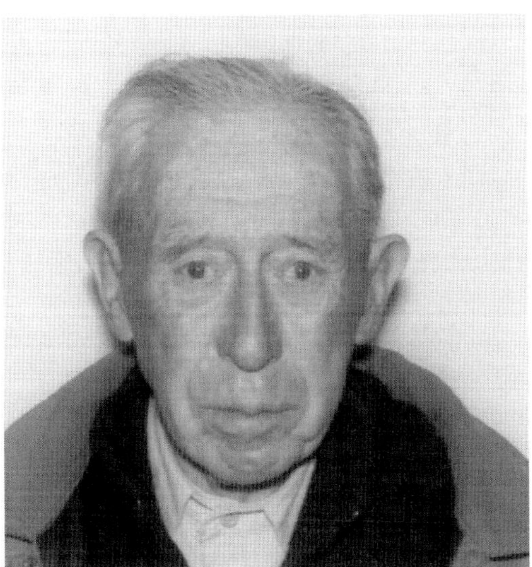

**S. Wickes Westcott**

"Mr. Wickes" is a 46-year board member of the Kent Soil & Water Conservation District and currently serves as the chairman. Westcott is involved in Kent County farming, and he and his family operate the Gregg Neck Boat Yard on the Sassafras River near Galena. Now in his 90s, he is involved every day in its operation. (Courtesy of S. Wickes Westcott.)

### The Gillespie Family

Gillespie & Son Inc. of Chestertown, a family-operated company selling ready-mix concrete and concrete products, was founded in 1922. It all started on the Sudlersville, Maryland, farm of George Edward Gillespie when he began making blocks to build a milk house from a form that he purchased from Sears & Roebuck. The demand for blocks, especially by the local farmers, led to the beginning of the operation. With the help of his son Victor, Gillespie & Son was established. The firm operated out of Dudley's Corner near Sudlersville for over 50 years. Shortly after World War II, Edward Stevens Gillespie joined his father and grandfather in their growing business. In 1963, Gillespie & Son purchased Kent Concrete in Chestertown and continued to serve from both locations until consolidating in 1971 to the Chestertown plant, where it still remains today. Sons Jim and Todd Gillespie became the fourth generation, joining the company in 1979 and 1993, respectively. Business continued to grow over the years, and they expanded their line into custom precast structures. In 2005, Jim founded Gillespie Precast, a subsidiary of Gillespie & Son and built a separate facility to keep up with production demands. Another precast plant was purchased in 2013 in Greenwood, Delaware, as they continued to expand their territory. Gillespie has incorporated the big red G as part of their logo, which is prominently displayed on all of their trucks and precast structures that can be seen in the Mid-Atlantic region, including Maryland, Delaware, Virginia, Washington, DC, Pennsylvania, and New Jersey market areas. The legacy continues as Andrew, Jim's son and the grandson of Edward Stevens Gillespie, has joined the team as a fifth-generation Gillespie to be involved in the business, with the possibility of more of his grandchildren to follow. Pictured here are, from left to right, Todd, Andrew, and Jim Gillespie with Edward Stevens Gillespie. (Courtesy of the Gillespie family.)

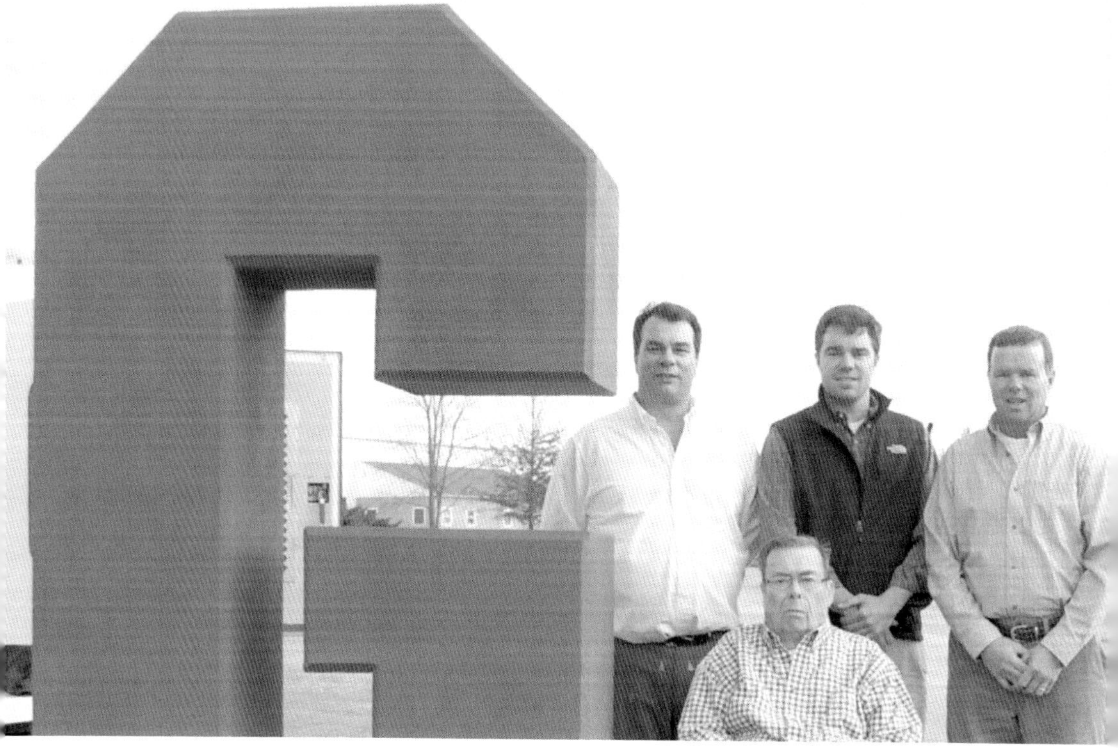

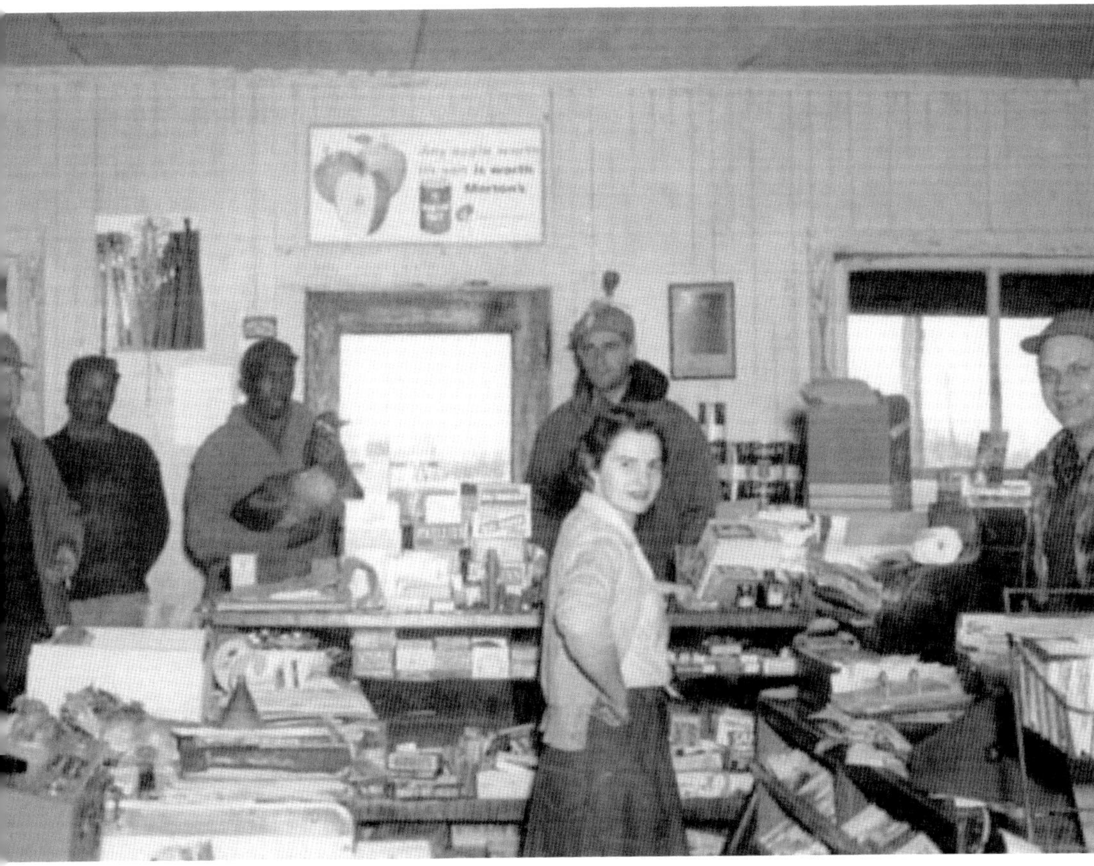

**Bob and Ruth Elliott**

The "Eastern Shore Sportsman" Bob Elliott and his wife, Ruth, operated Elliott's Sporting Goods and General Merchandise Store at Coleman's near Betterton for many years. Their store was stocked with all kinds of hunting and fishing gear and was popular with hunters and fishermen. Bob was a gunsmith and hunting guide and for several years wrote a hunting and fishing column for the local newspaper, the *Kent County News*. He developed and marketed the Chesapeake Electronic Game Call, a system that was banned by the federal government because of its effectiveness at pulling in ducks and geese. Bob and Ruth also bred, raised, and trained yellow Labrador retrievers. Their dogs were sought after for their hunting skills and gentle dispositions. He held a US Coast Guard Masters License and was known to his friends as "Cap'n Bob." He built a 43-foot wooden workboat in his backyard and named it the *Rubob*, now a fishing boat captained by their son Art. Pictured here from left to right are "Doc" Crothers, Jack Jones, Perry Wilson (holding the goose), Art Elliott, Ruth Elliott, and Bob Elliott. (Courtesy of Catharine Groves.)

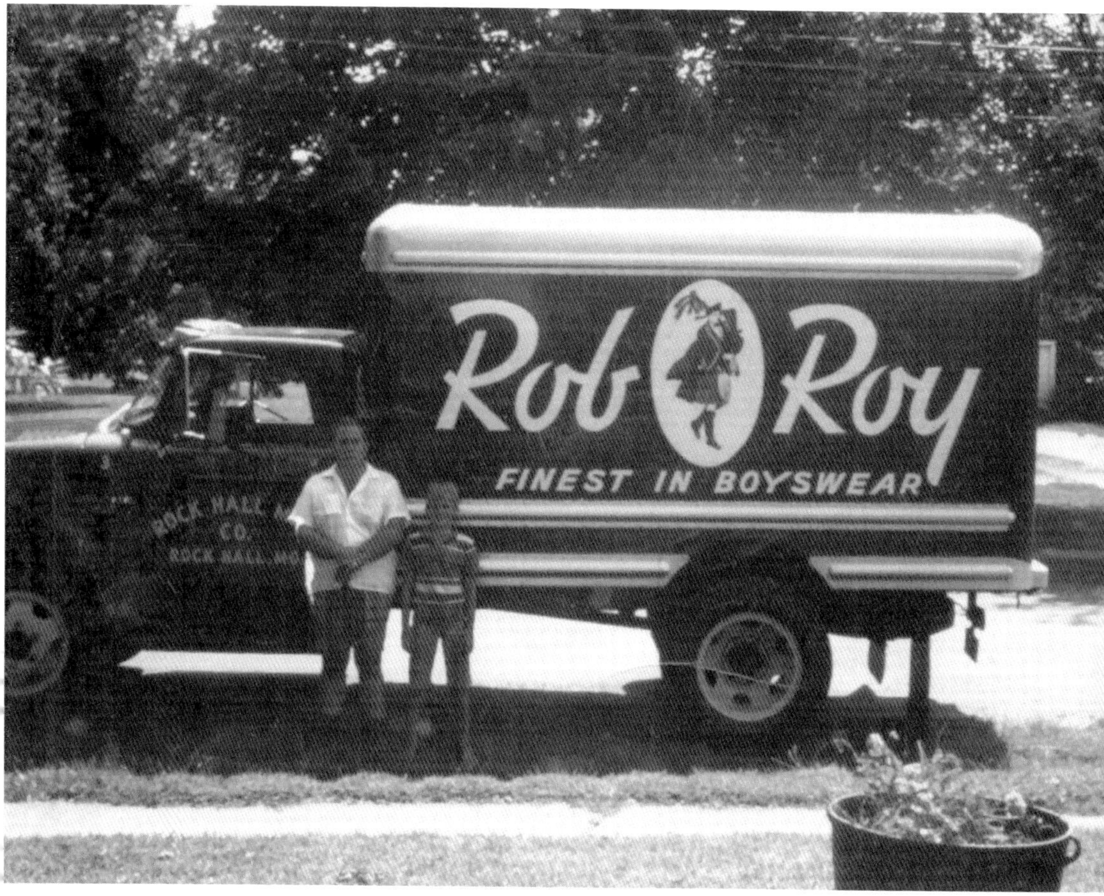


**The Elbourn Family**

The Rock Hall Manufacturing Company was owned and operated by the Elbourn family. Purnell Jump Elbourn opened the business in 1925 and made Marlboro men's shirts. About 1974, the company began making Rob Roy boys' shirts and later Queen Casual ladies' blouses. This was truly a family business. Daughter Norma E. Olson was secretary. Purnell's son Purnell Jay Elbourn (left) joined the business in 1950. His grandson Purnell Jay Elbourn Jr. (right) was also involved in the business, which offered employment to as many as 60 people. Other family members who worked in the business included Kim E. Conley, who took over the secretary's position when her Aunt Norma retired, son-in-law William H. Batchelor, who was floor manager, and grandson David Olson, who took care of the sewing machines. The business closed in 1986 after being in business for 60 years. Purnell Jay Elbourn was a successful candidate for mayor in 1972 and served two four-year terms. (Courtesy of Purnell Jay Elbourn.)

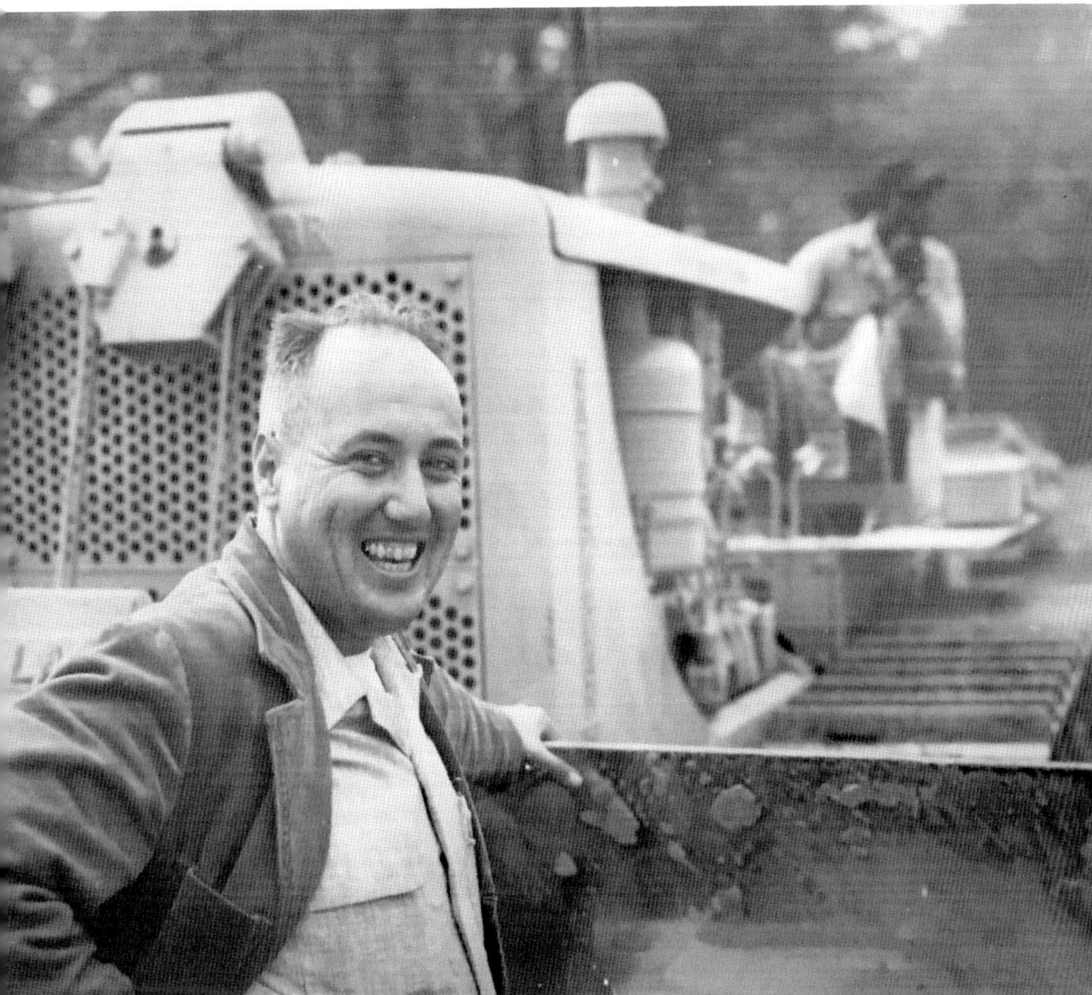

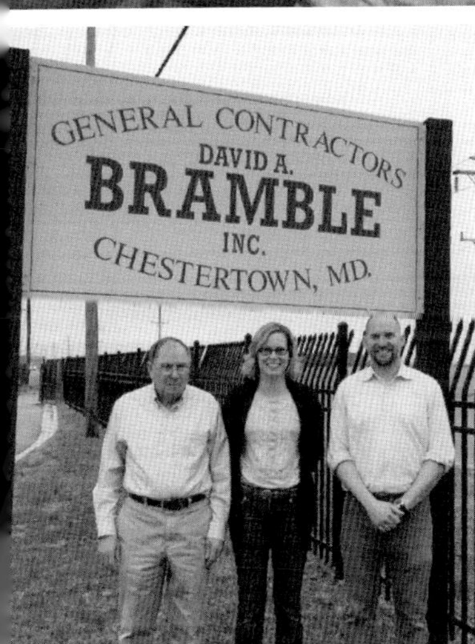


**David A. Bramble**

Lifelong Kent Countian David A. Bramble (above) operated a trucking business before enlisting in the Army Air Force in 1941. He became a pilot in the 8th Air Force during World War II, flying 25 combat missions aboard B-17 Flying Fortress bombers. He was awarded the Distinguished Flying Cross and Air Medal with three oak leaf clusters. He began a construction business after his discharge, eventually incorporated as David A. Bramble Inc. His son David C. Bramble purchased the business from his father. David A. Bramble Inc. remains a major contractor and is one of the largest employers in the upper Eastern Shore area. David C. Bramble's son Paul, a third-generation Bramble, has now joined the company along with his daughter Megan. Pictured here are, from left to right, David C. Bramble, Megan Bramble Owings, Esq., and Paul Bramble. (Both, courtesy of the Bramble family.)

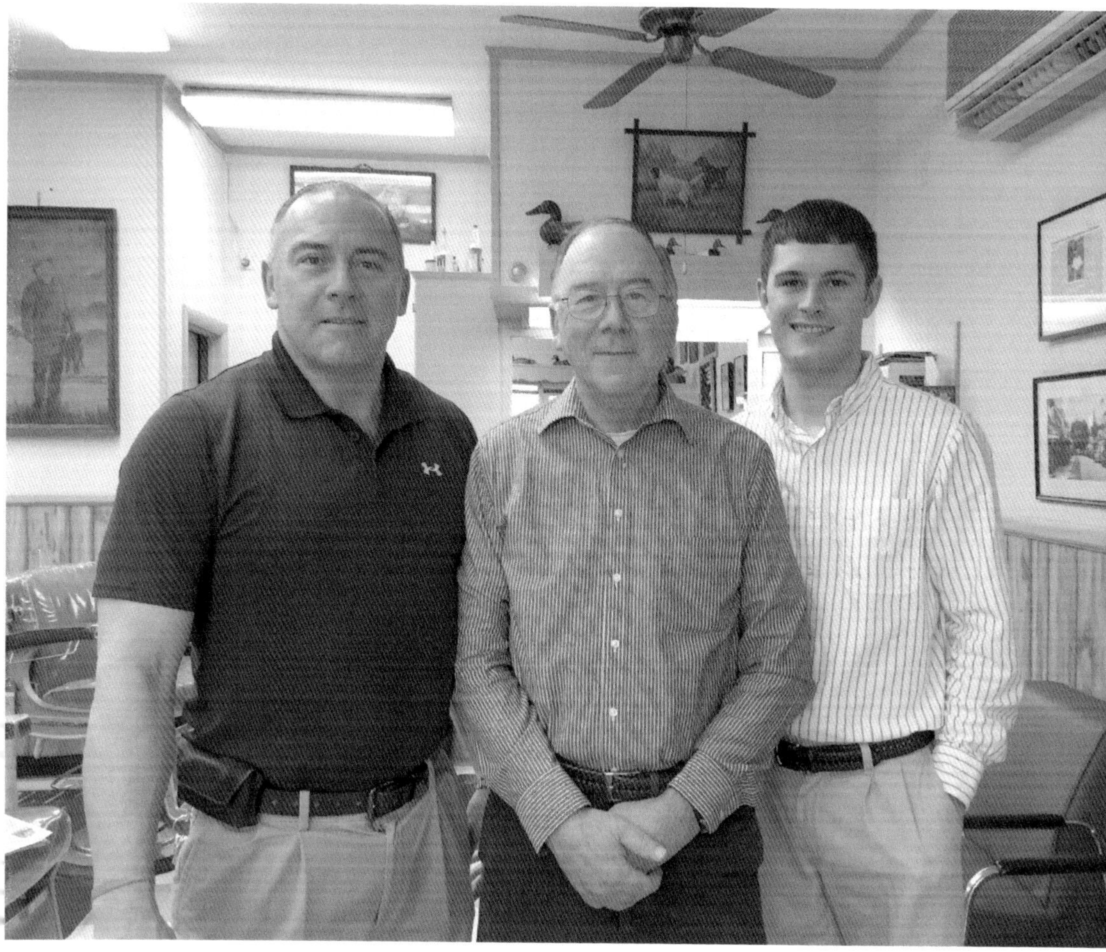

**Thompson Family of Barbers**

There have been barbers in five generations of the Thompson family. Andrew "Drew" Thompson, 21, of Rock Hall, is the fifth-generation barber at the College Heights Barbershop in Chestertown following in the footsteps of his father, John, grandfather Carroll, great-uncle Paul, great-grandfather John, and great-great-grandfather Jewell. Drew, his father, John Thompson, and his grandfather Carroll Thompson are all currently involved in the business in Chestertown. The Thompson barbershop had its beginnings in Rock Hall, where Drew's great-great grandfather Jewell Thompson first opened a barbershop. Jewell had two brothers, Carlton and Earl "Buck," who were also barbers. Buck barbered in Still Pond, and Carlton barbered in Florida. He had two sons, Paul and John. Drew's great-uncle Paul Thompson opened the College Heights Barbershop in Chestertown in 1959. Paul and Drew's great-grandfather John Cavendar Thompson first barbered in Rock Hall. Drew's grandfather Carroll was the first in the Thompson family to attend barber school. Drew's father, John, attended barber school in Baltimore, and Drew has completed his schooling in barbering. Pictured here from left to right are John Thompson, Carroll Thompson and Drew Thompson. (Author's collection.)

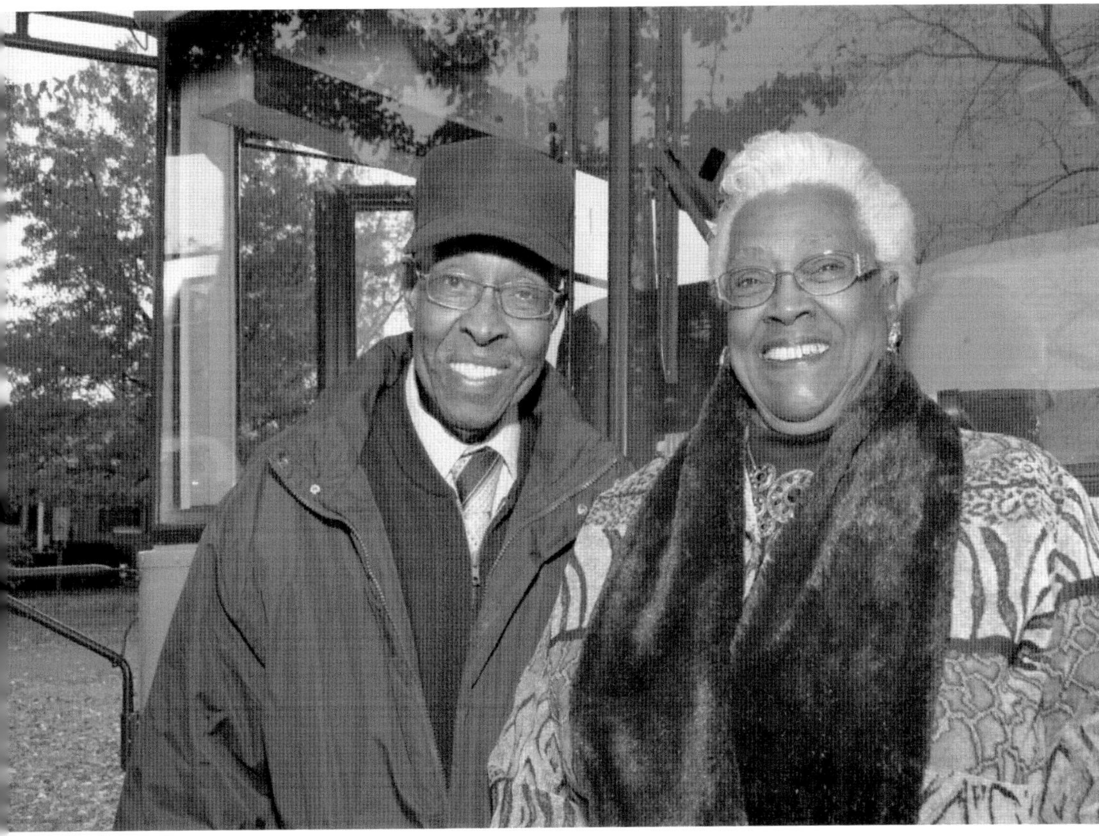

**Curtis and Anna Mae Dorsey**

Dorsey Bus Services was operated in Kent County by Curtis Dorsey and his wife, Anna Mae, for over 60 years. They retired in 2012. They purchased their first bus in 1958 and provided bus service to many generations of schoolchildren going to and from school and going to school events. They employed many local residents and trained future school-bus drivers. (Courtesy of C It Visually with CG Taylor.)

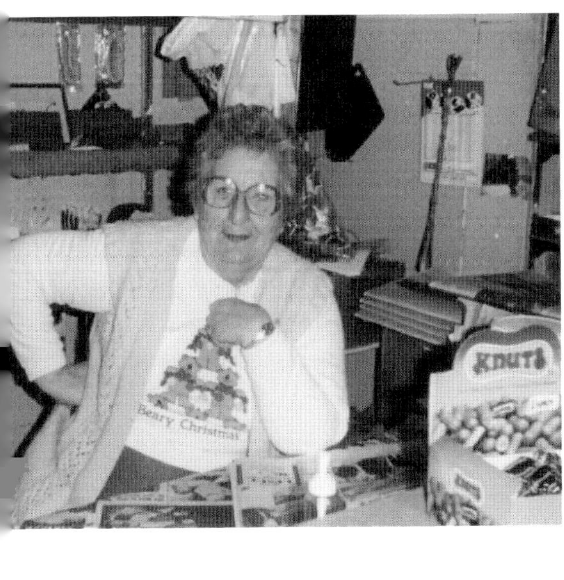

**Anna Scott Cole**

"Miss Anna" was born in Kent County. She started working at Fox's Five and Dime variety store on High Street in downtown Chestertown in 1944 when she was 16. She bought the Fox Family Shoe Store merchandise in 1974 and opened Scottie's Shoe Store. She added newspapers, magazines, cards, and consignment antiques. Cole had worked on High Street for 70 years when she closed her business in 2013. (Courtesy of Anna Scott Cole.)

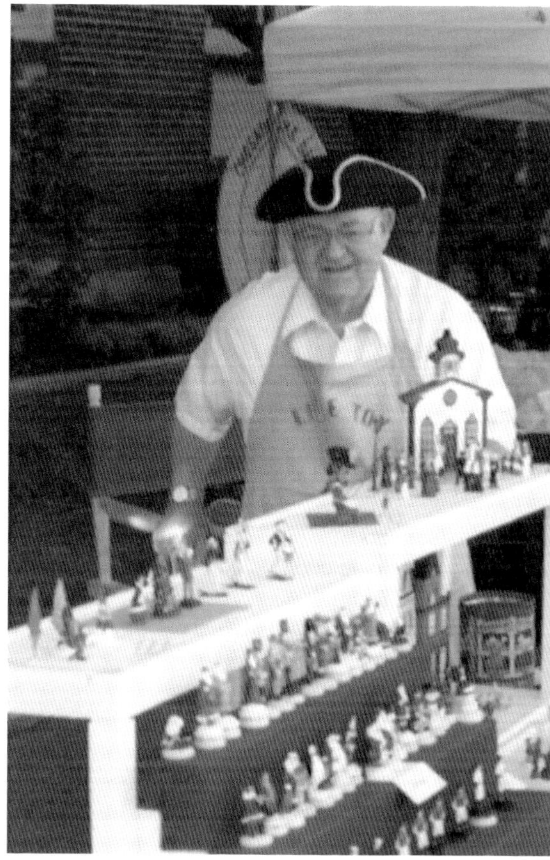

### William A. Biddle

The first president of the board of directors of Kent Youth Inc., which offered a nonresidential counseling program and a group home to boys for more than 32 years in Chestertown, was "Pat" Biddle. The board of Kent Youth named the Kent Youth building the Pat Biddle House in his honor. He is a retired school principal, enjoys singing with barbershop quartets, and is renowned as a maker of toy soldiers. (Courtesy of Glen Biddle.)

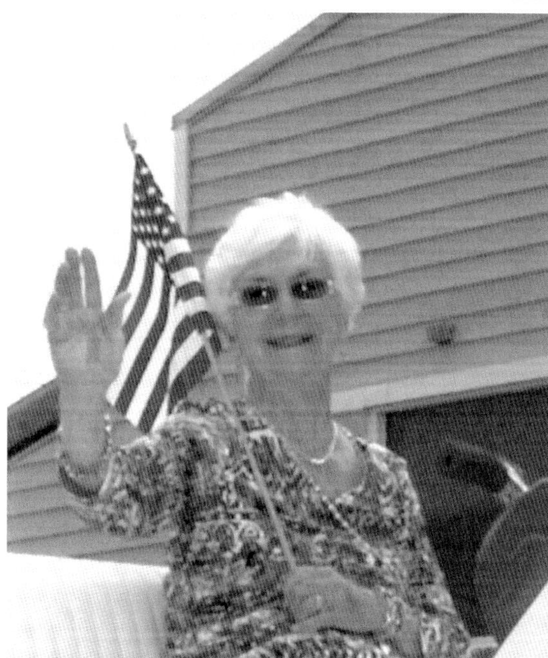

### Lois Crouch Wood

Wood loved every minute of her 32 years teaching in the Kent County Public School system. "Honey" is a lifelong resident of Rock Hall and has been a real estate agent for 30 years. She likes to share what she has learned in life; education, experience, and memories are things that no one can take away. She was honored as grand marshal of the Rock Hall Fourth of July parade in 2013. (Courtesy of Trisha McGee.)

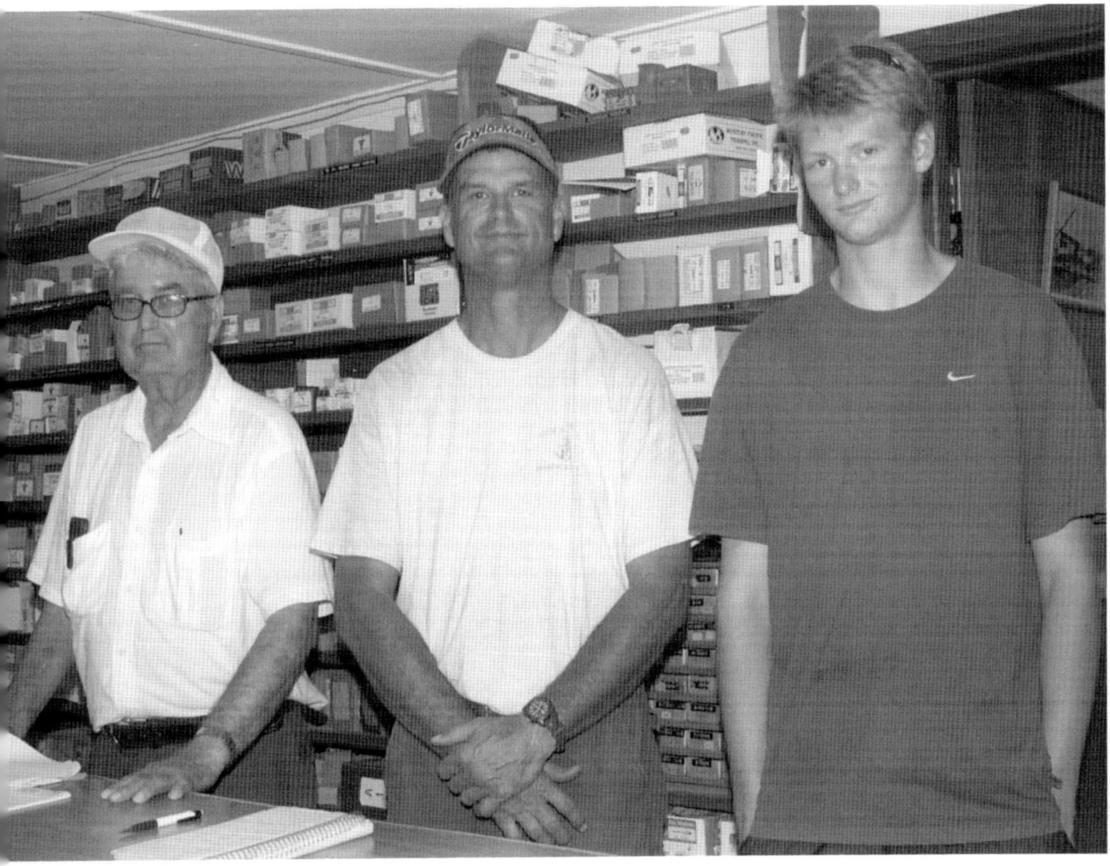

**Elmer Leary**

Elmer Leary and the Leary family have owned and operated the Rock Hall Marine Railway in the heart of Rock Hall harbor since 1928. They offer the only railway in the area, as well as three travel lifts that can accommodate boats up to 25 tons. They do marine repairs, offer boat slips and storage of boats, and operate a marine store. Ellsworth Leary started the railway business and passed it along to George Leary, who gave it to his son Elmer, the current owner. Along with his wife, Ann, Leary has been joined by his son Rick and grandson Tyler, the fifth generation of Learys to work in the business. Pictured here from left to right are Elmer Leary, Rick Leary, and Tyler Leary. (Courtesy of Trish McGee.)

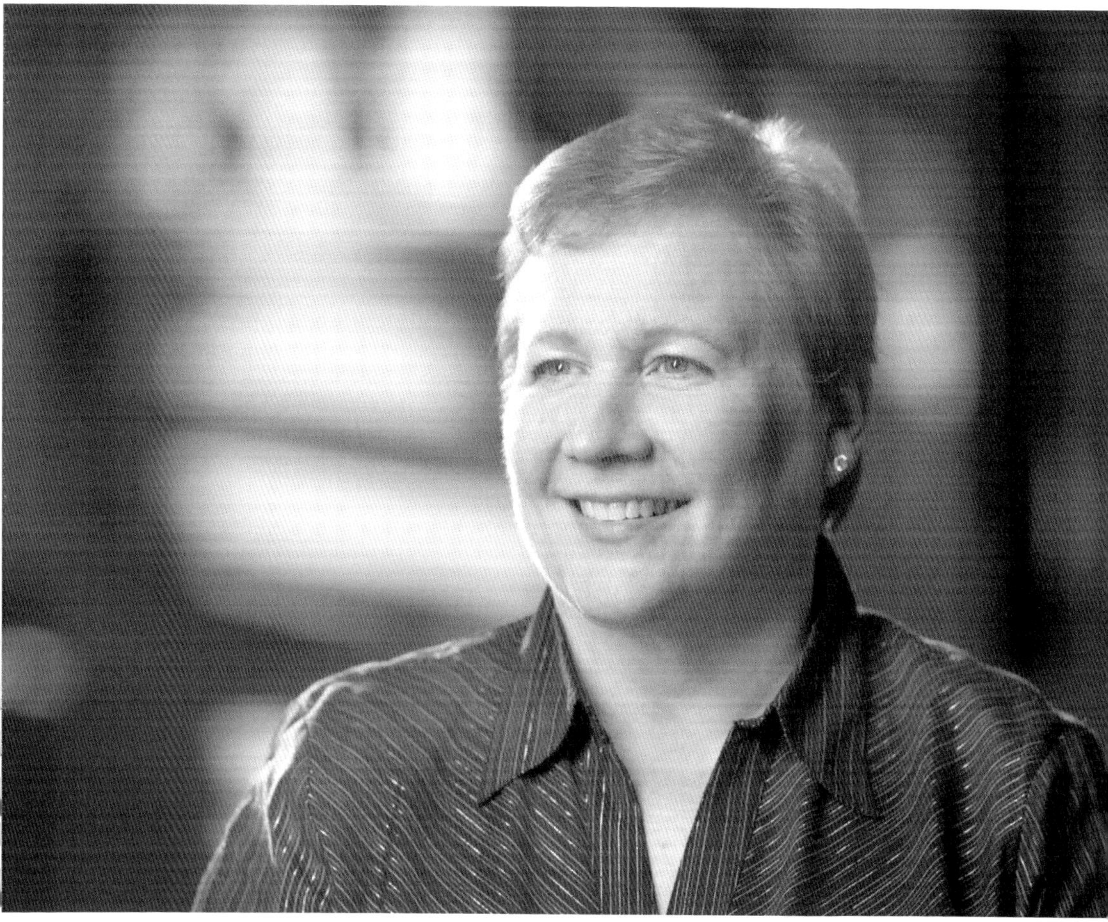

**Lillian Dierker Shockney**

A two-time breast cancer survivor, "Lillie," who was raised on a farm in Kent County, is a national expert and leader in the field of breast cancer. She is an associate professor in the Departments of Surgery and Gynecology and Obstetrics at the Johns Hopkins University School of Medicine, designated as the University Distinguished Service Associate Professor of Breast Cancer, and is the director of the Johns Hopkins Breast Center and director of Cancer Survivorship Programs. She is the only nurse at Hopkins to ever receive a physician distinguished service designation. Shockney, along with her mother, Charmayne Dierker, of Chestertown, cofounded the nonprofit Mothers Supporting Daughters with Breast Cancer. Author of 14 books and many articles in medical journals, she has received 41 national awards and four awards from Maryland. Shockney was inducted into the Maryland Women's Hall of Fame in 2010. In 2012, she was selected by Johnson & Johnson as the Most Amazing Nurse in America. (Courtesy of Keith Weller for Johns Hopkins.)

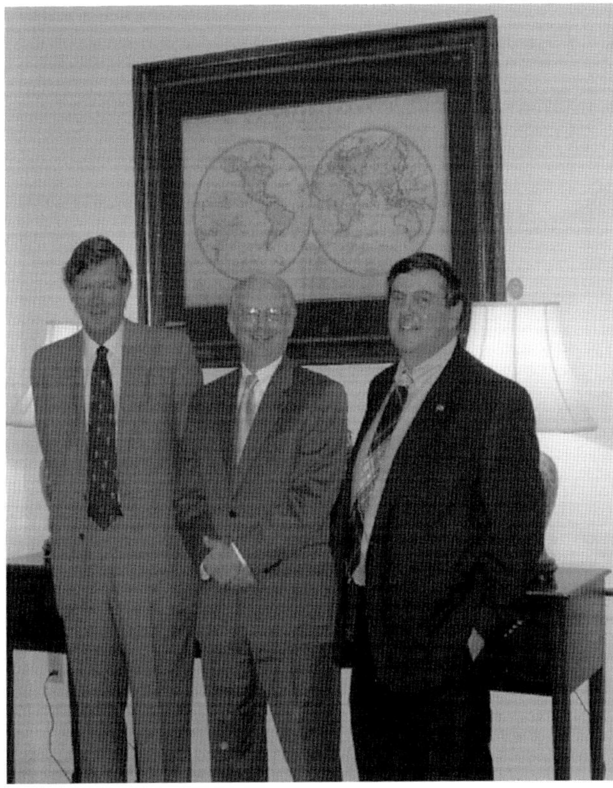

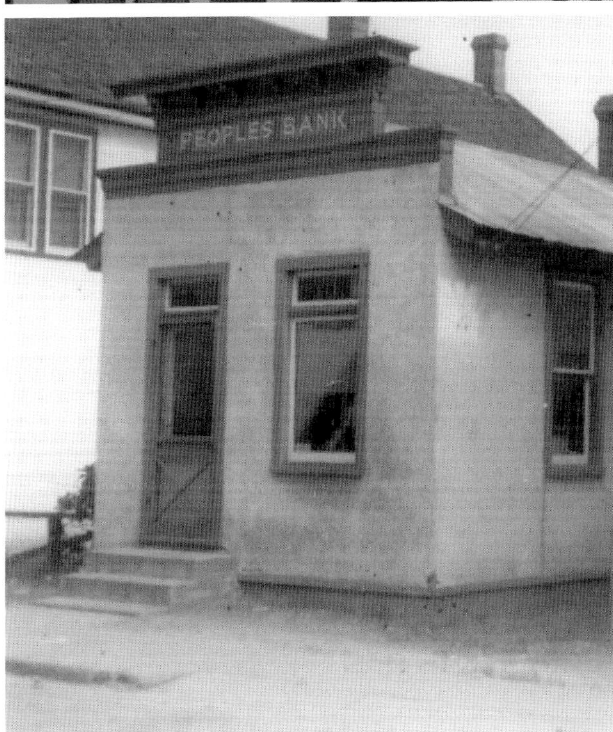


**Rasin, Wheatley, Rogers-Skipp Families**
The Rasin, Rogers-Skipp, and Wheatley families have been involved in the development of the Peoples Bank over the last 100 years. The bank was established in 1910, and these families played an integral part in the bank's formation and stature in the community. Many of the families from the original subscribers represented a general cross section of men and women in the area and are still present among the current stockholders. Pictured above from left to right are current board member Stefan Rogers Skipp, former board member Alexander P. Rasin III, and current board member William G. Wheatley. Pictured below, the Rock Hall branch of the Peoples Bank was opened in 1921. (Both, courtesy of the Peoples Bank.)

# INDEX

# INDEX